RENATA TEBALDI

❧Renata Tebaldi❧
THE VOICE OF AN ANGEL

by Carlamaria Casanova

translated and edited by
Connie Mandracchia DeCaro

BASKERVILLE
PUBLISHERS, INC.

Translation copyright ©1995 by Baskerville Publishers, Inc.
Originally published in Italian as
Renata Tebaldi: La Voce d'Angelo by Carlamaria Casanova

Baskerville Publishers, Inc.
7616 LBJ Freeway, Suite 220, Dallas, TX 75251-1008

Library of Congress Cataloging-in-Publication Data

Casanova, Carlamaria.
 [Renata Tebaldi : la voce d'angelo. English]
  Renata Tebaldi : the voice of an angel / by Carlamaria Casanova.
  p. cm. -- (Great Voices)
 Translation of: Renata Tebaldi, la voce d'angelo.
  Discography: p.
  Includes index.
  ISBN 1-880909-40-5 (alk. paper)
  1. Tebaldi, Renata. 2. Sopranos (Singers)--Biography.
 I. Title II. Series
 ML420.T28C413   1995
 782.6'6'092--dc20
 [B]   95-38387
                                          MN

Manufactured in the United States of America
First Printing, 1995

CD Program Information

1. The Jewel Song (1949)   *Faust* (Gounod)

2. Vissi d'arte (1949)   *Tosca* (Puccini)

3. Un bel di (1949)   *Madama Butterfly* (Puccini)

4. In quelle trine morbide (1949)   *Manon Lescaut* (Puccini)

5. Tacea la notte (1949)   *Il Trovatore* (Verdi)

6. O patria mia (1952)   *Aida* (Verdi)

7. Willow song - Ave Maria (1954)   *Otello* (Verdi)

8. Addio del passato (1954)   *La Traviata* (Verdi)

9. Porgi amor (1955)   *The Marriage of Figaro* (Mozart)

10. Poveri fiori (1955)   *Adriana Lecouvreur* (Cilea)

11. Selva opaca (1955)   *William Tell* (Rossini)

12. L'altra notte in fondo al mare (1955)   *Mefistofele* (Boito)

13. Suicidio (1964)   *La Gioconda* (Ponchielli)

14. Dolente immagine di figlia mia (1956)   Song (Bellini)

℗ 1949, 1952, 1954, 1955, 1956, 1964—The Decca Record Company, Ltd., London

Table of Contents

Table of Contents

✦Preface✦

The artist and the voice had enchanted me from behind the footlights and through recordings even before I met Renata Tebaldi. Becoming a friend of such an extraordinary person was a turning point for me. This great soprano and beautiful human being added a new dimension to my life. Together with a feeling of well-being, she brought me a more sensitive appreciation and understanding of life. Her inspiration has remained with me through these many years as our friendship has grown.

The many faces of Renata surface as I reflect back over the years: the glamorous diva whose voice and pathos overwhelmed her audiences around the world; the joyful and exuberant artist affectionately greeting the endless stream of admirers after a performance; the disturbed professional dissatisfied with an endeavor; the almost childlike enjoyment of the woman relaxing on a Sunday afternoon as she delighted in eating silver-dollar pancakes topped with maple syrup, or Carvel ice cream cones dipped in chocolate; and always the warm, unaffected, gentle, almost vulnerable personality who with a glance understands and with a smile says so much.

Much has been written of the impact Renata Tebaldi has

had on those who have heard her. Francis Robinson, the former Assistant Manager of the Metropolitan Opera House wrote in 1969, "Renata Tebaldi is an authentic star. She has the longest history of sold-out performances of any artist before the public today." He described his first contact with the singer by saying, "I fell in love with her from those first recordings which preceded her to this country by two or three years.... It was one of the sublime memories of a lifetime." More than a decade later he was to say, "Twelve years ago I wrote that her hold on the public amounted to veneration. It is more than the blue eyes and alabaster skin. It is some cleanness of mind and spirit beyond that of her voice which draws as surely as the moon does the tide." The renowned critic of *The New York Times*, Harold Schonberg, compared her to the "primavera" and said, "Botticelli would have rushed for his brushes." He also dubbed her "America's Sweetheart, your darling, my darling, everybody's darling." Guido Pannain of the Italian weekly, *Tempo*, said, "her voice expresses the inexpressible which is, after all, the expression of everything. Her radiance, her lack of affectation, the inner, perceptive force in her voice overwhelms the listener with emotion."

Renata's most frequent stage and recording partner, Mario Del Monaco, wrote to Tebaldi in 1979, "I began my career in 1936-37 and I have sung with the greatest singers of the past, but I have never heard another voice like yours. Your voice is unique.... Your Maddalena, Aida, and Floria Tosca are indelible.... I cannot forget the greatest Desdemona of all time."

What is the essence of this somewhat mystifying, extraordinary personality? Renata has said that the core of her existence, even beyond her music, is love, "love for her mother, love for her art, love for life as defined by her Christian faith." So we have a "cleanness of mind and spirit," a beauty which inspires, a voice which expresses the inexpressible, and love at the core. But the portrait of Renata would be incomplete without mentioning a subtle inner strength in moments of peril. She has had the strength to pull down the curtain on potentially destructive situations, deciding that she no longer wished to endure the pain, and by detaching herself, she endured.

She had the strength to overcome childhood polio myelitis which left her frail and vulnerable. It took courage to face a heartbreaking family situation during her teen years. It took resolution to put an end to a suffocating atmosphere at La Scala, but, in so doing, she endured. Courage was needed to detach herself from the man she loved when that love had become her torment, but, in so doing, she endured.

If the test of strength is the ability to endure, then Renata Tebaldi is formidable. Her strength has enabled her to remain at the peak of a superb career for 30 years, to remain in the hearts of the thousands who love her, and to remain, in her mature years, a woman whose expressive beauty reflects that inner love, pathos, and sincerity which made her inimitable voice the remarkable instrument that it is, capable of expressing the inexpressible.

With boundless admiration and affection,
Connie Mandracchia DeCaro

Many thanks to Stephanie Sundine, soprano, for her assistance with musical terminology.

xiii

❦ 1 ❧

Renata Tebaldi: Later

She laughs heartily and with evident pleasure. Her smile is luminous, intelligent, spontaneous, and captivating. Mystification is not part of her personal repertoire. Instead, the candor of her expression, of her glance, reveals her rare humanity.

Tall, beautiful, and radiant, regal and yet so approachable, Renata Tebaldi declares quietly, "I stopped singing without realizing it and without consciously wanting it. I made no decisions. One day I simply said to myself that I would not accept any commitments for a while. I wanted to rest. It was after my concert at La Scala benefiting the victims of the earthquake in Friuli in 1976. It was a strange and beautiful sensation to wake up without the responsibility of singing engagements and without concern for my voice. No more inhalations, pills, gargling! I did continue my daily vocalizing, but I stopped practicing with Maestro Müller who normally accompanied me every day. Then one morning I went even further. I thought about not vocalizing. And I stopped. From that day I haven't sung another note. I haven't suffered from it. I'll even go further and say that I've never even missed it. Singing is no longer part of me. When I sang I gave all that I had to give. Now that's past. I have no regrets. Have I lived my life for my art? Perhaps. Or better, without a doubt. But obviously my life wasn't only singing, since even without singing my life goes on. I have no family; I have no immediate artistic responsibilities, yet I'm fine. I have no complexes, I'm tranquil and at peace with myself. Many of my colleagues aren't as fortunate because they're not able to break away in time and they remain tragically ensnared by the limelight. They torment themselves when their audience diminishes or, even worse, abandons them. I'm grateful to my good fortune that I was never stage-struck."

But could you have been anything other than a singer?

"No! I could only sing. It gave me such enormous pleasure to know that through singing I could be loved by so many different people. So often as I strolled or shopped along the avenues of the world someone would touch my shoulder and thank me for the happiness that I had given him or her. That person's joy became my joy and that was the justification of my career, of my sacrifices, and of my existence. I've always derived great pleasure from giving, even more than in receiving. I would have sung for my public with my heart in my hands if I could have. More than once I sang with a fever, up from my bed, performed and returned to bed immediately after. My greatest concern when I wasn't well was that of disappointing my public and of inconveniencing management and colleagues."

Don't you miss the excitement and freedom that singing offered you?

"Not really. Often I truly did feel like a singing bird, free to sing as I wished, transported into an unreal world where I found marvelous spiritual gratification and profound emotion, which I was able to transmit simply because I found it there. Eventually I realized that it was not I who was singing but He who had given me my beautiful gift. That's why, now that I no longer sing, I often have the strange feeling that two beings existed in me and that the one who sang has gone far away and left me with many wonderful memories."

Do you believe in the hereafter?

"Yes. I believe that we will be judged, but in a different way than we are taught. I believe that God is, above all, just, and that it's not possible to deceive Him. We will be judged for our intentions, good or bad, and not for the effects of our actions. I believe that animals and plants have a soul, also, and I believe that after death, to the end of time, we will continue to circulate among the living. Often I feel the presence of loved ones who are no longer here near me."

Does the thought of death disturb you?

"No. It seems to me a logical consequence of life. I don't make it a problem. I know it will come and I await it serenely."

How do you view today's world and the future?

"It's not very beautiful because one no longer knows what to believe, especially the young don't know. They search in vain for something which makes life worth living. And they run to the psychiatrist. It makes me want to laugh, or better, cry. The truth instead is that we must solve our own problems. But by dint of wanting to discover the hidden I, we often end up by losing it completely. Nonetheless, I do hope for a better world, and with faith I await that God's Will be done."

Is the life of a celebrity difficult for a shy person?

"It can go to one's head. My life as a celebrity had no essential effect on me because I'm still the same person I was at the core. My friends tell me that I have never truly grasped the fact that I am a famous person. A celebrity. Truthfully, I've never grasped it. When my audiences applauded me clamorously and with overwhelming enthusiasm I was so happy. I felt them all so near me, but sometimes I felt uncomfortable because the applause seemed too much. It was difficult to understand that all of that was for me. And the applause I still receive today, at public appearances, both moves me and amazes me."

Is it painful to attend an opera performance with others singing?

"I suffer only if the opera is performed badly. I don't sadden myself by thinking of the way I used to sing this or that passage.... I listen very objectively as others sing. Surely I'm amazed at the ease with which voices are used today, fitting them to any role. But, the problem is probably a natural phenomenon. Since voices have grown smaller, we must accept the voices that we have or remove certain operas from the repertory."

Have you ever thought of teaching voice?

"No, not as a way of life. I become too involved with the subject, and then, patience is not my strength."

Your superb career continued its glorious crescendo in America. What caused Renata Tebaldi to return to Italy?

"My roots, which are here. I wept as I closed my house in New York to return to Milan, but my place now is here in my country."

"I have loved so much," "suffered so much," "worked so much," "sung so much," "laughed so much," "travelled so much": if you had to use one of these definitions to relate who you are, which would you select?

"All of them."

But if you had to select only one?

"I have sung."

Then after a moment Renata adds, "Love, too, is the essence of my life. Love for my mother, for my art, for life as defined by my Christian faith." With this reflection, the discussion concerning Renata Tebaldi could be closed. But, if the artist has taken her place in history, the person, precisely for her lack of posturing, ostentation, and eccentricities, provokes in us the desire to know more.

"I adore picnics. My dream was to travel in a trailer, but now that I have the time, it has become too dangerous! Just driving in today's chaotic traffic is a problem. I can't tell you how agitated I get. I'd like to drive around with my car window down, shouting out little profanities. I seldom go to the cinema anymore for what they're showing. And then, I don't enjoy going alone, and if Tina comes with me, New must remain home, and he will not remain home alone."

So, we have the picnics, the trailer, the profanities, the lack of cinema, the dog who will not stay home alone. Here, already, we begin to discover the unpublished Tebaldi.

"I'm a glutton for sweets, completely lacking self-control. Sometimes I would buy myself a quarter pound of chocolate and by the time I reached home, I'd already eaten all of it. I was raised on bread and chocolate. Harmful to the liver? To the skin? I wouldn't say so. For my snack at school my mother would send me off with a piece of dark chocolate, the hard, kitchen kind, and I would eat it with a half loaf of

5

French bread. I've never even had a pimple." So, here we have a childhood of bread and chocolate.

And yet, Renata Tebaldi was not a chubby, carefree child. If a happy life does not make "good copy," then certainly Renata's early years were an ideal scenario for a writer's interest, since they were very painful. Sometimes distressing. Ideal material for the biography of a star.

As to her artistic chronology, however, it was necessary to seek elsewhere from various sources because Renata confuses dates terribly, and she has never kept a record. She has forgotten the date of her debut in Rovigo. ("Was it the 12th or the 13th of May? It must have been the 13th because that's a number that has always brought me good luck." Then one discovers that it was the 23rd!) She doesn't remember the date of her opera debut at La Scala, nor the number of operas in her repertory ("It must have been 36.") or the year in which she sang *La Traviata* for the first time. Often, as she talks, her resonant and warm voice rises in pitch and is heard throughout the house—"Tina! Where are you? Do you remember how many years I stayed away from La Scala?" Then she sighs, "If Tina weren't here, nothing would be remembered!" It is precisely the unpretentious detachment from any adoration of her artistic past that amazes and excites one's curiosity concerning the person, Renata Tebaldi.

2

Childhood in Langhirano

The first contact Renata had with the outside world was a jolt of fear. One day when her mother was pregnant and walking along the shore in Pesaro, a frisky horse charged at her. The terrified woman was so traumatized by the frightening incident that her fear became her daughter's phobia in later years. During her career Renata suffered untold panic whenever her performance required proximity to a horse. In September of 1961, during a performance in Tokyo of *Andrea Chénier,* the horse drawing the cart with the condemned prisoners to the Bastille grew restless. Maddalena (Tebaldi) was supposed to climb onto the wagon with Chénier (Del Monaco). Sensing his colleague's panic, Del Monaco grabbed her firmly by the waist and supported her forcefully at the crucial moment. The scene conveyed fear and desperation so convincingly that the audience responded with eight minutes of enthusiastic applause. Tebaldi's comment was, "I had chosen the guillotine, but surely that was little punishment compared to my terror of that restless horse!"

All that, however, was a long way off when Renata Ersilia Clotilde Tebaldi was born at five in the afternoon on February 1st, 1922, under the sign of Aquarius. She was born in

Pesaro in Via XX settembre. Her father, Teobaldo Tebaldi, belonged to a family long-settled in the region known as Le Marche on the Adriatic Sea. His grandmother, Ersilia Guidini, was a celebrated beauty and singer. Renata's mother, Giuseppina Barbieri, was from Langhirano, a small town 24 kilometers from Parma. The Barbieris could also boast of musical precedents in their family. The most illustrious was Pietro Venturini, violinist and composer, who for 30 years was first violinist in the orchestra of the Carlo Felice Theater in Genoa. Even Giuseppina's father had a natural talent for music and had been one of the founders of the Langhirano band. Nonetheless, he was morally against Giuseppina's pursuing a career, despite her beautiful voice.

Denied a singing career, Giuseppina Barbieri, Renata's mother, beautiful, tall, and headstrong, wished to dedicate herself to medicine. Her sharp intelligence was not destined to be applied to medical studies, however, since family finances made that choice difficult. As a consequence, she turned to nursing. It was during this period that she met Teobaldo, a member of the Second Regiment of Grenadiers, when he was sent to Langhirano to convalesce from a leg wound suffered during World War I. It was the classic case of love at first sight between them. They were married and went to live in Pesaro in his family home. The year was 1920.

Teobaldo was a cellist by profession. He was six years younger than his bride, attractive and attracted to women. Tensions, aggravated by too much family intervention, soon intensified and the birth of little Renata failed to bring the couple together. Renata was three years old when her mother decided to return to her family in Langhirano.

In Langhirano the Barbieris had always had the franchise to run the local post office. Her grandfather owned a general store. There were uncles, aunts, cousins, and friends. There were the sparkling wine and the world-famous prosciutto from Parma. There was cheerful, pleasant conversation.

Above all, a home, friendship, and love were there for the young and disillusioned bride who had returned with her infant daughter. Among her own people Giuseppina reorganized her life; during the day in the store, in the evenings at home embroidering church vestments. The child was always near her. Langhirano has come to be cited often as Tebaldi's birthplace. She says of herself, "I have the spirit of contradiction and am difficult like the people of Le Marche, but on the whole, I identify myself with the people of Parma." She still owns a house and land there and her cousins, Luciana and Giorgio, live there.

When she was three years old, as she attempted to get out of bed one morning, Renata was unable to stand. The poliomyelitis which had afflicted her was to remain her Calvary for five interminable years. Five years of excruciating pain from injections, massages, thermal treatments, and physiotherapy followed the onset of this disease. Her skin was so punctured by injections that lying in bed became a terribly painful ordeal. She often spent the entire night in her mother's arms. She was so terrified of injections that just the sight of the doctor or nurse threw her into hysterics. Her family devised different strategies to distract her. One was the "strategy of the magic lantern" placed at the end of the corridor which created cascades of images for the child long enough to distract her as she was immobilzed on the cot for further medical treatments.

Renata's lack of appetite was an even more serious problem. She refused food and became very frail. The solution was the well-known Italian "Farina Lattea Mellin" which caused a miracle and she regained her appetite. This popular Mellin milk formula played another important role in Renata's childhood. As part of their advertising campaign, "after" photographs of chubby-cheeked children were published in the *Domenica del Corriere,* a weekly magazine. Renata's mother, hoping to attract the attention of her estranged husband, sent a picture of the now pink-cheeked child to the magazine to be published. And so it happened. Teobaldo saw his daughter's picture—a daughter whom he did not know—and he was touched. He wrote several animated letters to his wife, suggesting a visit. The Barbieri family thwarted a meeting that seemed to suggest only a temporary reconciliation.

In the meantime Renata had started school. She was, by her own admission, at eight years of age an "unbearable child." During the painful years of her illness, she had been pampered and spoiled, with the inevitable consequences. Her mother and relatives had sought ways to ease the anguish caused by her illness and her father's absence. She was not a sociable child and seldom took part in children's games. She often entertained herself by dressing in her mother's clothing and admiring herself in the mirror. She enjoyed "being the teacher" and often arranged rows of chairs, then striking them with a long stick! Having a sweet tooth at an early age, she often raided the little pastry shop in town. She had a weakness for *paste rosse* and devoured as many as possible by using the password, "Grandfather will pay," as he always did.

In the square, next to Renata's house, her grandparents owned a sweet shop which was a magnet for her. She would go behind the counter and devour chocolates unnoticed, and drop the wrappings under the counter where they would accumulate until someone swept. Then with a laugh or two the adults would understand the "mystery" of the "pilfered" candies.

When she exhausted her mother's patience, she was punished by being ordered to stand outside their front door until her mother came for her. After what seemed an eternity to the guilt-tormented mother, Giuseppina would hurry out to rescue her "punished" daughter, only to find her missing. The family would find her later exploring the town, oblivious of any anxiety she had prompted.

Renata was fascinated by dolls. She had only one, of pâpier-maché, which she loved passionately. One evening she left it on the terrace. It rained and the doll fell apart. Renata has never forgotten her distress over it, even though her mother made a financial sacrifice and tried to ease her daughter's heartache by buying her a new and far more beautiful doll. They named it Maria José because they thought she resembled the royal princess.

Renata preserves scattered but vivid images of those early years. She recalls those winter nights when, with the entire family seated together in the large kitchen, she was allowed to cook chestnut flour in thimbles on the coals, or to taste a new wine as though she knew her wines. She had even been affectionately nicknamed "basetti" which means drunkard in the dialect of Parma. Once, in the local church, preparations were made for Torricelli's operetta, *Il Talismano di Pim*. Renata, in the role of a boy, recited and sang to her heart's content, wearing blue pantaloons, white socks, red shoes, and a beret with a pompom on top.

It was at school during preparations for Christmas that Renata had perhaps the most brutal shock of her life. It had been Giuseppina's decision that her daughter should believe that her father was dead. She felt there would be time for explanations later when Renata would understand better. But, one morning in December when all her classmates were involved in writing Christmas letters to their parents, one child turned to Renata and asked why she was writing only to her mother. When Renata replied, "Because my father is dead," her classmate's prompt retort was, "That's not true, he's alive and lives in another city." After her show of bravura, the child stood there looking at Renata with proud impertinence. It was then that Renata sensed, in an obscure way, the presence in her life of something unnatural, almost monstrous, that she had not been conscious of before. She wanted to

11

strike out at her classmate, but succeeded only in wiping away tears of anger, shame, and pain. Her teacher understood everything and sent her home to her mother who dealt with the situation. The Barbieri household decided that it was imperative to contact Teobaldo.

Consequently, Renata's father reentered her life.

"But to have a father was not what I had thought it would be," Renata now reflects. "On the contrary, he became an intruder, a rival for my mother's heart which was no longer all mine. I agonized over suppressed sensations of resentment which caused me great pain."

Some moments of special tenderness with her father did emerge, but future events would put an end to them. It was their mutual love of music that brought them together happily as she practiced. By the age of ten Renata was already singing in church but her passion was the piano. Her grandfather had seen to it that she had lessons. Her father sat with her, and advised and shared his musical experience with her.

Events were taking shape, however, during this same period, as Giuseppina attempted to rekindle her husband's affections, which would cause the separation of father and daughter for almost all of the rest of their lives. Giuseppina was compelled to undergo facial surgery. During the operation, the doctors said later, a short circuit in the operating room caused the surgeon to accidentally cut one of the patient's facial nerves. "She entered the hospital a beautiful woman and they disfigured her. They had ruined her, my beautiful mother! I was furious. But the damage was done and it was irreversible." Renata's sadness can still be felt as she talks about this tragic time.

Giuseppina interpreted her misfortune as fate's way of destroying her last hope for marital harmony. Her jealousy and suspicions were rekindled, and they were not unfounded. In Parma Teobaldo had already met a woman ten years his junior. In the customary fashion, Teobaldo denied the existence of this new liaison to his wife and continued to deny it to Renata during their painful dialogue in Parma when Renata went, with her mother's approval, to confront her father openly. His denials did not alter the facts and Teobaldo was again lost to his family, and this time permanently.

When World War II started he was sent to Albania. By the time he returned, mother and daughter were established in Milan. Giuseppina and Teobaldo never saw each other again.

❦ 3 ❦

The Piano
The Voice

In 1935, as Renata was finishing her studies at school, her mother suggested several options for the future. She could join her grandparents in their general store or work at their post office. The other option depended on the extent of her passion for the piano. Spoiled and a bit arrogant, faced with the first major responsibility of her life, she selected the most difficult road. The piano meant rising at five in the morning, travelling two hours on the train from Langhirano to the Parma Conservatory, and then retracing her steps. As Renata reminisces, she explains her decision by saying, "I wasn't interested in fun and dances, or in the flirtations of my age group, so I selected the only thing that interested me. Once I decided, the sacrifices seemed only natural and I didn't mind the difficulties I had brought upon myself."

Winters in Parma are severe. Her trip on foot to the fable-like little train was long and difficult. When the fresh snow was deep, Renata walked in the mailman's footsteps. But as she stepped into his newly-made prints, they were so far apart that she often stumbled and sank into the still crunchy snow, and was often soaked to the skin by the time she arrived at the railway platform which provided no shelter. Eventually a

14

van was put into service which stopped in front of her house, and everything became simpler.

Renata studied long hours; she had few friends her age. At home she amused herself by selecting her favorite outfits from any magazines available and then in front of the mirror, in her mother's dresses, she would play at being the "lady." Her mother and family remained the lifeblood of her existence.

She was tall, timid, and a bit awkward. She wasn't aware until much later that she had a stupendous face. After she became "Tebaldi," journalists around the world would rave about her perfect complexion, her extraordinary blue eyes, the characteristic dimples, and her raven-black hair. But that was all in the future. At this time, her alabaster skin caused her only painful sunburns and she hadn't learned to style her hair yet.

Still to come was the discovery of the "Tebaldi voice" which was to bewitch her audiences around the world for years to come. She was 17 when her piano teacher heard her sing and sensed her extraordinary talent. Arrangements were made for her audition at the Conservatory where she was immediately placed in the advanced group taught by the renowned Ettore Campogalliani, who was one of the most sought-after vocal teachers of the time.

Campogalliani said that Tebaldi "was a scrupulous, perceptive student animated by an immense passion for music. She studied hard and always kept a certain distance between herself and others."

After two years of vocal and piano lessons, Renata realized that sitting at the piano keyboard placed pressure on her diaphragm, diminishing her breath control. Therefore, she slowly turned more and more exclusively to singing, disappointing her mother who had dreams of her becoming a concert pianist.

The meeting that was to hasten the start of her superb

career was soon to take place. At Christmastime in 1940, Giuseppina and Renata went to Pesaro to visit her father's relatives. An aunt, proud of her niece's artistic talent, arranged an audition with Carmen Melis, then a teacher at the Rossini Conservatory.

This fine singer, who was born in Cagliari in 1885, had had a successful international career which included performances at La Scala and Covent Garden. Her most celebrated interpretations were the two *Manons, Salome,* Santuzza in *Cavalleria Rusticana* and Minnie in *La Fanciulla del West,* which she studied with Puccini himself.

Renata's aunt had met Carmen Melis often. She owned a bakery which had become the magnet for the gluttons of the city, and Carmen Melis was one, just as her future student was. She readily agreed to hear Renata. At first she was amused by Renata's regional accent and teased her about it. That quickly passed as she became totally enchanted by the sound of her extraordinary voice. She suggested that they study some scores together during Renata's visit to Pesaro. And they did.

After this brief interlude Renata returned to her studies with Campogalliani at the Conservatory in Parma. It was then that her fellow students, who knew her voice well, were overwhelmed as they listened behind closed doors and wondered who this "new singer" was. The time had come to choose between Parma and continuing her studies with her new mentor in Pesaro. The decision was an important one and Giuseppina, needing further assurance, decided that Riccardo Zandonai, the Director of the Conservatory in Pesaro, should be the final judge. At her audition Renata prophetically sang *"Ebben ne andró lontana"* from *La Wally.* After a brief, emotional silence the maestro replied to Giuseppina's query by saying that to restrain the career of such a superb talent would be tragic.

❧ 4 ❧

First Recital
First Audition at La Scala
First Love
First Debut

In Pesaro Renata found more freedom than Langhirano had offered. Although she continued "not to go dancing" ("I've always felt ill at ease because I like to lead"), she did spend long hours at the beach sunbathing. Her long years of illness had left her with a desperate yearning to strengthen her body, which led to future summer pilgrimages to the Grand Hotel in Rimini and the beautiful spas at Montecatini, Abano, and Salsomaggiore. In Pesaro she paid for those moments of pleasure with excruciatingly painful sunburns which her mother tried to soothe with compresses of oil and water. And she continued to study.

By 1943, the war forced the closing of the Conservatory and the Tebaldis fled to Cartoceto, a nearby town. Their new lodgings were in a cinema which had been partitioned and used by families who had fled the bombs. Here, too, Renata continued to study, accompanied at the piano by a young friend, Tilde Bezzicari. She and her friend decided one day to organize Renata's first solo appearance in public. It was winter; one could hear the snow crunching underfoot. Blackouts were in effect. When Renata appeared on the small stage of the beautiful but icy little theater, the spectators were warm-

17

ing their freezing hands on the heating pans in their laps. The magic effect of this first recital spread rapidly and it was followed by an official concert, with a real, though tiny salary, in Urbino, at the Teatro Raffaello Sanzio. Maestro Riccardo Zandonai, who had been so encouraging, conducted. With her first earnings she bought a white dress from a Milan shopkeeper who had taken refuge in Urbino.

It was during their stay in Cartoceto that Renata had her first contact with La Scala. A friend, Novi Mengaroni, who for years was the chief costumer at La Scala, arranged an audition for her. The theater had been bombed and badly damaged, and to reach the stage Renata had to walk on a wooden plank mounted over the debris. Mr. Mataloni, the impresario, Maestro Gatti, Tancredi Pasero, the bass, and others were present when she sang. She selected *"Tacea la notte placida"* from *Il Trovatore*. "We'll contact you," they said. But the war continued to intensify, and La Scala had no need of anyone.

As the fury of war worsened, Giuseppina feared isolation from the rest of her family and decided to return to Langhirano. After their difficult and dangerous return trip, they learned that their home had been commandeered to house the homeless, but Giuseppina's sister, Marianna, quickly welcomed them into her home in Traversetolo. "In spite of the inconvenience of lodgings too small for three people, I felt at home again. Everything was familiar to me. I returned to the sites of my childhood. Not far from Traversetolo was the country home of the Pedretti family where I had spent carefree vacations as a child. There were two children in the family. One of them, Antonio, was my age. When I saw him again, I felt reassured..." Renata muses nostalgically about this young man who was her first love. "He was a tall, wholesome youth with curly hair. He was studying medicine. He was also a partisan. With strength and courage he jeopardized everything and was forced to divide his time between

18

his studies and hiding in the woods. We fell in love almost without realizing it. We would meet whenever we could, always in terror of the Germans. I was tormented at the thought of his being discovered, and Antonio was always fearful of reprisals against me, his fiancée. Antonio's cousin and their friends used to say with good humored skepticism that Antonio was a fool to be engaged to someone who wants to be a singer."

For the moment Renata's career seemed to be set aside. In a land under attack and in flames, the unknown voice of Renata Tebaldi had become a tenuous flame. But Carmen Melis was watching over the career of her star pupil, and in the spring of 1944 she sent word to Renata that she had secured an engagement for her in a "real theater, in a real performance." She was referring to the role of Elena in Boito's *Mefistofele* at the Teatro Sociale in Rovigo. The superlative cast included Tancredi Pasero, Onelia Fineschi, and Francesco Albanese, with Giuseppe del Campo conducting. Excitement and feverish preparation erupted within the family. Renata was to be accompanied by her mother, whose long journey around the world with her daughter, the singer, was just beginning.

The 70-mile trip from Traversetolo to Rovigo was a disastrous one. The station at Parma had been machine-gunned and the one in Mantua was in flames. Renata and her mother were driven by wagon to the train in open country where they boarded it. On their return trip the train was attacked. They continued on a truck which was later requisitioned at a checkpoint, and they stood for hours on the side of the road waiting to be rescued. Martial law prohibited hitchhiking but a good Samaritan slowed his car so mother and daughter, while still running and tripping, holding on to their luggage, could jump in. The distressed Giuseppina vowed never to move from Traversetolo again until the war was over.

In spite of it all, on the evening of May 23rd, 1944, in

Rovigo, Renata Tebaldi made her official debut. It was sensational and immediately attracted her first fans. No one in the excited audience was aware that this historic debut had been in danger of not taking place. Already seated on Elena's throne, in all her dignity, Renata suffered her first moment of stage fright as she heard the rustling of the stage curtain. She frantically searched in the wings for an escape route but her eyes met, instead, the fiery gaze of Carmen Melis, who was there for her student's debut. Any further thought of flight was out of the question. Thus, riveted to her throne, Renata commenced her career.

The next day, the *Rovigo Daily* spoke of her "auspicious performance in the difficult role of Elena which signaled the prelude of a luminous career." The only protest was that a voice such as hers should have sung the role of Margherita, the protagonist, and not Elena, a secondary role. It was not long after that she made her debut in the role of Margherita, first at the Sport Palace in Milan on August 3rd, 1946, and then on February 8th, 1948, at the Teatro Regio, in Parma.

After the performance she was shown a wall plaque inscribed with the names of great singers who had sung at the theater. Two famous debuts which preceeded hers were of Beniamino Gigli and Rosetta Pampanini. The impresario's comment was, "One day we'll glory in your name, too," perhaps not fully realizing the extent of his prophecy. She smiled, almost frightened, unable to imagine it herself. With her earnings she paid for her room and board and for a rosary.

Later, in January of 1945, Renata made her debut as Mimi in *La Bohème* in Parma's Teatro Ducale. Tension and apprehension pervaded the atmosphere since Armando Borgioli, the baritone who was to have sung Marcello, was killed when his car was bombed on the Via Emilia as he was driving towards Parma. The baritone who replaced him in the role was injured alongside Armando Borgioli and sang with his nose bandaged. Mafalda Favero, with whom they had both sung a performance of *La Bohème* at the Cercano Theater in Milan the previous evening, was also in the automobile with them.

Despite the war, some opera performances continued in Italy. Parma's Teatro Regio was preparing brief, dazzling seasons with such names as Francesco Merli, Cloe Elmo, Onelia Fineschi, and the young Mario Del Monaco.

The renowned Teatro Regio beckoned Renata to its footlights in February of 1945, inviting her to sing Mimi in *La Bohème,* followed by two performances of *L'Amico Fritz* in April. On April 2nd, during the afternoon performance of *L'Amico Fritz,* Parma was under aerial attack. The objective of the bombings was the Mulinetto on the periphery of the city, but to zero in on the target, the bombs were launched over the theater. The journalist, Piermaria Paoletti, stationed himself by the little window of the restroom where he continuously assessed the danger and then, running into the theater, declared that all was well. As Renata and Luigi Infantino sang that the *"ciliege"* were *"giá mature,"* the whistle of the bombs could be heard splitting the air. Showing a contempt for life worthy of the great stoics of antiquity, the agitated audience encouraged them on with "Don't stop! Nothing will happen! We're watching!"

The following week Renata sang her first Maddalena in *Andrea Chénier* replacing Mercedes Fortunati who was a favorite in Parma. Fortunati was a beautiful blonde, graceful and appealing on stage. Renata was vulnerable in her inexperience. The blonde wig which was to cover her dark hair was not at all becoming. In the theater, groups of fans were determined to hinder the "intruder." As Renata sang, however, the explosive applause, not bombs or detractors, brought down the house. In September 1948, after her Maddalena debut at La Scala, the review in Milano's *Il Tempo* spoke of the superb interpretation of the soprano Renata Tebaldi, as Maddalena di Coigny, her marvelous vocal qualities, intelli-

21

gence, and dramatic impact, and the much deserved enthusiastic ovation.

It was very early in her career that Renata was to discover the intrigues of the theater. She was preparing to make her debut as Desdemona in *Otello* in Trieste in December of 1945. The musical director wanted to place his protégée in Renata's role. Two of her colleagues, Francesco Merli and Piero Biasini objected violently to the deception and, thanks to them, Renata continued with her debut. Furthermore, she was such a success that the management called her back at a later date to replace the protégée who was the cover for Franca Somigli as Maddalena in *Andrea Chénier* but with whom Maestro Quadri, the conductor, refused to work. So Renata returned to sing with only a piano rehearsal or two. For her debut performance as Desdemona Renata had not had time to have costumes made and Franca Somigli loaned her her costumes and every evening she arrived in her young colleague's dressing room to help her dress and make up.

"I already knew Tebaldi from my days in Pesaro," Mario Del Monaco, her Trieste Otello, recalls. "A cousin of hers and childhood friend of mine, Renato Alberini, had spoken to me about her. Since my career had already taken off a year or two earlier, he asked if I would hear her sing and give my opinion. I listened to Renata as I accompanied her on the piano. She sang '*L'altra notte in fondo al mare*' and '*Io sono l'umile ancella.*' Renata was about 20 years old then. I was immediately aware of a voice of incomparable purity and brilliance. I urged her to continue studying and told her that if she succeeded in achieving perfect uniformity throughout her vocal range, she would enter the operatic world as an exceptional singer. And so it was that a year or two later Renata made her operatic debut and her ascent was rapid, triumphant and inevitable. We were partners in many operas and concerts in the major theaters of the world, and the vast discography that we have left behind is testimony enough of

22

the compatibility of our voices and justification enough for our being internationally proclaimed the couple of the century."

During this time Renata was living in Parma with the Pagani family, patrons of the arts, who were devoted to helping young artists. "Those were happy days," Renata recalls. "My career was developing rapidly, and my stay at the Paganis spared me from having to eat at the opera canteen!"

The increasingly solid affirmations of her career put Renata face to face with the reality of settling in Milan. Her fiancé, Antonio, facilitated the move with some financial assistance. In Milan, Renata and her mother found lodgings with a woman who rented rooms at 13 Via Broggi. The landlady was from a fine, wealthy family, now in need of money. She was strange, rather unpleasant, and she never had any fondness for Renata. It annoyed her so when Renata's mother asked for the hot water heater that Giuseppina took to warming the bath water on a heater which she kept in their room.

❧ 5 ❧

The Audition with Toscanini
The Debut at La Scala

In 1945 the rite of passage for singers great and small was the Alci Agency of Liduino Bonardi on Via Mazzini and then Via Santa Radegonda in Milan. It was appropriately renamed "purgatory" by all who came to audition. Liduino appeared to them as the mythological Minos whose serpent's coils bound his trembling victims, and according to voice and talent assigned them to the various levels of Dante's *Inferno*. Their destinations were the modest stages of the provinces or the renowned theaters of the world. He determined salaries, settled contracts, assigned roles. Above all he was noted for his "combinations" which in record time launched many future stars. His tactics were well-known. "Do you want Onelia Fineschi? Then you'll take Tebaldi for two performances. She's young but she has a very beautiful voice," or "I'll give you Prandelli only if you give the young Di Stefano a performance. He'll make it if he has an opportunity to be heard."

A torrential rain accompanied Renata on the day of her audition with him. She was drenched and unnerved. After she sang, Liduino made, perhaps, the only blunder of his career. 1945 was a year of financial difficulties for him, and accepting Renata would have meant financing her studies, since she had no income. He decided against placing her under contract. With him, fortunately, were Messieurs Scalvini, Malinverni, and Gatti, as well as members of the agency. They quickly opposed his veto and the agency assumed responsibility for the young Tebaldi. Lessons were arranged for her with Maestro Giuseppe Pais, a fine gentleman and a musical expert. It would be Maestro Pais who would conduct Renata's Catania debut in *Tosca* in October 1946. The gears were beginning to turn—Parma, Genoa, Brescia, Catania, Bologna....

When Renata and Giacinto Prandelli were in Brescia singing *L'Amico Fritz*, the tenor was called for an audition with Arturo Toscanini, who had just returned from his political exile in America. Maestro Toscanini was searching for voices for the coming season at La Scala and for the gala concert inaugurating the newly rebuilt opera house. Following his audition, Prandelli received a telephone call informing him that the Maestro (as Toscanini was always called) had chosen him for Beethoven's Ninth and asked him to inform Renata Tebaldi that the Maestro would like to hear her as soon as she returned to Milan.

Renata has forgotten most of the details of her career, but she remembers every particular about that fateful Saturday. "I left the house that morning at eight o'clock for the short walk to La Scala. The audition was at ten. I took a longer, circuitous route trying to calm myself with agitated glances into store windows. At 9:30 I was in the Galleria with nowhere else to go. I finally summoned enough courage to approach the stage entrance. I was the first one there, soon followed by a few others who all seemed much calmer than I. We were asked to wait outside the Red Room. Promptly at ten an usher appeared, and asked for Renato Tebaldi. I jumped up, almost incensed at the indignity. 'There must be some mistake.... Renata, not Renato! I am Renata Tebaldi!' The usher was not impressed. My audition was the first and I was in an indescribable state. If I had had the courage, I would have taken to my heels and run, but instead, terrified and almost numb, I was escorted into the Red Room. The Maestro sat at the end of a long table with his son, Walter. Dr. Antonio Ghiringhelli, and, I believe, Dr. Luigi Oldani were seated near him. At that moment, I thought of my debut at the age of eight, when I sang and danced in the church wearing my beret with the red pompom. The Maestro asked me where I came from and with whom I had studied. Even though I felt lost, I felt that he was pleased with my answer (I, too, came from Parma, and I had studied with Carmen Melis). I sang 'La mamma morta' from Andrea Chénier since I had recently sung the role of Maddalena on stage and had it in my voice. I had decided before the audition that if the Maestro requested a second aria the battle would be almost won. When he did request another one, I joyfully proposed the 'Ave Maria' from Otello. The maestro glanced at me skeptically, almost annoyed, but made no comment."

In retrospect, the scene that followed might seem amusing, but at the time it was almost disastrous. Renata stood near the piano, facing the Maestro, and began. "I started with the recitative, 'La canzone del calice!' The Maestro was not satisfied with the accompanist's tempo and started correcting it with his hand. I adjusted quickly, but the pianist had his back to the Maestro. My accompanist tried desperately to warn me that we were not together and, in turn, I rolled my eyes towards the Maestro hoping to make my accompanist aware of the Maestro's wishes. At last, the accompanist realized the problem and slowly shifted the piano and his beat. With God's mercy, it was finally over."

Silence followed. Then the Maestro motioned to his son, Walter, to make note of Tebaldi's name. He turned to her and said the now famous "Brava! Brava!"

Maestro Del Campo was outside the door waiting to hear

the outcome of Renata's audition. He was in a wheelchair, paralyzed, but still a fine music coach. He had been her musical godfather, conducting her Rovigo debut. Now, he was the first to know that Toscanini had accepted her.

"My joy was such that as slowly as I had walked to my audition, now I wanted to fly home, and the tram seemed to crawl." Renata knew that the first big trial of her life had been won, and she wished to share her joy with her mother who was at home praying for her. The happiness shared in Via Broggi on that day can only be imagined.

Two days after the audition Toscanini's secretary informed her that the Maestro wanted her for the inaugural concert at the newly rebuilt La Scala. She would sing the Prayer from *Moses* by Rossini and Verdi's *Te Deum*. In the *Te Deum* she had an entrance marked "a voice from heaven" where she was to pick up the trumpet's last note. She was standing in the midst of a double chorus on risers. After repeated rehearsals, Toscanini still was not satisfied. He decided to place Renata at the top above the chorus. "I want this voice of an angel to truly descend from heaven!" he exclaimed. With his words, Renata's Tebaldi's legendary "voice of an angel" was born.

The concert at La Scala was heard around the world via radio and in Milano's Piazza del Duomo via loudspeakers. The piazza was overflowing with people enthusiastically waiting to share in this historic musical event.

It had been with great sadness that Renata first viewed the destruction caused by a bomb and fire which left the roof and interior of her beloved opera house destroyed. The rebuilding was accomplished in less than two years. She was overjoyed at the sight of the faithful reconstruction by architects who meticulously followed the original design down to the last detail. One insurmountable problem was the replacement of wood panels carved by artisans of the past. In fact, the acoustics were not as exceptional as in the old house.

Emotions ran high on the evening of the inauguration, and the audience erupted in rapturous applause as Toscanini appeared at exactly 9 p.m. with a tricolored baton in hand. An interminable ovation left him so moved that he remained motionless for a long time on the podium facing his audience. "It was an evening of unforgettable emotions and long ovations," Renata reminisces. Franco Abbiati of the *Corriere della Sera* wrote that Toscanini united the audience in a spiritual and joyful frenzy, and they responded with an overwhelming outburst of admiration.

At the inauguration supper after the concert, Renata was seated next to the Maestro, as he had requested. Soon after, he arranged for her to sing the Verdi *Requiem*. He followed her career closely and convinced her to prepare *Aida*. To this day, Renata proudly displays Toscanini's framed letter with his affectionate dedication to her on her grand piano at home in Milan.

After the triumph of that memorable evening came Renata's first disillusionment. She was contracted to sing two performances of Maddalena in *Andrea Chénier* at the Lyric Theater in Milan. The arrangements had been made by a company that, unknown to her, was on its way to bankruptcy. According to custom, artists were paid halfway through a performance, during the first or second intermission. Unfortunately, during the first performance payment wasn't made until the end of the evening and Renata, not wanting to miss the last tram home, left quickly expecting to collect for both performances during the second one. By then bankruptcy had been declared, and the management had fled with the cash. The Lyric Theater management, in spite of it all, decided that the show would go on, and Renata sang two performances gratis.

At La Scala Renata quickly plunged into an active schedule. During its short summer season at the Palazzo dello Sport, she sang Elena, the role of her debut in Rovigo. In subse-

28

quent performances she replaced Onelia Fineschi in the role of Margherita, the protagonist in *Mefistofele*. She also sang Elsa in *Lohengrin*, after her debut in the role at the Teatro Regio in Parma in January of 1946. Her performance of Elsa was described in *L'Avvenire d'Italia* on March 15th, 1948, as "exquisitely delicate and caressingly melodious in its subtleties," and again on July 5th, 1949, in *Momento-Sera,* as "magnificent for her vigorous, intensive breath capacity, and brilliant tone color."

Early in her career Renata already had fans who waited for her at the stage entrance to see and greet this vocal phenomenon in person. She would smilingly thank them as she tried to free herself quickly in order to catch the last tram home. Her lifestyle was still so uncomplicated that she continued to pack the few necessary items in a simple carry-all net of the sort popular soon after the war.

It was already evident, however, that the meteoric rise of her brilliant career would have no limits and, as a result, she was faced with the distressing dilemma of deciding between her love for Antonio Pedretti and her love for her art.

❧ 6 ❧

Nicola Rossi-Lemeni
The Arena di Verona
Lisbon: The Joyful First Tour

The moment had arrived when Antonio, the fiancé she had left behind in Parma, confronted Renata with having to make a decision. Now an established physician, Antonio was eager to have her near him, to marry, have children, and live tranquilly amidst all that had been precious and familiar to them since childhood. But Renata's destiny was to sing, and she expressed this openly and emotionally to him. It was a moment of gentle communication and great sadness which ended with their parting. Renata suffered as she left him, but she never questioned her decision. She was too completely involved in her future and there was no time for regrets.

Her engagements became increasingly pressing and she had many roles to learn. This was the period of *Otello*, *Lohengrin*, *Mefistofele*, *Tosca*, *Andrea Chénier*, and Verdi's *Te Deum*. Her debuts in *I Maestri Cantori*, *Faust*, and *Lohengrin* were imminent. In May of 1947 Renata sang the role of Eva in *I Maestri Cantori* at La Scala. Soon after, during the summer season at the Arena di Verona, Renata sang her first Margherita in Gounod's *Faust*. That same season at the arena Maria Callas sang her first Gioconda.

Vulnerable because of her recent painful break with Antonio, Renata quickly was attracted by the attentions of a new suitor. The festive atmosphere of the opera season heightened her susceptibility to this attractive colleague, Nicola Rossi-Lemeni. He was a fascinating artist as well as a fine bass, and, above all, he was entertaining and gallant. Whenever Renata and Nicola walked together in the square they aroused pleasurable curiosity among the townspeople.

For the young Renata emerging from a sentimental heartache and now completely devoted to her music, this new suitor was a cure with no side effects. He seemed ideal for her. Using every approach available to him to his advantage, including the artful costumes of Mefistofele, he strove to win over his guileless Margherita on stage and off. Verona, with its legendary, pervasive romanticism, provided him with a more than adequate backdrop.

Nicola's father was Italian. His mother, capricious and authoritarian, was Russian and boasted of Romanoff ancestry. Nourishing an obsessive love for her only son, she laid down a rigid schedule for him, especially his evening curfew. Although her control was confining, Nicola did nothing to free himself. Any intrusion in this mother-son relationship would have been unwelcome, and Renata, inexperienced and respectful, would not dream of doing battle with such a rival. In spite of this, their relationship ran its happy course, helped along by their many professional engagements together. In Florence it was Rossi-Lemeni in *Khovanshchina* and Renata in *Lohengrin,* Rome heard them together in *Mefistofele* in the Summer of 1948, and they sang *Tannhäuser* in Naples, Trieste, and Venice later that year. All this served as the inspirational setting for the various stages of their love. The two mothers were in the wings, Renata's looking on with sorrowful insight, while Nicola's mother cast a shadow of continuous and aggressive disapproval on him.

Then unexpectedly Nicola met Vittoria Serafin, the daughter of the celebrated Maestro Serafin. She was beautiful, so-

31

phisticated, self-assured, a member of the international jet set. When she saw Nicola it was love at first sight. Whether or not his mother would make Vittoria welcome in their home did not concern her. When artistic commitments took Nicola to Buenos Aires for the opera season at the Colon Opera House, Vittoria followed him. Vittoria's courage gave him the freedom he had never before enjoyed. On their way home from Argentina, they visited Mexico and were married there.

Since theirs had been a lighthearted affair, the relationship between Renata and Nicola changed without anger into a cordial friendship, especially when Renata took the first steps to reassure him. Vittoria, who was accustomed to jealous feuds between women, was suspicious and reserved, but Renata knew how to calm her fears. Vittoria's love story was not "forever after" however. It came to an end in 1957 when the irresistible green eyes of the soprano, Virginia Zeani, singing Cleopatra to Nicola's Antony in Handel's *Giulio Cesare*, stole his heart. They were married in Milan in church since his Mexican marriage to the divorced Vittoria was not valid in Italy. While Maestro Serafin found many opportunites to unleash his fury against his ex son-in-law on stage during performances, Renata, ironically, was the one person with whom Vittoria confided during her moments of marital anguish.

In November of 1947 Renata began a long-lasting artistic partnership and affectionate friendship with Carlo Bergonzi. Renata sang Mimi in Catania and her former fellow-student from the Parma Conservatory sang Marcello. Carlo Bergonzi started his career as a baritone, but soon changed to tenor roles, and he and Renata became partners through a lifetime of performances. Renata has many fond memories of carefree New Year's Eves spent at the Bergonzi inn and restaurant, I Due Foscari, in Busseto, Verdi's hometown. In the company of good friends, surrounded by an abundance of delectable dishes and sipping champagne, they would frolic and sing until dawn, and then, happy and exhausted, they would all finally retire.

1947 was the year Renata debuted as Violetta, and later as Elizabeth in *Tannhäuser*. She sang *La Traviata* in Catania in November of that year, followed by further performances in Parma, Venice, Bologna, Ravenna, and in February of 1948 in Naples. Her audition the previous year with Maestro Francesco Siciliani, the artistic director of the San Carlo Opera, and Pasquale Di Costanzo, the manager, clinched her 1948 debut in Naples. The two men were enchanted immediately by the young singer's appearance, and they became profoundly moved when she started to sing. Maestro Siciliani engaged her on the spot for *La Traviata* and with a bold move he engaged her for *Tannhäuser* as well.

"Renata entered the audition hall dressed in a simple blouse and white frock," Siciliani recalled. "She wore her hair loose, no trace of makeup on her face. An expression of intelligence and candor permeated her being. It seemed to me that I was witnessing the entrance of Elizabeth in *Tannhäuser*. It was as though she were the personification of sacred love. Most important of all was that her voice was perfect for the role. It was extraordinary and gifted with natural pitch and color." In spite of his very favorable first impression, engaging a young and unknown Tebaldi for *Tannhäuser* (especially since Karl Böhm was conducting) seemed quite hazardous, and so it appeared to Di Costanzo. After the audition, Siciliani and Di Costanzo walked out together. Finally, a very taciturn Di Costanzo stopped, turned and asked, "Maestro are you absolutely sure about this Tebaldi? You know, we have Maria Caniglia, and Ebe Stignani at San Carlo. We're spoiled." "Don't worry, Commendatore, trust me," was Siciliani's reply. They resumed walking but soon Di Costanzo stopped again. "Maestro, are you engaging someone for the opera or for the cinema?" "Commendatore, you're absolutely right. Tebaldi would be perfect for films,

but don't worry, she'll be perfect for your opera house, too...."
Many years later, the renowned Karl Böhm admitted to Maestro Siciliani that there had been many Elizabeths, but he
had never been able to find another one like Tebaldi!

After her debut as Desdemona in Verdi's *Otello* at the
Teatro Verdi in Trieste on December 30th, 1945, many other
glorious performances followed in Bologna, Venice, Rome,
Verona, Caracalla and Cesena. In February of 1949, for her
debut as Desdemona, La Scala presented Tebaldi with a star-
studded cast which included Ramon Vinay and Gino Bechi,
under the baton of Vittorio De Sabata. "A performance conducted by De Sabata started punctually but never ended at
the same time. Maestro De Sabata was very capricious with
his *tempi* and every evening was a surprise...," Renata recalls.

Ramon Vinay was her Otello again that summer at the
Arena di Verona. It was during a third-act rehearsal that the
Chilean tenor, a man of great temperament, flung himself
with such force on Renata during the *"Giura e ti danna!"*
that she fell like a dead weight on the edge of the steps. Her
pain was so great that the words, *"Esterefatta fisso,"* never
left her throat. Vinay, realizing what he had done, was so
mortified that during subsequent performances he attempted
to make amends by excessive kindness and special attention.
To keep her from sliding off the bed in her satin nightgown,
he suggested that she be tied to the bed in the last act, as she
lay there suffocated. While he stood over her, strangling her
ferociously, he whispered warmly, "Renata, you sang like an
angel."

There was much preparation for her first tour abroad to
Lisbon, scheduled for March 1949. Her new audience would
hear her in *Faust*, the *Stabat Mater* of Rossini, *Falstaff*, and
La Traviata. During their tour in Lisbon, the Italian colleagues
got along beautifully. Giulio Neri, the bass, was one of the
biggest pranksters in the world of opera, playing countless

tricks, and everyone at one time or another became his victim. Most common were the plastic flies and cockroaches which showed up in someone's soup. Occasionally his pranks were very embarrassing, such as the noise-maker he placed under Renata's chair in the last act of *La Traviata*. *"Oh! come son mutata! Ma il Dottor a sperar pure m'esorta!"* Renata sang with heartrending emotion as she looked in the mirror of her dressing table, but as she sat down she heard odd sounds and understood quickly that this time the joke was on *her*. While her fellow singers were splitting their sides with laughter in the wings, she was forced to proceed with *"Ah, con tal morbo ogni speranza e' morta!"* She continued with *"Addio del passato,"* barely touching the seat of her chair. When Annina arrived to advise her of Alfredo's imminent arrival, she sprang from her seat with a rapidity and enthusiasm seldom seen on any stage!

In those early years of stardom Renata had many happy experiences. The occasional painful experience emerged, too. In the Summer of 1950, the Arena in Verona set the stage for the first tumultuous experience of her career. Always concerned about her partner's height, she was reassured by the management that Giacinto Prandelli would be her tenor in *Mefistofele*. Renata's concern was justified. Being five feet nine inches tall, she was frequently embarrassed by having to sing next to a "short partner." She feared that the lovers, one tall and one short, would evoke hilarity rather than tenderness in the audience. As luck would have it, pressure on the theater's management resulted in the replacement of Prandelli with a local favorite, who was short. Even though the stage director attempted a solution for the duet sung by Faust and Margherita in the garden, the result was grotesque. He had the tenor stand next to the well where he could lift himself onto its base as Renata remained firmly anchored to the floor. Unfortunately, he was not only short of leg, he was also short of voice. By then, the conductor, Maestro Capuana, resigned in protest. A more daring Maestro Questa, substituting for Capuana, refused to conduct if the tenor remained. Forced to recall Prandelli, the management discovered that he had already accepted an engagement with the Rome Opera. After much pleading by the management and altruism on the part of the Rome Opera, Prandelli was released from his contract and departed quickly for Verona, arriving just in time for the performance.

Meanwhile, in the wings, word had spread about the soprano's refusal to sing with the tenor because he was too short, and some of the townspeople pointed at her as they called her the "tall one." Their resentment surfaced in the arena on opening night of the 28th season. Many agitators were present in the audience, and they turned the scene into mass confusion. The police had to be called in to restore order, and the house lights were left on during the entire first act. The scandalous behavior finally ended during Act III as Renata sang Margherita's aria, "*L'altra notte in fondo al mare.*" A calmer audience finally noticed that the "notorious" Tebaldi sang superlatively. The huge amphitheater erupted into thunderous admiration as the audience pleaded for an encore. Her adoring fans admonished indignantly, "Don't! They don't deserve an encore!" Even though Renata did grant a repeat of the aria, she did not step into the Arena again until 1957.

Another Verdi opera which could not remain outside Tebaldi's repertory for long was *Aida*—her voice had all the necessary volume, the color, and the *chiaroscuro* that the complex role called for. La Scala suggested the opera to Renata, and Toscanini convinced her to sing it. The Maestro asked her to come to his home in Via Durini with her score.

"I know why you're hesitating," he said. "You're worrying about the *recitativi*, and 'Ritorna vincitor.' The *concertati* bother you. You feel at home, instead, in the second and third acts...." And that was exactly how she felt. "It's an

36

opera for you," he insisted, and then added, "Aida is not a fiery, passionate woman. She's a gentle person. Until now this role has never been interpreted as Verdi wrote it. Everyone insists on expressing dramatic intensity by agitated and loud singing. What is needed is nostalgia, expression and diction! Aida is not a heroic role, it's a human one. If you understand this, you'll sing the role of Aida as it should be sung."

Renata had already studied the score with Carmen Melis. Now, in order to approach the technical difficulties gradually, she studied the opera backwards, starting with the fourth act first.

La Scala added *Aida* to its roster for Tebaldi on the 12th of February, 1950. The unmatchable cast included Mario Del Monaco, Fedora Barbieri, Cesare Siepi, and Raffael de Falchi, with Antonino Votto conducting. The outcome was a triumph. Tebaldi sang seven performances. Because of engagements in Lisbon, she was unable to sing the last three performances scheduled, and was replaced by Maria Callas, the "new one" about whom much was being said, who by then had married and added Meneghini to her name.

❦7❧

1950: First Tour of La Scala Abroad
An Admirer: Ernestina Viganò
San Francisco Debut

The first post-war tour abroad to Edinburgh and London was planned by La Scala for September 1950. It was a giant move which included the entire orchestra, chorus, corps de ballet, soloists, plus carpenters, electricians, technicians, and La Scala's personal photographer. Three conductors, Vittorio De Sabata, Guido Cantelli, and Ernesto Capuana, also travelled with the group. A very ambitious program was prepared which, for Renata, included *Otello*, *Aida*, the Verdi *Requiem*, and the Mozart *Requiem*. Opening night was reserved for Tebaldi in *Otello* opposite Ramon Vinay and Gino Bechi.

The sensational outcome of Renata's London debut left her with a firm following which through the years has continued to grow. Recently invited to England by London Records, Tebaldi was thrilled to discover that not only were her many fans from the past there to greet her, but that so many young admirers were among the many honoring her.

From the time Renata debuted in Rovigo, when her career began to take her further and further away from home, Renata's mother became her travel companion. She would help with Renata's costumes, her hair, and her makeup. She became a familiar sight in the wings during Renata's performances, with her rosary in one hand and a red horn for good luck in the other. Renata's fans had become numerous and always more enthusiastic, and her mother assumed the responsibility of shielding her daughter whenever necessary. The fans could be found everywhere, particularly at every stage door, with flowers, gifts, smiles, and joyful enthusiasm.

A member of this ever-growing group was a thin, shy girl from Monza called Tina Viganò. Always accompanied to La Scala by her brother she would slip into the family circle and listen with score in hand, often unable to see any part of the stage. So it happened with a performance of *Otello*. She had no idea who was singing, but as soon as she heard the first notes sung by the soprano, *"Mio superbo guerrier,"* in the duet of Act I, Tina immediately recognized the voice as the one she had heard only once before during a radio broadcast of *La Bohème*. "It was unmistakably that voice, unlike any other! Impossible not to recognize!" was Tina's emphatic response.

Once she knew the soprano's name, she never missed a Tebaldi performance in Italy. She also could be found at the pier, at the airport, at the train station waiting to see her favorite soprano as she arrived home from out of town. One evening after a performance, as Renata was leaving the theater, Tina offered her a drawing of Saint Cecilia, the patron saint of singers, which she had sketched. Tebaldi was amazed to learn that this unassuming admirer was a remarkably talented miniaturist.

Anyone visiting Tebaldi today sees evidence of Tina's art. A marvelous portrait of Tebaldi as Desdemona is on the grand piano amidst her many cherished photographs and other memorabilia such as an inscribed photograph of Puccini and one of Tebaldi at the White House with President and Mrs. John Kennedy.

"Tina's art is very good." Renata says, "She has so many

other paintings inside. In America she was offered a great deal of money for a professional production, but she wasn't interested." Renata calls to Tina to bring in some of her drawings and Tina appears with several sketches, many of them reproductions of famous paintings. She is equally comfortable with pastels and watercolors. Tina replies to the many questions and amazement with "I've studied a bit, and I've learned."

Then tea is served ("Would you prefer cocoa? Tina has a special recipe.") with delicious pies and pastries all baked by Tina who worked in a bakery for thirteen years. She also cooks, drives, packs, irons expertly, gives injections, cares for the dog, and wraps Christmas presents beautifully. She even paints the shutters ("La Signorina doesn't want me to because she's afraid I'll fall, but I do it anyway."), cleans the windows, and washes the leaves of the many plants sent as expressions of continuous devotion to Tebaldi by her fans. Tina is a skilled dressmaker; she sews everything by hand.

In America Tina had great fun sewing all the tiny outfits for New II, Renata's poodle, matching the costumes worn by his mistress on stage. New II even had a little western outfit put together from the leather cuttings left from Tebaldi's costume as Minnie in *La Fanciulla del West,* holster and pistol included. The success of the outfit almost rivalled Tebaldi's on stage. The cast members clamored for photographs with New. One Christmas Tina even made a Santa Claus costume for New including a red hood trimmed with white fur. On Christmas morning she sent New in, dressed as Santa, to waken Renata, as he carried her Christmas present in his mouth. But all that was yet to come.

It was not until several years after Tina had introduced herself to Renata that she, by then a diva at the Metropolitan Opera House, would receive a letter from Ernestina Viganò and a photograph of herself dressed as a maid with the inscription, "This is my dream." At first bewildered,

Renata soon started to consider employing this strange, discreet girl who was persistent but was always respectful and loyal. Renata's mother was an obstacle to be overcome since she had become Renata's factotum and guarded that responsibility tenaciously. In the opera houses she was known as the gendarme. To Renata's amazement, as soon as she mentioned Tina's name, Mamma Tebaldi was in agreement. Tina left for America with Renata in January 1957, and has never left her side since.

In 1950, however, after her great success with La Scala in England, Tebaldi embarked on her first journey across the ocean for her American debut in San Francisco, accompanied only by her mother. She had been contacted, sight unseen, by Gaetano Merola, the artistic director of the San Francisco Opera. After hearing one of her recordings, he was convinced that what he had heard was enough to judge a voice like hers. The contract was for *Aida* and *Otello*.

Tebaldi and her mother arrived in San Francisco with mixed emotions. There was the exhilaration of her American debut. There was also the emptiness of not knowing the language amidst new surroundings. They had no friends or interests other than her singing engagements. Renata was not fond of parties or of public appearances. Although Renata's photographs appeared in all the newspapers, she, gently but firmly, never allowed anything to be known about her beyond her date and place of birth, the famous story of Toscanini dubbing her the voice of an angel, and her debut at La Scala.

"It was difficult to remain in my shell," Tebaldi would say later. "In New York, too, invitations would pile up. At first, for a while, I attended some cocktail parties, receptions, dinner parties. I would meet many celebrities from the arts, politics, and the jet set. But as a rule the talk was superficial and impersonal, and, therefore, uninteresting to me. I soon made up my mind that this life was not for me and that everyone should know quickly. I began to turn down all invitations. At first people were annoyed. Later they accepted me as I am and everything went well." This became Tebaldi's way of life throughout her entire career.

Renata plunged into preparations for her *Aida* debut, scheduled for September 26. The cast included Mario Del Monaco, Elena Nikolai, Robert Weede, and Italo Tajo, and was conducted by Fausto Cleva. As always after rehearsals were completed, Tebaldi's ritual of withdrawing into herself a day or two prior to a debut performance began, and she would remain alone and nurture her role. Rudolf Bing, the director of the Metropolitan Opera, landed in San Francisco on the evening before the first *Aida*. The following evening, Bing poked his head into Tebaldi's dressing room, exclaimed "Wonderful!" and offered her a contract with the Metropolitan for two unscheduled, non-subscription performances inserted for her during the season already in progress. Tebaldi, astute enough to understand that making her debut at the Metropolitan Opera House in midseason would deprive her of all the advance publicity appropriate for such an event, promptly replied, "I don't feel quite ready yet, but I certainly look forward to singing in your theater in the near future." The words, accompanied by the twenty-eight-year-old singer's radiant smile, captivated the renowned impresario who later reverentially dubbed her *"primadonna assoluta."* He was referring not only to her exceptional voice but also to the strength of character concealed by her winning, dimpled smile which he, from then on, jestingly called "iron dimples."

Renata recalls the delightful visit to Hollywood and 20th Century Studios during her stay in Los Angeles. Her guide was her frequent stage partner and popular tenor, Giuseppe Di Stefano, or "Pippo" as he was affectionately called by his friends. The singers were received by Danny Kaye who, at one point, began singing a parody of *La Bohème* in their honor, with hilarious results! At the studio Renata finally met the man who would have been a perfect stage partner for her, at least in height. She beamed at Gregory Peck as she took in his tall, slender frame and ecstatically proclaimed, "He's endless!"

Richard Conti, Jennifer Jones, and Betty Grable were also there to meet the singers. Mario Lanza invited Renata to hear the soundtrack of *The Great Caruso*. Of that experience she says, "His voice split the air" and he was "spectacular." Of her meeting with Joan Fontaine Renata fondly remembers, "I had always considered her the most feminine of actresses, and when she said 'How do you do' in her deep voice, I was floored!" (Tebaldi had never heard her real voice in films, and the voice dubbed in Italian was higher-pitched).

After this first thrilling American experience of 1950, Renata's homeward passage was booked on the *Saturnia*, departing from New York. During the crossing the ship ran into a hurricane and their arrival in Naples was delayed two days. Waiting for her at the pier was the chauffeured limousine sent by Pasquale Di Costanzo, the director of the San Carlo Opera, and she was rushed off to Naples for rehearsals. She was to sing the Verdi *Requiem* on December 6 at the Teatro San Carlo with a cast including Ebe Stignani, Gianni Poggi, and Nicola Rossi-Lemeni, under the baton of Tullio Serafin.

A second, non-subscription performance of the Verdi *Requiem* was added to satisfy the endless demand for tickets. The second performance took place on December 7, in the church of San Francesco di Paola, with the same cast that had sung at San Carlo.

For the young soprano, 1950 ended triumphantly as she sang Desdemona in *Otello* on opening night, December 26, at La Scala in Milan.

❦ 8 ❧

1951: The Fateful Year
La Traviata at La Scala

1951, one of the most pivotal years of Tebaldi's career, brought her many triumphs and some distress. The year started busily in Milan with performances of *Otello*, *La Bohème*, and *Andrea Chénier* (with Filippeschi and Tagliabue), followed by *La Traviata* also at La Scala on February 1st.

La Traviata was not a new opera for Renata. After her November 1947 debut in Catania, she performed it again in 1948 in Parma, Venice, Bologna, Ravenna, and Rome (with dazzling success, singing with Giacinto Prandelli and Carlo Tagliabue), and then in Lisbon in 1950. The music critic, Guido Pannain, did include some negative opinions in *Tempo* (April 16, 1948) when he wrote, "Without a doubt, Renata Tebaldi has unique talent but also some serious weaknesses. She excels in her high and low notes but is weak in her middle range. She has a beautiful voice, thrilling, powerful high notes, exquisite and expressive subtle colors (*mezze tinte*) and velvet-like phrasing. But her voice is unpleasantly uneven; her middle range is without resonance, particularly in the transition passages. But she is young; she has temperament, and if she trains herself well, she will not fail." A few years later, the same critic triumphantly set the record straight, "Tebaldi is truly an exceptional singer.... She must have treasured the advice we directed at her from these pages." For *La Traviata* at La Scala, the Rome cast was reassembled, with Maestro De Sabata conducting. Along with preparations for this opera, Renata also had two performances of the Verdi *Requiem*, preceded by two performances of *Andrea Chénier* in Naples, on the 18th and 20th of January. As a consequence, her voice was placed into the *verismo* repertory and then the Verdi repertory, causing a shuffling of difficult "*messe in gola*," or placement of the roles in the voice.

Rehearsals at La Scala followed one another in a frenetic, difficult pace. On the 27th of January *La Traviata* was rehearsed in the afternoon; that evening the first of two performances of the *Requiem* was performed. The second followed on the 29th of January. *La Traviata* was scheduled for the first of February with a general rehearsal on the 30th of January. Maestro De Sabata realized what a burden such a tight schedule would be for the soprano. He moved the first *Traviata* to February 3rd. The dress rehearsal was held on February 1st and was a splendid success. "Your Tebaldi really outdid herself this time!" the music coach reported to her waiting fans at the stage entrance. The rehearsal had been closed to the public.

The vocal and physical stress Renata had been under surfaced on the evening of the first performance. It was an unlucky performance from the start. Champagne corks that went flying into the orchestra pit during the "*Brindisi*" stirred some laughter. Scenery fell on two stagehands, causing concern, and the prima ballerina made her entrance gliding on her buttocks during the gypsy dance in Act III. Since Tebaldi was wearing a diadem, necklace, and bracelet of diamonds and rubies which had belonged to a tsarina, a substantial number of policemen were in the theater, increasing the tension.

Tebaldi missed the two *gioir* in Act I. Then in the last act her voice cracked in the A of the "*Addio del passato*," an

45

aria which had always been one of her most successful. There were no protests, only murmurs of surprise and disappointment.

"That was even more painful for me. It was as though I had betrayed my audience, and they, out of love for me, dared not express disapproval...." Renata's reaction to this first unfortunate incident of her career was drastic: absolute rest and then a *"remessa in gola"* from the beginning. She cancelled her remaining performances of *La Traviata* and the scheduled performances of *Aida*. More than a month passed before she resumed them.

"I wasn't running away, nor was I afraid of the role," Tebaldi explains. "In fact, I mounted the same horse that had thrown me, and when I returned to the stage, thanks also to Pasquale Di Costanzo of the San Carlo Opera who had faith in me and offered me the opportunity, I sang *La Traviata* again and it was the most beautiful I had ever sung."

Di Costanzo's admiration for Tebaldi bordered on affection. ("Was he in love with me? Yes, most probably he was. His attentions toward me went beyond the ordinary, even if his behavior was always professional. Di Costanzo gave his heart to the theater.") For this *Traviata* he wanted a sensational production. It was his idea to cover the drop curtain with fresh camellias and Di Costanzo, himself, worked with the others to attach them to the curtain. The costumes were sumptuous.

"But even more extraordinary were the stage sets of *La Traviata* at the Arena Flegrea a year or two later," says Tebaldi. "I can't remember anything like it in my entire career. Elegant horse-drawn carriages were driven through double rows of cypress trees. It was more like a movie set than a stage performance!"

After the *La Traviata* incident, Renata Tebaldi's return to the stage in March created a great deal of suspense. A colleague who had eyes on the role for herself showed up in Mr.

Di Costanzo's office to inform him that in case Tebaldi should cancel ("You never can tell after what happened at La Scala!"), she would be standing by to step in. Her "generosity" was rather poorly received by Di Costanzo, who got rid of her brusquely, while making, as any good Neapolitan would, all the necessary incantations to ward off bad luck. The contract called for four performances. Including those sung in 1952, there was a total of 16 performances of *La Traviata*.

One mishap did occur in one of the later performances, but it was not vocal. In the second act, after the duet with Germont in the garden, Renata was in danger of losing her skirt and ending up in her *panier*. It was a very delicate situation. Violetta had just made the greatest sacrifice of her life by renouncing her beloved Alfredo. The moment had come to write the horrendous letter which would reunite her with the Baron. Violetta was desperate and as she prepared to sing the climactic point of the opera, "*Amami Alfredo,*" it certainly was not time to be caught in one's underwear! Renata's mother, who always watched from the wings, understood the problem and quickly called the dressmaker. Tebaldi remained boldly seated in front of Germont until "*Siate felice, addio.*" Then, taking advantage of a pause, she rushed offstage holding onto her skirt with both hands. She was pinned back together again just in time for her tempestuous entrance as she sang "*Dammi tu forza o cielo!*" No one in the audience was ever aware of the problem. The tension was not interrupted and "*Amami Alfredo*" was sung with the perfect balance of pathos and pain.

Reminiscing about *La Traviata* Renata explains that "*Amami Alfredo*" must be prepared for, both musically and dramatically; it must be a crescendo of tensions concluding in a final outburst. "*Amami Alfredo*" must incite an encore just as Cavaradossi's "*Vittoria*" in the second act of *Tosca* must. The encore need not be granted, but even if it is sung better than the first time, the result is always less successful, precisely because the dramatic tension is missing."

In June the San Carlo Opera went to Paris for the 50th anniversary of the death of Verdi. (It was the first foreign opera company to be invited to the Paris Opera after World War II.) Renata Tebaldi sang the title role in *Giovanna d'Arco,* as well as performances of the Verdi *Requiem* at the Church of the Madeleine. Again, Di Costanzo paid special attention to Renata. It was his wish that Joan of Arc in the Paris Opera posters resemble Renata. After the first Paris performance of *Giovanna d'Arco,* Georges Braque, the French cubist painter, could be seen applauding wildly amidst a thrilled audience.

❦9❦

The South American Tour
The Callas-Tebaldi Feud Begins

After their first very casual meeting at the Arena di Verona in August 1947, contact between Maria Callas and Renata Tebaldi was rare and impersonal. In January of the following year, at the Fenice Theater in Venice where Tebaldi was singing *La Traviata*, she heard Callas in *Tristan*. She went backstage to congratulate her, saying generously, "If I had sung that role, I would have come apart at the seams." In October, in Rovigo, their performances alternated between Callas in *Aida* and Tebaldi in *Chénier*. In 1950 Tebaldi sang several performances of *Aida* at La Scala, and Callas sang later ones after Tebaldi left town.

Rio de Janeiro became their battleground. They were on tour with a group of young, but already well-known, Italian artists. The occasion was a benefit concert organized by Barreto Pinto, the impresario and owner of several opera houses in Brazil. That evening Paolo Silveri, the baritone, and Boris Christoff, the bass, were singing with the two sopranos. Tebaldi and Callas, and later Gianbattista Meneghini in his book, gave their versions of the facts, which were contradictory. Callas said, "We had agreed; in fact, Tebaldi suggested that we not sing any encores. Then, when the audience

49

wanted one after her aria, she gave them two!" Tebaldi's reply to this: "We hadn't agreed on anything and when the audience wanted an encore, I agreed. That Callas later decided not to follow suit was no concern of mine."

That incident was followed by the famous dinner at a restaurant. Tebaldi and her mother were seated at the table of Elena Nicolai, the mezzo-soprano. When Callas and Meneghini entered, Elena invited them to sit at her table, too. The Callas version of what happened: "Renata started to talk about her unfortunate *Traviata* and to speak badly of La Scala, which I found exceedingly unpleasant since I was making my official debut there three months later." Tebaldi said, "Callas started judging my *Traviata* at La Scala, saying that she was upset by what had happened, then giving me advice on how to sing. In fact, she advised me not to sing *La Traviata* at all, and to sing fewer performances in general, since it is best to make an audience desire you. She became so loud that Meneghini occasionally poked her arm to calm her, but without success."

La Traviata, Aida, and *Tosca* were the three operas in which Callas and Tebaldi heatedly competed with one another. And it was here in Rio during that summer tour of 1951 that the *Tosca* incident occurred. Renata was in São Paolo singing the role of Maddalena in *Andrea Chénier* while Callas was in Rio singing *La Tosca*. During the first performance, Callas had a vocal mishap. The audience reacted noisily and started shouting the name of Elizabeth Barbato, a local favorite. The next morning Barreto Pinto sent word to Tebaldi to return from São Paolo.

The 28-year-old Callas was not one to be set aside without fighting back, which she did literally. As she herself admitted, and Meneghini later confirmed in his book, the impetuous singer fell upon the impresario in his office, abusing him, threatening him with a large, bronze inkwell, and even unleashing a knee-kick to his stomach. She certainly would have injured him badly if Meneghini had not dragged her back to the hotel, where, two hours later, flight tickets back to Italy were delivered to them from Barreto Pinto.

In the meantime, Renata arrived from São Paolo unaware of what was happening. She accepted Pinto's offer of additional performances happily because they now made it possible for her to buy a pair of earrings, which she previously felt she couldn't afford.

The abruptness of these events made preparation of proper costumes impossible, and those that were made for Tebaldi within 24 hours were clumsy and approximate. But Renata went through with the performances and had a resounding success. Maria Callas learned of it immediately and said (and probably believed) that the whole thing had been planned for a long time. Resentments finally surfaced at that point with a declaration of war—a war which joined the roster of earlier primadonna feuds, such as Maria Malibran vs. Henriette Sontag and Giuditta Pasta vs. Giulia Grisi!

This new battle of the primadonnas exploded unexpectedly as friends, detractors, journalists, and fans all contributed to fuel it. "In truth, many things were said that we had no knowledge of, which were attributed to one or the other. Endless gossip, naturally unpleasant, was reported...," says Tebaldi.

One thing is certain: some years later, Callas made the statement which appeared in *Time* magazine (November 1956): "The day that my dear friend Renata Tebaldi sings *Norma* or *Lucia* or *Anna Bolena* one night and *La Traviata*, *La Gioconda,* or *Medea* the next, then and only then will I consider her a rival. Otherwise, it would be like comparing champagne with cognac, or better, with Coca Cola!" Tebaldi did not honor that remark with a reply, but the same journalist from *Time* magazine commented, favoring the Italian soprano: "It's true that Callas has a voice of champagne but it is also true that champagne easily turns sour, as more than

one opera buff who has heard Callas sing several consecu-
tive performances can attest."

In that same article, Callas detoured from professional
comments to attack her rival's vulnerability as a woman saying that Renata, "poor thing, lacked a good husband," and
that she hoped with all her heart that she would find one
quickly. She concluded by saying that Tebaldi had left La
Scala in order to avoid confrontation with her because Tebaldi
was "a woman without a backbone."

This time Renata replied, as always, via the press, "It
could be, but I have something that she doesn't have: a heart."
No agent in the world could have created more publicity for
her than this reply did.

By this time, known internationally as "the angel"
(Tebaldi) and "the devil" (Callas), the two primadonnas were
trailed by their respective earthly angels and devils: their fol-
lowers. It cannot be said that all of Renata's fans were an-
gelic, though! One of her more persistent fans supplied her
idol with every newspaper clipping pertaining to her; she also
included anything unfavorable referring to Callas, upon which
she would comment with sarcasm, "The voluminous Callas
misfired!" after a performance of *The Barber of Seville* or
"The Piemonte is flooded, we have tornadoes and a crisis in
the Government and that...Gronchi confers the order of
knighthood on Callas! Absolutely ridiculous...." Tebaldi also
received a newspaper clipping on which the angry fan wrote
"scoundrel" in the margin, because Mario Del Monaco denied having been kicked in the shins by Callas and said she
was a great lady.

Another article mentioned that Callas had received a
gentle turtledove in a cage after a performance of *La
Sonnambula* at La Scala. Since it was an anonymous gift it
was thought to be a practical joke played on her by Tebaldi's
fans. A copy of the same article was sent to Tebaldi by one of
her fans with the comment, "We don't know anything about

this." Tebaldi's fans were even less innocent on the evening of January 19th, 1956, when Callas was singing *La Traviata* and a bunch of radishes were thrown at her. Because of her myopia, she gathered them in her arms with all the flowers and carried them to the footlights. To avenge the offense, a Callas fan planted herself in the Teatro Manzoni at a Tebaldi concert, and after the explosion of applause had subsided, she shouted, "Maria!" for all to hear. She was almost killed.

A very unusual project was undertaken by one of Maria's fans who was bold enough to love Renata, too. Working with incredible precision, she reconstructed a *Turandot* with the two rival voices singing—Callas as Turandot and Tebaldi as Liù—using their respective recordings (Columbia 1957 and Decca 1953). Patiently cutting and splicing tapes for months on end, this impassioned, work-addicted opera buff from Milan succeeded in creating an unpublished experiment which, onstage, would have been the operatic event of the century.

However, attempts such as this one to please both artists were rare and poorly received by the opposing forces who preferred clashes to peaceful coexistence. It can never be said that the two artists, who usually became aware of such schemes only long after they had occurred, had a hand in suggesting them. And if Maria Callas often verbally attacked her rival during interviews, Renata Tebaldi categorically refused to comment in public. In so doing, they tacitly perpetuated the "devil" and "angel" myth, not without some pleasure.

❧10❧

Beniamino Gigli
Triumphs in Rio de Janeiro
Stifling Atmosphere at La Scala

Tebaldi had a deeply emotional experience before she completed her hectic tour of South America. She sang *Andrea Chénier* together with the legendary Beniamino Gigli in São Paolo, Brazil. Reminiscing about the celebrated tenor, Renata says, "Gigli had a very unique style which he enhanced by his use of sobs. He used them as a means of expression but above all to relax himself, to rest his voice. The success of that performance in São Paolo is difficult to describe. At the end of Act II everyone stood and cheered." After the performance, this seasoned and mature tenor embraced his young colleague and said, "Thank you, my dear, for making me feel 20 years younger...."

This triumph was followed by a gala evening in their honor attended by all of São Paolo's elite society. The celebration continued the next day with a Tebaldi recital and ended the following day, October 1, 1951, with a performance of the *Requiem* for a Verdi commemoration. The cast included Tebaldi, Barbieri, Gigli, and Giulio Neri, with Tullio Serafin conducting.

The return trip to Italy was disastrous. The plane carrying Renata and her mother developed serious engine malfunction and was forced to land in Senegal. The passengers were taken to Dakar, where they spent an unbearable night because of excessive heat and humidity. They were scheduled to depart on another aircraft the next morning, but the plane never arrived. The malfunctioning engine was repaired and the passengers continued their flight on that plane. Already unnerved, they boarded with prophetic apprehension and soon found themselves trapped in a menacing cyclone. The airplane navigated over and through monstrous clouds. The terrified passengers cried out desperately or prayed silently. When they finally landed in Lisbon, their first European stop, Renata kissed the ground and swore never to set foot in a plane again. Her decision upset her mother who enjoyed flying and preferred it to sea travel and the seasickness that accompanied it, but Renata was immovable and she was the one who decided these things.

"They would say that Mamma was a gendarme," Renata recalls. "She certainly took good care of me, but she never forced her will on me. She accepted whatever my career brought, saying that we were like an army: she was the troops and I the general, and when it was necessary for me to make a decision she always adapted to it. It was her nature to detest continuous change, poor Mamma, but my career had become the sole purpose of her life, and my success was her only happiness."

At the end of October 1951, Renata Tebaldi reentered the Italian scene with a memorable performance of *Falstaff* sung in Parma with Mariano Stabile as Falstaff. Piero de Palma, a young tenor from Genova, was Dr. Cajus, the same Piero de Palma who, 30 years later, in the 1980-81 opening night performance at La Scala, sang the role again with great dignity.

Opening night at La Scala was held on December 7th, the Feast of St. Ambreus which replaced the traditional December 16th opening. The inaugural performance was *I Vespri*

Siciliani with Maria Callas. *Norma* followed in January and February, 1952, and *The Abduction from the Seraglio* in April. Callas had already been engaged to open the 1952-53 season with *Macbeth,* conducted by Victor De Sabata, and *La Gioconda* at the end of the year. *Mefistofele* (seven performances) and *Falstaff* (three performances), both conducted by Victor De Sabata, were the operas that Tebaldi sang at La Scala during the 1952 season.

The atmosphere at La Scala was becoming more and more disquieting, and Tebaldi decided to distance herself from the Milan opera house. During a very busy 1952 she sang *The Siege of Corinth, La Traviata, Otello,* and *Adriana Lecouvreur* in Naples, *The Marriage of Figaro* in Rome, *La Traviata* in Genoa, Trieste, and Bari, Rossini's *William Tell* and *Stabat Mater* in Florence, and returned to Rio de Janeiro for *La Traviata, Andrea Chénier,* and *Tosca.*

It was in August 1952 that Tebaldi arrived in Rio de Janeiro on the *SS Giulio Cesare.* On board was the Chilean Nobel Prize-winning poet, Pablo Neruda, who, after several years of exile in Italy, was returning to Chile to take part in the International Congress of Culture in Santiago. There was a moment of tension as the ship entered the port. Some youths had dived into the sea and were swimming swiftly towards the liner shouting as they neared. It was feared they were coming for Neruda. Soon it was evident that they were fans coming to greet Renata Tebaldi with a reception similar to Claudia Muzio's many years before. It was at the Teatro Municipal that Tebaldi sang *La Traviata, La Bohème,* and *Aida.*

1953 began with Tebaldi's debut at the San Carlo in Naples in a contemporary opera, *Cecilia* by Licinio Refice, who also conducted the performances. This debut was followed by performances of *Mefistofele* at the Teatro Massimo in Palermo, *Tosca* in Regio Emilia and Brescia. She returned to Naples for five performances of *Aida* and then appeared in Monte Carlo at the Grand Théâtre in *La Traviata*. She returned to La Scala in April 1953 for several performances of *Tosca* with Victor De Sabata conducting, and *Adriana Lecouvreur* with Carlo Maria Giulini conducting. Five performances of *La Forza del Destino* followed at the Maggio Musicale Fiorentino with a stellar cast including Mario Del Monaco, Cesare Siepi, Fedora Barbieri and Renato Capecchi. On the podium was Dimitri Mitropoulos who wanted some rather unusual *tempi*. The singers felt uncomfortable with their roles and were finally compelled to return to the score to study as young students would. It seemed as though no one knew how to sing anymore, and the rehearsal rooms of the Teatro Comunale were occupied by the principal singers for private coaching.

The Austrian stage director, George Pabst, had decided to set this *Forza* in Spain during the 1936 revolution where he intended to include modern cannons and arms. Tebaldi, as Leonora, would be a camp aide. The cast rebelled and Pabst finally was forced into doing a more acceptable setting. Sixteenth century Spain was agreed upon finally, and there were no further objections.

In July of 1953 Renata set sail again for South America, this time for her debut at the Teatro Colon in Buenos Aires. "It is the most beautiful theater in the world," she says, "perhaps even the largest, with five tiers of boxes and two family circles. The orchestra seats are extremely comfortable, the acoustics in the theater and on stage are perfect, and the administration is stupendous.... It's marvelous to work there!" Renata has memories of a unique audience in Buenos Aires. "During my career I've received innumerable letters from my admirers. Unfortunately, I've had to discard many of them for lack of space, but I've never had the courage to do away with the letters from Argentina. For the most part they were from Italians who had emigrated, and they thanked me for having brought memories of their homeland to them. After a performance they would come to kiss my hand as though I were a saint. They would stop to caress the ship when I was leaving."

The *Aida* of her debut at the Teatro Colon was not an exceptional spectacle since the sets were old and the orchestra not very exciting, but of Tebaldi, however, it was written, "When all singers start to interpret Verdi with the same dignity (we do not begin to hope for similar vocal beauty) that Renata Tebaldi brings to the role, the public will again start to appreciate opera as they did in the past."

After Buenos Aires there was Rio with *Otello*, *La Bohème*, *Tosca*, and *La Traviata*. Then in November came the opening night performance of *La Traviata* in Barcelona.

Renata had just turned 30. Her position as beloved artist in the world of opera was by now clearly defined. Her charismatic personality, spontaneous and devoid of artifice, enchanted those near her. A journalist in Barcelona described her very accurately when he said, "Tebaldi is tall, young, beautiful, and not very photogenic; she has a bright expression and a ready smile; when she speaks, her voice is almost as exceptional as her singing voice...." To this same journalist Renata revealed what can be considered her professional motto: "The pain of giving oneself totally to one's art is the greatest happiness for an artist."

Tebaldi returned to La Scala in December for the inauguration of the 1953-54 season. It was Catalani's *La Wally* on December 7th, with Mario Del Monaco, Giangiacomo Guelfi, and Giorgio Tozzi. Renata Scotto made her Scala debut as Walter. Carlo Maria Giulini was on the podium for all six performances. Quickly following, on the 10th of December, was Cherubini's *Medea* with Maria Callas and Gino Penno, with Leonard Bernstein on the podium.

Interest in the revival of the Cherubini opera imbued this performance with the excitement of a gala opening. The outstanding production and the tumultuous performance by

Callas (*Medea* became the hallmark of her career) was one of the most sensational events of the season at La Scala.

La Wally was an extraordinary success. Rarely has an opera been cast so ideally. Tebaldi and Del Monaco, both in splendid voice, created their roles to perfection. And still it could be said that the echo of *Wally* was swept away by the avalanche. The die was cast and the era of revivals began.

In the planning stages for Callas for the 1954 season were *Lucia di Lammermoor* and *Alceste* (revival conducted by Giulini). There was talk of the following year's opening with *La Vestale* by Spontini. For Tebaldi, the new production of Tchaikovsky's *Eugene Onegin* was prepared for May of 1954. Tebaldi made her debut as Tatiana with Giuseppe Di Stefano, Cloe Elmo, and Ettore Bastianini also in the cast. Artur Rodzinski conducted. During that season at La Scala, Tebaldi also sang several performances of *Otello* and *Tosca* alternating with commitments in Naples, Rome, South America, and Spain, where she sang *La Wally, The Marriage of Figaro, Andrea Chénier, Otello, Tosca, La Traviata, La Forza del Destino, La Bohème,* and *Lohengrin.* In Rio that year she sang *Cecilia* by Licinio Refice again.

In previous years Tebaldi had successfully performed several important revivals such as Rossini's *The Siege of Corinth* in 1949, Spontini's *Olympia* and Handel's *Giulio Cesare* in 1950, Verdi's *Giovanna d'Arco* in 1951, and Rossini's *William Tell* in 1952. From the contemporary repertory she performed Casavola's *Salammbò* in 1948, and Refice's *Cecilia* in 1953 and 1954. Tebaldi, in truth, preferred avoiding experimentation because of her intensive work schedule and perhaps because of laziness, too. Later in her career, for nine years, Decca urged her to record Verdi's *Requiem,* and even though she had said yes, she never did find the right moment. Looking back on her career, Renata now has some regrets. "Considering how anyone will sing anything these days, my past scruples make me angry now. For years, Maestro Serafin urged me to sing *Norma,* but I was convinced that after Gina Cigna's splendid Norma, there was little that I could add to the role. Maestro Serafin insisted, saying that in six months we would have prepared it perfectly. 'You will create your own Norma, different from all the others,' he used to say. But I was never convinced. I felt the same way about *Un Ballo in Maschera* and *Don Carlo.* After Maria Caniglia, what could I add to those roles?" Fortunately, Tebaldi did record *Don Carlo* with Carlo Bergonzi, and *Un Ballo in Maschera* with Luciano Pavarotti, both for London, before concluding her recording career.

Renata Tebaldi always refused to sing in French or German. "French is too nasal and German is too guttural and I was afraid of ruining the quality of my voice. I could have compromised the diction and saved the sound, but I wouldn't do that. Requests for me to sing the Marschallin in *Der Rosenkavalier* were frequent, but I worried about the consequences of singing the role. It would require changing my way of singing. I'm convinced that only Germans and Austrians can truly sing Strauss, and I'd even go as far as saying that of Mozart, too. There are Italian operas that were tempting to me, but I didn't dare because I felt that they were not for me. Then, after all, there were so many other beautiful operas for me to sing that were suitable for my voice!"

So Tebaldi, the consummate professional, after performing some revivals and contemporary opera, returned to her preferred repertory where she had no rivals. Callas, with her various voices, beautiful and ugly, enticing and dramatic, and with her penchant for publicity, stirred a new interest in reviving rarely performed operas.

Tebaldi handled this course of events by remaining in control of the situation. Instinctively and wisely she quickly eliminated any direct confrontations and instead chose the opposite approach, perpetuating her role of "angel" which was becoming to her, and leaving Maria Callas to grapple with the perhaps more exciting, but certainly more insidious, role of "devil."

Tebaldi's artistic and personal qualities revealed a beautiful woman who at 32 years of age had succeeded in remaining captivatingly unassuming in spite of her intense artistic life, the travelling, the grand hotels, the admirers, and fans. Not yet overcome by love or great passions, she lived in her own serene world, protected by her mother's warm guidance. In an almost symbiotic existence, they had, until then, travelled the entire route of Renata's artistic journey together. She was a primadonna on stage, but once her costumes were put away, Renata ignored most banquets and parties where she would have been the honored guest, and quickly returned to her hotel. There, her mother had ready not a "dish of spaghetti," as the American press enjoyed saying, but rather, "two slices of prosciutto, from Langhirano, naturally."

Renata's love for beautiful jewelry, furs, and clothing was legendary. She happily enjoyed her long walks, finding time within her busy schedule to explore the many shops and boutiques along her route. She would often mentally note an item for a return visit, or she would enter and, amidst a flurry of attention and pleasure by the salespersons, add something new to her already impressive collections.

Her natural timidity and her preference for innocent pastimes—reading, long walks, crossword puzzles, collecting native dolls, and supper with good friends—surprisingly added to the mystique of the celebrated Tebaldi of the operatic stage, who rigorously refused to take part in the indiscretions that fueled the flames of gossip in cultural and operatic circles. Deeply religious, Renata went to church to pray as did Floria Tosca, her favorite operatic character.

Renata knew exactly where she stood artistically. She was in her vocal prime and at the apex of her career. Any contractual request was respected. Harold Schonberg of *The New York Times* wrote that "Tebaldi asks for and gets the highest fees since Caruso." There wasn't an opera house in the world (except perhaps La Scala during the Callas commotion) that wasn't eager to confer on her the greatest honors.

So at the height of her career, confronted with an unbearable situation, yet never losing control, Renata Tebaldi decided to remain true to herself. "The atmosphere at La Scala had become stifling. Undoubtedly, the administration at the opera house favored Maria, but I decided that I did not want to endure it, so I accepted the offer from Rudolf Bing, who for years had been inviting me to sing at the Metropolitan."

"I decided that I did not want to endure it" is perhaps the key to the "mystery" of Renata Tebaldi. Years later, when she finally fell seriously in love and was confronted with new kinds of distressing problems that offered no solutions, she found herself at the outer limits of her endurance. Again she decided to "not suffer any longer" and saved herself by closing the door forever.

PART TWO

❧ 11 ❧

1955: Debut at the Metropolitan Opera House

On January 6th, 1955, Tebaldi and her mother sailed on the *Andrea Doria* from Naples to New York. Her debut in *Otello* took place on January 31st. Mario Del Monaco sang Otello and Leonard Warren was Iago. One of the pillars of the Metropolitan, Maestro Stiedry, conducted.

Tebaldi's photograph appeared on the cover of New York newspapers. They named her "America's new opera sensation" and she became front-page news from the first evening. The opera audience fell in love with her and adopted her. The music critic of *The New York Times*, Olin Downes, wrote, "At the start one sensed that she was nervous and pressured, but the voice quickly revealed its beauty. Tebaldi's appearance is enchanting: as beautiful [last evening] as an antique Florentine painting. She has great musicality, technique, and tasteful interpretation. Her conscientiousness and her extraordinary transmission of emotion have much impressed us...."

During the first two months of 1955, New York was to experience three events considered among the most important in the city's musical history. Two weeks before Tebaldi's debut, Marian Anderson became the first black person to sing at the Metropolitan Opera House after years of humili-

65

ating racial discrimination. She sang Ulrica in *Un Ballo In Maschera*. Two weeks after Tebaldi's debut, Kirsten Flagstad returned to New York for two recitals, twenty years after her legendary debut. She was 59 years old and succeeded once again in thrilling her audience.

Renata loved New York immediately. With the help of an interpreter, she expressed her feelings very simply to the press. "This is really America! New York is so impressive. At first I was intimidated by the frantic pace, by the wealth, by the dynamic strength of the city. I felt so insignificant. Then I began to notice an informality which surprised me, but which I liked. For example, women think nothing of wearing expensive furs and boots and a kerchief covering their hair, sometimes barely hiding hairpins and rollers. An Italian woman would never do that. On the other hand, I find this way of life practical and intelligent." Someone asked her if she would enjoy living in New York always, and Renata, the Italian, the Emiliana, the homebody, answered in Italian without hesitating, "Why not? My life isn't set on any definite path yet. Who knows?" Renata also added, "I could even stop singing. I've sung everywhere in Italy, I've sung in the most important cities of the world: Paris, London, Rio, Buenos Aires, Lisbon, Barcelona, Los Angeles, San Francisco, and now New York. I would like to sing in Vienna. After that? What else can I do that's different?"

Her words were interpreted by some as a subconscious (or perhaps conscious) desire for marriage and children. The search was on to uncover the tenor who could represent a love interest for Tebaldi. But none was found. In fact, he didn't exist. Found among her countless admirers, instead, was the son of a Texan oil magnate, who, after seeing her perform, invited her to a lavish affair in his sumptuous villa in Dallas to sing for his friends. What did he offer her in return? A blank check and his private plane to fly her back and forth. To add further gallantry to the affair, he also offered himself in marriage as part of the bargain. Renata declined both the invitation and his hand in marriage, declaring candidly that "the trip woud be too tiring and she preferred an Italian husband."

While in New York, Renata was often asked about her relationship with Maria Callas. She would reply that "the rivalry between us is mostly the result of gossip among our fans. There's more than enough work for both of us, and, in any case, our voices are very different. I am a *lirico spinto*, not a *coloratura* soprano."

Members of the press who ventured to her hotel without an interpreter had a difficult time. "Miss Tebaldi's English is very good, her pronunciation is clear," one of them wrote later on, "but unfortunately, it consists of only seven words: 'Thank you,' 'Please be seated,' 'Hello,' and 'Goodbye.'"

Whether or not Renata spoke English, New York found her enchanting. Throughout her career, articles about Renata Tebaldi invariably were captioned "Diva Serena," "Diva Simpatica," "Diva without Tantrums," and reporters were always extremely protective, never indiscreet. Perhaps the reason was that Tebaldi, despite her luminous smile, her natural courtesy, and her professional availability, was the rare artist who "kept her distance." Her appearance was reassuring, serene, beautiful. Her nose had a lovely upward tilt (When I'm angry my nose points even further upwards."), her clear, blue eyes, her perfect alabaster complexion, and the flirtatious dimples were all so appealing. Even her stubborn unwillingness to speak anything but Italian created a certain tenderness and increasing adoration of her.

Tebaldi's popularity inspired Chef Muller of the Met's Louis Sherry restaurant to create an entree in her honor, Chicken Breast alla Renata, which he included on the menu two evenings before her debut in *Otello*. It consisted of grilled prosciutto seasoned with a piquant sauce, topped with grilled chicken breast and mushrooms, and covered with the sauce.

Renata's first engagement at the Metropolitan Opera lasted three months. Besides her debut as Desdemona, she also sang Mimi, Maddalena in *Andrea Chénier*, and *Tosca*. *Aida,* which she had to cancel due to illness, was postponed until the following November. On the 27th of February she sang in concert with Mario Del Monaco and Ettore Bastianini. Fausto Cleva conducted.

At the Metropolitan Opera, Renata found that work schedules were prepared quite differently than in Italy and were closely controlled by the iron discipline of the opera's director, the Viennese-born Rudolf Bing. He had come to the Metropolitan from England where, as a British citizen, he had started his career, first directing the Festival at Edinburgh, and then at Glyndebourne. Since 1950 he was at the Met where he worked a fourteen-hour day, lunching on a sandwich and a cup of tea in the Metropolitan cafeteria or in his office.

Bing, by then a naturalized American citizen, was respected as the ultimate diplomat. When he invited Tebaldi to sing at the Metropolitan, Zinka Milanov, the Yugoslavian soprano reigned. After several years as a leading soprano in Zagreb, where she sang over three hundred performances in the Croatian language, she made her debut at the Metropolitan in 1937 as Leonora in *Il Trovatore*. Although she was often away because of engagements around the country and abroad, Milanov was the Metropolitan's uncontested leading soprano—until Renata Tebaldi arrived. In spite of this, Bing succeeded in keeping the two artists under one roof without friction. But that wasn't enough for him. He also wanted to include Maria Callas on the billboards for the 1956-1957 season, and he did.

Within a few days, historic photographs of the signing of contracts appeared in the daily papers. Bing had obtained Callas's signature by flying to Chicago and offering her *Norma* on opening night. He obtained Tebaldi's signature by enticing her with a new production of *La Traviata*. To Milanov he promised a new *Ernani*.

"The three girls are happy, the manager of the opera house is happy, the public is happy, so why worry about Bing's methods?" was the wise comment which appeared in one of the weekly magazines.

Mr. Bing did have a problem with Zinka Milanov when she decided to make her entrance into the audience at precisely the same moment that Maria Callas was making hers on stage during the first performance of *Norma,* and thus detract from Maria's moment. Bing's comment later was that he had succeeded in stopping her. In fact, however, Milanov did follow through with her plan and the two singers did make their entrances simultaneously. While there was some murmuring and some applause for Milanov in the audience, from onstage Maria Callas interpreted it as being for her. Fortunately a disaster was averted, but Mr. Bing must have had some moments of anxiety.

Rudolf Bing was as firm as he was diplomatic. He did not hesitate, years later, to show Callas the door when she refused to alternate performances of *La Traviata* and *Macbeth* because of their very different *tessituras*, declaring that "her voice was not an elevator." It was thought, instead, that Callas was using that as an excuse for not complying with her contract. "Bing was unbending in his professional decisions. He was often very demanding, but he was fair, and for me he was the greatest," says Tebaldi. "The Met's system of scheduling didn't allow any laxity in discipline. Operas, roles, and singers were alternated with the greatest ease. While Italian opera houses emphasized the entire production, in the States, voices and singers were more important. In Italy everyone rehearsed together, and the same cast appeared in all the performances which were given within one block of time. Then that opera was removed for the season and another was performed. The Metropolitan alternated operas, offering many of them throughout the entire season with different casts. Having various operas to perform within a given period kept us from tiring of a particular role, but it was certainly more dangerous for the voice. One also felt the pressure of being at one's best at all performances because critics review every performance that has even a minor cast change."

Discipline was evident on all fronts. Being late for rehearsals and especially performances was inexcusable. On the other hand, artists were given a calendar of their performances, rehearsals, and costume fittings one year in advance. The organization was so efficient that most problems were averted. On February 16th, 1955, Tebaldi informed the Metropolitan eight hours before curtain time that she was indisposed and could not sing *Aida*. Even though there was no standby for her, the public still saw a performance. The Verdi opera was replaced by *Tosca* with Zinka Milanov in the starring role.

❧12❧

Milan: Piazza Guastalla
New York: First Christmas Away From Home
"Miss Sold-out"

At the end of March 1955, elated by the homage and in-creasing fame, Tebaldi returned to Piazza Guastalla, to her apartment in an elegant, new condominium-complex which she tastefully decorated in greens and ivory. She carefully selected each of the exquisite antiques which so beautifully grace her home.

Because of her very busy singing schedule which included Florence, Rome, London, San Francisco, Los Angeles, Chicago, Philadelphia, and New York through the end of 1955, her visit to Milan was all too brief, just long enough for five performances of *La Forza del Destino* at La Scala. Then she was off to Florence for five performances of *Otello* and two of *Falstaff*, before departing for London and the U.S.A.

At the Maggio Musicale in Florence, Tebaldi's Iago was Tito Gobbi. The performances of *Otello* were followed in rapid succession by two performances of *Falstaff* in which Gobbi sang the title role. By the last *Falstaff*, Gobbi was completely exhausted and he cancelled. At the last moment the management was forced to find a replacement. Mariano Stabile, considered by many the greatest interpreter of the role, was contacted by phone. He was found at home indulging

71

himself in a gourmet meal which would have delighted Sir John Falstaff! By 2:15 p.m. he was on the express train to Florence where he arrived at 7 p.m. Two hours later, when the curtain went up over the Inn of the Garter and Sir John launched his invective, "*L'onore, ladri!*" the surprised audience recognized the most celebrated Falstaff in history under wig, makeup, and potbelly, and enthusiastically applauded him.

In June and July, the British applauded Tebaldi in *Tosca* with Ferruccio Tagliavini and Tito Gobbi at Covent Garden. By September, she was again crossing the Atlantic for her now celebrated visits to New York and San Francisco. On September 5th she was in New York for a "Telephone Hour" concert on NBC-TV. On the 28th of September she joined soprano Elisabeth Schwarzkopf in a concert at the San Francisco Opera, followed by an intensive schedule of performances in Los Angeles and San Francisco. During a non-subscription performance of *Tosca* in San Francisco, after Tosca's aria, "*Vissi d'arte*," Tebaldi's overwhelmed audience gave her a seven-minute standing ovation, and she felt compelled to encore the aria. Since tradition forbade encores in major opera houses, the news almost caused a scandal. Not since Tito Schipa's "*Le Rêve*" from *Manon* had a similar ovation for an encore occurred at that opera house. On November 1st, Tebaldi made her Chicago debut at the Lyric Opera House with two performances each of *Aida* and *La Bohème*. "When the role requires it, Tebaldi is equally impressive as slave or Ethopian princess," voiced the *Chicago Tribune* of her *Aida*.

Several exciting events occurred in December 1955. Tebaldi appeared in a recital in Carnegie Hall on the 18th with Martin Katz accompanying, and again on the 20th in joint recital with Jussi Björling, with the erudite Leonard Bernstein at the piano. On the 23rd of December, Tebaldi appeared in concert on New York TV's "Telephone Hour."

For the first time since the war, Renata and her mother

72

were spending Christmas away from Langhirano. "My happiest days were those spent with the whole family, when I was a child," recalls Renata. "I did try to follow tradition by avoiding professional commitments away from Italy during the Christmas season. After 1955 I had to give up the pleasure of Christmas at home, and from then on, the day was like any other. However, regardless of where we were, while Mamma was alive, there was warmth. Then it became a sad recurrence...." In 1969 on Christmas Eve while in New York, Renata wrote to a friend, "Everyone is so excited about the holidays here, and, as usual, I wish they'd never come! I had a dress rehearsal of *Tosca* today, and a performance on New Year's Eve, so you can see that I won't have time for anything special, not even to eat my sweets! (I guess it's better that way so I don't gain weight!)" Then on December 26th she wrote, "Christmas is over, Thank God!"

The Metropolitan Opera traditionally ushers in the new year with a performance of *Die Fledermaus* including surprise guests who sing at Prince Orlofsky's party in Act II. On December 31st, 1955, Tebaldi was one of the surprise guests and sang *"Io sono l'umile ancella"* from *Adriana Lecouvreur*, much to the delight of a thrilled audience.

Andrea Chénier with Richard Tucker was her first performance of 1956 at the Metropolitan, followed by a gala benefit concert on the 5th of January presented by *La Follia,* the Italian magazine published in New York. The event featured Tebaldi, Tucker, Regina Resnick, Mario Ortica, and Jerome Hines. Posters publicizing the concert presented Tebaldi's name in large letters, while the names Tucker and Hines were underneath hers, in smaller letters. While this did not perturb Hines, Tucker, a leading tenor at the Metropolitan, was quite offended. "I agreed to sing gratis, but I also expected equally generous treatment in return!" he complained. He sent a contribution to the association but refused to sing at the gala.

"Richard was touchy at times but he was a magnificent colleague. At performance time he was usually relaxed and calmed everyone. He always felt well and he was always satisfied. Whenever I asked him how he felt, he invariably answered, 'Terrific!' so eventually I nicknamed him Mr. Terrific," Renata reminisces about her former leading man.

On the 27th of January, 1956, Renata participated in a gala concert with many other outstanding artists including Jussi Björling, Artur Rubinstein, Marian Anderson, Isaac Stern, Roberta Peters, Leonard Warren, and Zinka Milanov. This unusual event, at Massey Hall in Toronto, featured so many stars that the public, overwhelmed by the display, almost resented their being packed into one evening which prevented a true appreciation of any one star!

Within a year of her debut at the Metropolitan Opera House, Tebaldi was America's uncontested primadonna. "She started at the top and she remained there," wrote Harold Schonberg. In 1956 the mayor of Hartford, Joseph Cronin, named the Renata Tebaldi Square in her honor.

In a New York cab on their way to the Metropolitan Opera, where they were scheduled to appear that season, two prominent singers were talking to a cab driver who was saying ecstatically, "Metropolitan? Tebaldi! Tebaldi!" The tenor, a bit nettled, replied, "Tebaldi, yes, but I am—" The cab driver appeared not to understand and repeated "Tebaldi! Tebaldi!" While the female singer, a good friend of Renata's, enjoyed the scene fully, the tenor's pique increased.

When Tebaldi embarked on the *Andrea Doria* to return to Italy, a throng of admirers, disregarding the final blast of the siren as they said their final goodbyes to their beloved soprano, almost risked jumping into the sea just to remain with her a bit longer.

In the meantime, as her engagements in the US increased, her appearances in Italy became rarer. In April and May of 1955 her commitments at La Scala ended after five outstanding performances in *La Forza del Destino*. The *Corriere d'Informazione* on April 27 had this to say, "Tebaldi has given us an interpretation which will not be easy to equal." She would not appear at La Scala again for four years. During 1956, a busy schedule in New York, Boston, Philadelphia, Newark, and Toronto was followed by several performances of *Tosca* and *La Forza del Destino* at the Teatro Massimo in Palermo. After performances of *William Tell* in Naples and *Tosca* in Rome during April, she participated in the XIX Maggio Musicale Fiorentino.

The repertory selection for the Maggio Fiorentino for the 1956 season had been belabored. The original plan was to start with a Mozart revival, but government subsidy was denied, as were the plans to premiere a new work, usually an important yearly feature of the Maggio. Maestro Francesco Siciliani, the artistic director, had submitted a carefully planned repertory which included Busoni's *La Sposa Sorteggiata*, Strauss's *Salome*, Debussy's *Pelléas et Mélisande*, Schönberg's *La Mano Felice*, and Janacek's *Katia Kabanova*. Included also was a contemporary work and Puccini's *Manon Lescaut* to be sung by Tebaldi for the first time in Italy, conducted by Dimitri Mitropoulos. Zandonai's *Francesca da Rimini* was also planned for Tebaldi. Unfortunately nothing came of this challenging and culturally rewarding program.

Attempting to keep their commitment to progress, the Maggio set forth a new outline, a comparison of Mozart and Rossini. Government authorities declared that Mozart lacked the popularity to draw crowds and sell tickets. A compromise was reached finally with the "anti-Scala" opening night performance of Tebaldi in *La Traviata* conducted by Tullio Serafin, which was to compete with the controversial Callas *Traviata* at La Scala, directed by Lucchino Visconti.

All the Tebaldi enthusiasts of Italy converged on Florence for the occasion to hear their beloved soprano. She sang seven performances that May and June in Florence. Tebaldi had a veritable triumph. During the first performance, Tebaldi granted an encore of "*Amami Alfredo,*" and at the end of the opera a unanimous cry of "To La Scala! To La Scala!" rang out in the theater.

In *Il Nuovo Corriere* on May 7th, 1956, Virgilio Doplicher spoke of "the splendor of Tebaldi's pure vocal tones and harmonic adaptability," saying that "from the carefree fickleness of Act I, to the dramatic duet with Germont, the distressing card scene, and the scene preceding her death, the expressive accent given by the intensity of her musically modulated sound revealed those qualities which make this soprano famous."

Maestro Siciliani shared in her triumph. He had been one of her first and greatest supporters and had encouraged her to use her tremendous vocal powers to explore rarely performed repertory. "Renata sang *coloratura* in the early years," says Maestro Siciliani, "and I was the one to select *The Siege of Corinth* for her debut in Florence. I also convinced her to do *Olympia* and *William Tell,* which were great successes. The *Traviata* that Renata sang in 1956 at the Maggio Fiorentino was the last one there under my direction. I left for La Scala soon after."

Italy's desire to have Renata Tebaldi back in her homeland was a well-deserved victory for her. Now she enjoyed the pleasure of taking her time. Her "exile" in America was golden and her reign more secure than ever. In the States she was now often called "Miss Sold-out" and she was considered so "at home" that she was asked to participate in the "I Am An American" ceremony which was held every year at Golden Gate Park in San Francisco. She shared the honor with the legendary Ezio Pinza, who was no longer singing by then.

In the States, Giuseppina Tebaldi enjoyed near-celebrity status. Her constant presence as affectionate and protective "gendarme" had caused tenderness for her among Renata's

American admirers. Very frequently, articles about Tebaldi included some mention of her mother, too. Letters written to Tebaldi always included kindest regards for her. *The New York Times* devoted a long article to her emphasizing her savory recipes. "Mrs. Tebaldi prepares almost all of her daughter's meals when they are in New York. She keeps them very simple. She shops on Mulberry and Bleecker Streets in Little Italy, and does her cooking on a small burner in her apartment at the Buckingham Hotel. Mrs. Tebaldi's favorite dish for her daughter is her roast chicken which she flavors with sage, rosemary, salt and olive oil. She also makes a strong espresso, with no sugar, no milk, and no whipped cream. Spaghetti and desserts are forbidden. If Tebaldi has a performance, her mother avoids cooking with garlic and onions! When she is asked whether her daughter is a good cook or not, she answers with a shake of the head, saying, 'She's certainly a better singer!'"

Renata loved dogs and wanted one of her own, a middle-sized gray poodle. Occasionally, a particularly adorable one would attract Renata and she would follow, walking behind it for a while, just enjoying the sight. She knew that she would have a dog one day, but for the present there wasn't much hope since her mother was very much against it. Renata quickly clarified the point saying that "Mamma loved animals very much and at home in Langhirano there were always dogs, cats, and birds. Each time one died, its death caused so much pain that Mamma used to say there was already so much pain in life, why add to it?" Her resistance would end soon.

In San Francisco in September Tebaldi sang a concert with Giorgio Tozzi and performed *Tosca*, both at the San Francisco Opera. This was followed by a concert at Golden Gate Park and another concert with Elisabeth Schwarzkopf at the San Francisco Opera. She was heard for the first time in Verdi's *Simon Boccanegra* in San Francisco, singing two performances which prompted enthusiastic reviews, including Patterson Green's in the *Examiner:* "Magnificent is the only way to describe this singer, magnificent of voice, appearance, artistry... Her Amelia Grimaldi is one of the miracles of opera!" She sang another performance of this opera at the Shrine Auditorium in Los Angeles.

Some years later, at the Metropolitan, tickets to *Simon Boccanegra* was the prize won by a contestant on the TV show, "Queen for a Day." Janet, the winner, was selected because in reply to how she would spend an evening as "queen" she wished that Renata Tebaldi would sing for her fiancé, Steve, who had polio and was unable to get to the opera house to hear her sing. Janet's request was judged the most worthy by the jury. Arrangements were made and Steve was transported to the Metropolitan Opera House. Before the curtain went up, the management announced that Renata Tebaldi would sing for Steve who was in the audience happily sharing Janet's wish for him.

Zandonai's *Francesca da Rimini,* which had been cancelled from the season's program at the Maggio Musicale Fiorentino the previous spring, was planned for September in San Francisco and then cancelled. Not having sung *Francesca da Rimini* remains one of the few regrets Tebaldi has about her career. It was probably no coincidence that she chose a chalet in Gabicce Monte on the Adriatic coast, for summer vacations, which has a transcendent view of Gradara, the setting, according to the legend, of the tragic love between Paolo and Francesca.

"There is a phrase," Renata muses, "in the love scene in Act III in which Francesca makes a final attempt to resist before giving in to Paolo's embrace, kissing him on the mouth and saying, '*Guardate il mare come si fa bianco!*' And that is exactly what happens. As the sun sets, the flame-red sky grows pale and the sea loses all its color and becomes white. From my chalet I can see the whiteness and I feel as though I were watching it from Francesca's room in the castle."

A very busy 1956 ended with performances of *Tosca, La Forza del Destino, La Bohème*, a concert with Ettore Bastianini and Giulietta Simionato under the baton of Georg Solti at the Chicago Lyric Opera, and performances of *Tosca, Aida*, and a concert at the Teatro Liceo in Barcelona.

❧13❧

Concert at the Teatro Manzoni, Milan
Nini Castiglioni: Press Agent

On January 3rd, 1957, Tebaldi was scheduled to appear at the Teatro Manzoni which was just a short distance from La Scala. The proximity to La Scala and a press conference announced by Tebaldi had caused a stir in Milan. She had decided on a press conference hoping to put an end to any gossip arising from an article about Maria Callas in *Time* magazine. She also hoped to clarify any new developments in their rivalry. The unexpected arrival of Callas from New York on the heels of her noisy dispute at the Met with the baritone, Enzo Sordello, created more of a sensation. It was said that she wanted to be in town during Tebaldi's conference and available for immediate reply.

After careful consideration, Tebaldi decided to follow her instincts and fight with a weapon more powerful than words: her vocal merits. She cancelled the press conference. On January 3rd, for the UNICEF benefit concert, with Giorgio Favaretto accompanying her at the piano, Tebaldi sang to an ecstatic capacity audience. She was elegant in a lavish white gown, her radiant face exultant and emotional. To end her program she sang eight encores. During the last one, overcome by fatigue and emotion, Tebaldi's final note of the "*Ave*

Maria" from *Otello* was not perfectly clear. After the briefest hesitation, the audience exploded in tumultuous applause. Her audience kept her on stage for a 35-minute ovation. Although a torch-light procession planned by her fans was prohibited by the authorities, it remained an evening of incendiary emotions. Tebaldi's limousine with her in it was pushed to the entrance of La Scala.

The day after the concert, Antonio Ghiringhelli, the manager of La Scala, met Giulietta Simionato as she was having lunch at the Biffi Scala. He unabashedly asked her about the concert the previous evening. Her reply was "Stupendous! I was amazed you weren't there!" His lame reply was, "I sent flowers." She snapped back boldly, "Fine! But you should have been there!"

Following Tebaldi's enormous success, a skit was aired on RAI[1] on a late evening program which featured satire. The sketch humorously described Callas's reaction to Tebaldi's extraordinarily successful concert. It had an angered Callas hastily sending her rival a book entitled *Io Ti Ucciderò!*[2] In the background, a Callas recording of Rossini's aria from *The Barber of Seville,* "*...una vipera sarò'...e cento trappole...,*"[3] played softly.

Tebaldi's not quite limpid note at the end of the "*Ave Maria*" resulted in an intense review by the music critic, Teodoro Celli. By tacit agreement, benefit concerts and, above all, encores, are never subjected to negative criticism. Celli's judgment was resented by Renata's colleagues and saddened her. The following year her disaffection was lessened during a meeting with Celli arranged by her press agent, Nini Castiglioni. The meeting took place over dinner in a Florentine restaurant. After a moment or two of uneasiness, they were

---

[1] Radio Italiana

[2] *I'll Kill You!*

[3] "...I'll become a viper...and a hundred traps..."

comfortably on common ground discussing singing, high notes, and technical difficulties. Celli commented on Tebaldi's *Tosca* saying that *"Davanti a lui tremava tutta Roma"*[4] had to be sung by her, not declaimed, because her voice was one of the rare ones able to sustain those notes musically. She treasured the advice. When she returned to La Scala in December of 1959, she sang the famous phrase, and the result was that in front of her *"tremava tutta Milan."*[5] Celli, very flattered, wrote a beautiful article about Tebaldi and sent a congratulatory telegram to her, saying "Superb!"

To Nini Castiglioni, Renata was an old acquaintance. In 1940 she already was enthusiastic about the voice she had heard for the first time at the Parma Conservatory. On May 23rd, 1944, as the war raged, she went to Rovigo to hear the young Tebaldi debut in *Mefistofele*. After that performance, enchanted by her voice, she attended almost every Tebaldi performance.

Nini Castiglioni became an institution to whom the operatic world was beholden. Most singers, Italian or foreign, went through her office if only briefly. Few people knew as well as she the mysteries and subterfuges behind the triumphs and scandals in opera. After 40 years in the business, she identified her career with three names: Del Monaco, Simionato, and Tebaldi; but the "lightning bolt" that turned her into a passionate opera enthusiast was Tebaldi.

Tebaldi sang a concert sponsored by Martini & Rossi with Ettore Bastianini, conducted by Oliviero De Fabritiis, at Studio RAI in Milan on January 7th, and a performance of *Andrea Chénier* at the Teatro Regio in Parma on January 13th. Having completed these engagements, she undertook the challenging task of preparing for a transatlantic voyage to the US and commitments in major American cities, Toronto,

---

[4] "All of Rome trembled at the sight of him"

[5] "All Milan trembled"

and Havana, Cuba from the 8th of February to the 27th of June. After a dizzying schedule, performances at the Arena di Verona in August and a summer vacation awaited her.

❦ 14 ❧

New Production of *La Traviata* at the Metropolitan
Elsa Maxwell

Tebaldi's expedition to the United States at the end of January 1957, included her mother, her secretary, Linda Barone, and Tina Viganò travelling with her for the first time. A great deal of luggage accompanied them.

For some time now, Giuseppina Tebaldi had agreed with Renata that it would be opportune to have someone they could rely on to assist them, and Tina's name kept turning up. Perhaps she had a premonition that she would soon yield her role as her daughter's guardian angel.

But there was no sadness as they embarked on the *Queen Elizabeth* at Le Havre. In fact, they shared a lingering feeling of euphoria from the affectionate send-off by Tebaldi's admirers at the Milan Central Station. Their gift to her was a talisman for her trip, a blue angel with a very wide wing span! As soon as they were out of the harbor, the liner started to rock alarmingly. Mother, daughter, and Tina buried themselves in their cabins and were not seen again. Only Linda Barone, unaffected, rambled through the ship comfortably and calmly.

"With what little courage I had I'd occasionally waddle over to the porthole only to see a mountain of water coming at me. I was terrified by the thought that the ship would mount another crest and then pitch and roll again and I'd wait there petrified," is Renata's account of the ordeal. It wasn't until the fifth day of the crossing that Renata finally emerged unnerved and exhausted, but relieved by the calmer waters.

Waiting to greet her warmly and in full force as she arrived in New York was the Tebaldi Fan Club. The customs officers at the pier waved her through with her numerous trunks and valises with an emphatic "Welcome home, Miss Tebaldi!"

La Traviata at the Metropolitan was scheduled for February 21st and anticipation had become feverish. Mr. Bing, wishing to take advantage of Tebaldi's arrival, scheduled a non-subscription performance of *La Bohème* on February 8, which included Richard Tucker, Ettore Bastianini, and Giorgio Tozzi, with Thomas Schippers conducting. That performance, which ended at eleven, produced such congestion in the area around the opera house that it was well after midnight before pedestrians and automobiles were dispersed. On her way out, Renata was blocked by throngs of fans on the brink of hysteria ready to tear her affectionately to pieces if she tried to hail a taxi herself and not allow them to do so. Finally, three very tall police officers arrived. Elbowing a path for her through the crowd, they eventually succeeded in escorting Tebaldi out of the theater and into a waiting cab after many interruptions as she lingered to talk with her admirers.

Putting aside her usual modesty, Renata sent a cable to Nini Castiglioni informing her of the performance: "*La Bohème* causes wild ovations. Endless curtain calls. Tucker forced by public demand to let me take solo calls. Historic evening."

Rudolf Bing captured the favorable moment and the public's enthusiasm by scheduling another *La Bohème* for March 13 and a *Tosca* with Jussi Björling and Leonard

Warren for February 27. After *"Vissi d'arte,"* Maestro Mitropoulos interrupted the performance and waited seven minutes until the applause finally ended. Renata, in her customary cable to Italy to her press office, mentioned that Maestro Mitropoulos had been *"molto carino"* (very sweet).

The second *Bohème* was followed by a sumptuous reception hosted by Elsa Maxwell with Tebaldi as guest of honor. She had become an enthusiastic admirer from the moment of Tebaldi's debut at the Metropolitan, and, often since then, gave lavish parties for her, as she did for other friends. These parties were often paid for by some wealthy acquaintance of the columnist who, happy to be seated at the famous gossip columnist's table, was willing to pay for everyone.

In her newspaper column she would report at length, "Yesterday I hosted a party for my friend, Renata Tebaldi. Among my guests were the Ambassador from Spain, Princess Caetani, the Ambassador from Italy, Prince Lobkowicz, Igor Markevitch.... Yesterday the diva was a dream. She has shed 25 pounds. Her black satin gown was marvelously chic. Her new hairdo made her look younger and even more beautiful. I said to her, 'Not another pound less, Renata!' and the diva's reassuring reply was 'Of course not.' She was the favorite topic of conversation the entire evening." Maxwell's column further magnified the anticipation of the event of February 21st, 1957.

Rudolf Bing engaged Giuseppe Campora and Leonard Warren to sing with Tebaldi for this new production of *Traviata,* with Fausto Cleva conducting. Maestro Cleva spent most of his career at the Metropolitan, starting as stand-by conductor in 1920, then chorus master and, finally, in 1950, conductor of the Italian repertory. He died in Athens in 1971. The director was Tyrone Guthrie (known at the Metropolitan for his successful *Carmen*), Oliver Smith was the set designer, and Rolf Gérard designed the costumes.

Tyrone Guthrie was difficult to work with, and was unpleasant about New York to the press. Even Tebaldi, eventually, had a confrontation with him, and that was such extraordinary news that the incident was quickly picked up by the newspapers. "Miss Tebaldi did well to argue with Guthrie," they wrote. "In fact, she should have put her foot down not only about that scene...."

The disagreement arose about the arrangement of the guests during the party in Act I. Tebaldi was lost in the crowd and became annoyed with the scene. She finally protested, "But, after all, who's giving this party anyway? Who's the hostess?" Mr. Bing was called on stage and settled the dispute by spreading the guests out and leaving more room for Violetta.

Tebaldi, who was very restless during the rehearsals of the opera, tried objecting to the yellow gown—she detests yellow—designed for her for Act II. Mr. Bing was forced to intervene again. His opening remark was, "You know, you're very stubborn! Sit in the orchestra and see for yourself what a beautiful effect your gown makes on stage with the right lighting." As she sat in the orchestra, very annoyed at having been told to do so, she was determined not to budge an inch. Then she caught sight of someone on stage wearing her yellow gown, wig, wide-brimmed hat, and gloves. The person had a very bizarre way of walking. As soon as that "someone" was recognized as Mr. Bing, laughter resounded in the theater and Renata, laughing too, had to yield. He had won again.

Disguises were not new to Rudolf Bing. During the Metropolitan tours, he often had fun appearing as a stage extra. In Act I of *Tosca* he would be recognized under the bishops mitre. In *Cavalleria Rusticana* he would disguise himself as a peasant. His appearances were unannounced, and there was always the risk that the singers would burst into laughter at the sight of him standing in front of them, in costume and makeup.

The critics had many reservations about the direction, sets, and costumes of Guthrie's *Traviata*. Rolf Gérard had imposed a dominant color on each act to underscore the musical and psychological atmosphere. Act I was blue and white, Act II pale autumnal yellow, Act III violent contrasts of black, brown, and strong tones, and Act IV blue-gray—tableaux not appreciated by all. Furthermore, Act III was overpowered by a grand staircase with the action occurring up and down the steps, which was tiring to the singers. Act IV, an unadorned Parisian bedroom, became instead a Hollywood-style bedroom. The scenes were cluttered, the costumes too cumbersome and overpowering. Violetta's costume for Flora's party, prepared in a Parisian *atelier*, and costing $8,000, caused some controversy. Finally, Tebaldi, in spite of her 25-pound weight loss, didn't look fragile enough for her role as a consumptive. Some people felt that a different approach to the stage direction would have prevented such problems.

Despite these objections, *Traviata* was an unparalleled success. It was a rare event. The Metropolitan tried to enforce its traditional veto of solo curtain calls. The artists were expected to appear on stage holding one another firmly by the hand. Giuseppe Campora and Leonard Warren were well aware of this tradition but they repeatedly tried to send Renata out alone to receive the ovation she deserved. When she finally did make a solo bow, the result was an event not frequently experienced at the Metropolitan. She was showered with flowers as a spontaneous manifestation of affection and admiration emanated warmly from the thrilled audience. Louis Biancolli of the New York *World Telegram* wrote that she was "a Violetta irresistible to the eyes, to the ears, to the heart."

After the performance, policemen, some on horseback, worked at restraining the crowd of admirers waiting for Tebaldi to exit the theater. When she finally freed herself from the adoring crowd, she left with her mother, Tina, and Linda Barone for her hotel on 57th Street. There, tranquil and happy, she ate her usual portion of prosciutto.

The battle at the Metropolitan had been won. The Sunday *News* expressed it the day after the performance in an article headed, "Renata is champ."

Mr. Bing had engaged Maria Callas for the opening night of *Norma* while scheduling Tebaldi for the important new production of *La Traviata* in the same year. He planned carefully so that their schedules in New York would not coincide.

Maria Callas arrived, sang to a sold-out house, was greeted by crowds of fans at the stage entrance after every performance, but her press reviews were less than enthusiastic. *Time* magazine said, "Callas has come and gone, leaving the field to her great rival, Renata Tebaldi." In the Sunday *News* John Chapman simply revised American history by saying, "The first conquest of Manhattan occurred through peaceful negotiations between whites and redskins. Today the battle for Manhattan was fought between two women, Maria Meneghini Callas and Renata Tebaldi. Tebaldi won!"

Though the Tebaldi-Callas conflict at La Scala ended with Tebaldi's decision to leave ("A chicken coop cannot house two roosters; I preferred to live in peace, so I left."), things went differently at the Metropolitan where Renata was hailed as queen, a position she held for more than 15 years. A New York newspaper wrote, "Now Miss Tebaldi could open a school for angels."

❦15❦

Art Subsidy under Attack
First Tour with the Metropolitan
Letter to Elsa Maxwell

Government subsidy of the Arts, a favorite target of legisla-
tive budget slashing, came under attack again in Italy in 1957.
The most vulnerable were the astronomical fees asked for by
the superstars. On April 19 of that year, Gianfranco Piazzesi
wrote in *Nazione* that opponents of government subsidy of
opera now had a trump card because "Callas and Tebaldi
receive 700,000 to one million lire per performance," he went
on to write, "now that fanaticism for opera has diminished."

Tebaldi, abroad, received a copy of the article a few days
after its publication and immediately wrote her reply to the
editor of the newspaper: "The entire blame can't be placed
on demands made by the opera singers, and furthermore, I'd
like to clarify a misconception which may obscure my integ-
rity as an artist. It isn't at all true that I receive 700,000 to
one million lire per performance. Mr Piazzesi's statement is
inaccurate. I have never requested more than 500,000 lire
from any Italian opera house or organization, although they
would have offerred me the same fee given to other artists
who are in no way superior to me. My assertions can be
substantiated by those same theaters and my agency, ALCI. I
have never exploited my voice, and I am more than con-

90

vinced that it is pure art and not large fees that enhances an artist's worth. I'm certainly not adding deficits to the budget. The three singers who are demanding the above-mentioned fees are Callas, Del Monaco and Di Stefano. But that in no way makes them artistically superior to me. Kindly leave me in peace and stop involving me in a controversy which obscures my reputation as a true artist." This letter was handwritten by Tebaldi on stationery from the Cleveland Hotel where she stayed from April 22 to April 28 during the Metropolitan's 1957 tour.

The tour, following nine performances of *La Traviata* and two of *Tosca* at the Metropolitan plus several concerts all performed from February through April, would take her to eleven cities in the States with final performances in Toronto and Montreal.

This was Tebaldi's first appearance in most of the tour cities, and everywhere she sang the same phenomenon was repeated: sold-out theaters overflowing with thrilled audiences eager to hear her.

For her Baltimore debut on April 1st, Renata had a bit of bad luck. A cold, probably caused by excessive air conditioning, kept her performance uncertain and her stand-by waiting in the wings until close to curtain time. In spite of the cold, Tebaldi did get through the performance which was attended by the legendary soprano, Rosa Ponselle. The next day the press reported that although they could not totally evaluate the voice, they were truly overwhelmed by its exceptional beauty. (Years later, in March of 1966, after a magnificent concert by Tebaldi, in that same city, a smiling Rosa Ponselle was heard by this translator saying, "This is the first time I am standing in line to congratulate a diva!" as she held an enormous corsage of orchids which she then warmly presented to her younger colleague.)

In Houston there was again a sold-out theater. Tebaldi, always in the company of her mother, Tina, Linda Barone, and 28 pieces of luggage, arrived at the Rice Hotel. This time Mamma Giuseppina, fearing that her daughter would catch another cold as she had in Baltimore, plugged all the air conditioning vents in their rooms with cotton. After Tebaldi's Houston performance of *Tosca* she was reverentially linked to the great divas of the past who had sung there: Adelina Patti, Mary Garden, Geraldine Farrar, and Claudia Muzio.

Following the Metropolitan tour, Tebaldi visited Cuba, making her debut in Havana in *La Traviata*, *Tosca*, and *Aida*. Tebaldi remembers that the heat and humidity were dreadful. During performances her makeup had to be reapplied between each act. In her dressing room, even with air conditioning, which Mamma Tebaldi left on this time regardless of possible harm to her daughter's voice, most things left out on the dressing table melted, including pills.

In Havana, a series of gala parties hosted by the rich elite in their fairy-tale villas followed one another. In fact, the Cuban opera season was sponsored by a group of wealthy ladies who consulted with the Metropolitan Opera for the scheduling of their season, and cost was of no concern. Castro's arrival in Cuba would soon end that.

Her tour behind her, Tebaldi returned to New York on June 27, the day before her departure for Italy on the *Cristoforo Colombo* for her performances at the Arena di Verona and her customary summer vacation. Arrangements for a pre-departure concert at Lewissohn Stadium by their beloved Tebaldi had been spontaneously set in motion by throngs of opera lovers with the support of their music clubs and organizations. The evening of the 27th was the only time available for a concert since their very bizarre petition to delay the departure of the *Cristoforo Colombo* was turned down.

Tebaldi accepted this time- and weather-defying challenge. There was no time for a rain date. The fans, committed to their last breath, offered an assurance from the good Lord by affixing "good weather guaranteed" on concert billboards. When the ship arrived from Cuba in the late afternoon, a limousine and a motorcycle escort sped Tebaldi uptown to the stadium. With only enough time to change, she made her entrance onstage, regal as an Olympian goddess in emerald green and the result was rapture and delight throughout the huge stadium. She sang arias from *Il Trovatore, La Forza Del Destino,* and *Otello.* As she concluded her program, the 20,000 spectators, in a standing ovation, shouted for encores. They were granted two, and kisses were thrown to them with much *allegria.*

Renata had another reason for being happy that day. Her mother had finally agreed to her having a poodle. While she was enjoying her triumph on stage, Tina was speeding towards New Jersey to pick up the puppy, a grey poodle, and that evening New I entered the Tebaldi household.

On August 20th Tebaldi returned to the Arena di Verona where she had not appeared since the turbulent *Mefistofele* of 1950. "The Arena is frightening because of its size," says Renata. "Conductors are forced to use a musical strategy, an almost imperceptible anticipation of the tempi, to try to minimize the effect the vast distance between the stage and the orchestra pit has on the singers. Certainly, the acoustics are perfect and the voice travels to the farthest recesses of the Arena. The greatest inconvenience is that singing outdoors is harmful to the vocal cords, especially in the evening when the throat is warmest and humidity sets in."

For this non-subscription performance of *La Bohème,* fans arrived from Parma, Modena, Milan, Rome, Naples, Palermo, and elsewhere, some even on bicycles, carrying banners acclaiming their Renata.

For the occasion, Elsa Maxwell, who was in Venice at the time, sent a note of best wishes to Renata. She excused herself at great length for her absence, which she blamed on a cold. She expressed her desire to see Renata soon in New

York and closed her note with "all my love." But in fact, the old gossip had "joined the enemy." Elsa Maxwell, who had written of Callas's debut at the Metropolitan in October 1956, "the '*Casta Diva*' of Madame Callas was a great disappointment," and who had continuously attacked Callas without pity after all her performances, quite suddenly changed her attitude. It happened at a costume ball at the Waldorf Astoria. Callas, dressed as Cleopatra and wearing close to $1,000,000 in jewelry, asked to be introduced to Elsa Maxwell. Veiling any anger she might have felt over Maxwell's vehement press attacks, Callas greeted her affectionately. When the columnist asked Callas her opinion of Tebaldi, she was heard to reply, "I'm a great admirer of Tebaldi!" Then she glanced at Maxwell with her large, magnetic eyes and Elsa melted.

In the Spring of 1957, Elsa Maxwell was in Italy for the publication of her book, *I Married The World*. On the pretext of getting to know the singer better and bringing about a reconciliation with Tebaldi, she accepted Callas's hospitality to visit her at her villa in Sirmione. "At 73 I am tired of speaking ill of people. I wish only to speak well...," she said, along with announcing her intentions of bringing peace to the two rivals. This sudden desire to light the flame of peace in the world was, in reality, her way of masking the sudden burning attraction she felt for Callas. It was in fact in her honor that Elsa Maxwell hosted a gala ball in Venice which Callas attended even though it meant cancelling her final performance of *La Sonnambula* in England.

When Tebaldi, during an interview for an article she was writing in the magazine, *Oggi,* good-naturedly alluded to her friend's fickle behavior, Maxwell replied with biting sarcasm in another magazine, *Europeo*. Tebaldi remained calm; she wrote her a long reply via the *Europeo:*

Dear Elsa,

I want to start my letter, which I wish to make public, by congratulating you on your now frequent contributions to such a prestigious Italian magazine. I know of no other American writer similarly engaged. I would also like you to know that I was surprised and saddened by your words. As you well know, I'm not a writer. The three biographical articles written for another magazine (*Oggi*) are my first literary attempts. You, on the other hand, who have been writing articles and books for many years, quickly crushed my brief essay and contradicted everything I wrote about you. I'm distressed by this because during my long visits to the United States you always showed me friendship and I'll always be grateful to you for that.

I have no desire to argue with anyone, least of all with you, who so frequently gave me proof of your exquisite courtesy and admiration for my art. But it's necessary for me to explain to you and to all my friends in Italy that I've never been disloyal to you, nor ever will be. I called you a gossip only because all the newspapers call you one and not because I think of you as one. If I wrote that you went to Milan to find a publisher for your new book, it's because I read as much in the Italian newspapers. I was on tour with the Metropolitan at the time. I'm sorry if I've erred in some details but you're too well known everywhere to think that I would try to diminish your popularity maliciously. I've been with you at the theater, at public affairs; everyone knows you and seeks your autograph. I'm well aware that you're a personality, and the dinner you gave for me at the Colony, with so many ambassadors and other influential people attending, attests to that.

Your being photographed together with Maria Callas, obviously a wise publicity move, was quite an achievement. You are an unbeatable combination and both of you are expert in attracting the attention of the press. When you had not yet learned to appreciate my colleague, I remember your telling me, in the presence of others, "Callas sent me flowers. How can I say how many? It's impossible." Perhaps the various times you mentioned these flowers they were always the same flowers.

I thank God that I'm a singer and not a writer. I thought that my articles were of little importance. I see, instead, that even you read them, in Italian. I'll stop writing, Elsa, but I'll go on singing because it is in singing that I find that happiness that you wish me. I have not had an easy life, as you well know, and the sacrifices to succeed have been many. God has helped me and continues to do so. The satisfactions are immense, but they don't make me forget my friends. I have no social ambitions because I don't have time for them. All my thoughts, my energy, my efforts are devoted to honoring the responsibility that my name carries with it. This is a burden even if it is accompanied by much joy.

Elsa, perhaps you haven't understood me, you with your enthusiasm, your irrepressible joy of life, your worldly experience. I've only one desire, to live and let live. My philosophy consists of those marvelous words spoken by Beatrice to Dante at the beginning of the *Divine Comedy*, *"Temer si dée di sole quelle cose/Ch'hanno potenza di far altrui male;/Dell'altre no, ché non son paurose."*[6]

Thanks for all your kindness and the beautiful things you have written about me. Don't search for disloyalty or insincerity in me because you won't find

---

[6] "One must fear only those things/That have the power to hurt others;/Of the rest, do not fear, for they are not frightening."

96

any. Perhaps I'm a bad journalist, but I'm a good friend. I repeat what I said in my last article, 'I'll always be happy to see you.' Renata Tebaldi

This time Elsa Maxwell was completely disarmed. She sent Tebaldi an enormous bouquet of flowers and confirmed her friendship "with all my love."

❦16❦

The Death of Mamma Tebaldi

Tebaldi was beset by illness during her performances at the Chicago Lyric in the Fall of 1957. After a glorious success on opening night, with Mario Del Monaco as her Otello and Tito Gobbi as Iago, the Asiatic flu caused her to cancel. Maria Kuhn arrived from Philadelphia to replace her after the second *Otello*. (Mamma Tebaldi and Tina soon came down with the flu, too.) The first performance of *Manon Lescaut*, which Renata was debuting in Chicago, was postponed until late in October. She sang a total of three performances of *Manon Lescaut* in Chicago that season which was the rare occasion that paired Tebaldi with Jussi Björling. Two performances of *Andrea Chénier* followed, with Del Monaco and Gobbi under the baton of Gianandrea Gavazzeni.

Adriana Lecouvreur, which had caused a tug-of-war with Rudolf Bing, ended the 1957 season for Tebaldi at the Chicago Lyric. She had wanted to sing the opera at the Metropolitan, but Mr. Bing would not agree to its inclusion in the repertory. With her unyielding stubbornness, she suggested it to the Chicago opera comapany with success. The opera was prepared for her. Renata sang two performances with Giuseppe Di Stefano, Tito Gobbi, and Giulietta Simionato.

Here, too, there were problems. Simionato fell on stage, twisted an ankle and finished the performance in a wheelchair.

Immediately following her Chicago performances, Renata left for New York with her mother and Tina. A busy schedule had been planned for her at the Metropolitan. She was to have sung *Tosca*, *Aida*, *La Bohème*, *Andrea Chénier*, *La Traviata*, and *La Forza del Destino*.

On the 18th of November, Mamma Tebaldi's 68th birthday was celebrated quietly with a few friends. The next day she complained of not feeling well, and a physician who was called in quickly defined her malaise as negligible. The diagnosis by Renata's long-time friend, Dr. Claudio Gerbi, was altogether different. He recognized the problem as coronary thrombosis. The gravity of the problem became apparent immediately. Mamma Tebaldi should have been hospitalized, but the management at the Buckingham Hotel made it possible for her to remain in the hotel, and a room was prepared where oxygen could be administered.

Tebaldi cancelled her November 21st performance of *Tosca* and Antonietta Stella was brought in as her replacement. She also cancelled her performance on November 24th at a benefit concert. She and Tina and two nurses took turns at Mamma Tebaldi's bedside. After a day or two her condition seemed improved, and Renata announced to the management at the Metropolitan that she would sing *Aida* at the matinee on November 30th. Maria Curtis Verna had been called in for the last two dress rehearsals.

On the evening of the 29th, Mamma Tebaldi had another crisis. She lapsed into a coma and passed away on Saturday, November 30th, at 5 a.m. At the matinee performance of *Aida*, Rudolf Bing appeared on the Met stage to announce to the audience the absence of Renata Tebaldi. He said, "I am certain that all of you join us in sharing Madame Tebaldi's deep sorrow and in expressing our deepest sympathy and condolences."

A requiem mass was officiated by Cardinal Spellman at St. Patrick's Cathedral on the morning of December 3rd. Learning of the gravity of Mamma Tebaldi's illness, the Cardinal had gone personally each day to the Buckingham Hotel to visit her. At a much happier time earlier in the year, Cardinal Spellman had awarded Renata Tebaldi the Great Cross of the Order of the Dames of the Holy Sepulcher. On that occasion Princess Grace and Prince Ranier were present.

On the morning of the requiem a silent crowd accompanied the funeral procession along the entire route from the Hotel to the Cathedral. Renata, despite her vow never to travel by plane again, decided to accompany her mother's remains home to Italy. Because of stringent regulations, the coffin was loaded onto a TWA cargo plane. Renata, with Tina and one of her oldest friends, Luigi Rovescala, who had flown in immediately from Italy, were to follow on an Alitalia flight.

A blizzard delayed the flights for two days. Later, at Shannon airport, the coffin was transferred to another cargo plane. When Renata finally arrived in Milan, no news was available. Dense fog had delayed the arrival of the cargo plane and forced it to land in Torino instead of Milan. Tebaldi was notified that it was necessary to identify the body before its transfer to Milan. Nini Castiglioni, who had waited all night at Malpensa airport in Milan for the cargo plane, rushed to Torino. She did not, at first glance, recognize the body which, contrary to Italian custom, had been embalmed (in America). Dazed because of the delays and fatigue, Nini was confused until she noticed a few roses that she, herself, had ordered, still in the hands of Mamma Tebaldi.

The body was taken to Milan and then to Langhirano. Twice during the trip the hearse took the wrong turn. At last the trip ended at the little cemetery of Mataleto. All of Langhirano accompanied Renata, along with many friends from Milan and elsewhere.

The next day Renata returned home to Piazzetta Guastalla. With her were Tina and Aunt Marianna (who had welcomed Mamma Tebaldi and her niece into her home during the war). The rooms looked large, empty, and sinister. All that had happened seemed incredible. Everything had happened so fast. Renata wasn't even certain that she would sing again.

In Elsa Maxwell's column in the Sunday *News*, a paragraph bordered in black announced the death: "The music world is saddened by the news of the death of Renata Tebaldi's mother. Miss Tebaldi loved her mother very deeply and it is hard to imagine the grief this splendid singer has endured during these last two weeks."

❧17❧

Return to the Stage: *Butterfly*
Vienna Debut
Giuseppe Di Stefano

It was a cold evening in Barcelona on January 23rd, 1958, as a huge crowd filled the artists' exit of the Teatro Liceo. It was a quiet, almost embarrassed group. They had come to greet Tebaldi after her debut in *Madama Butterfly*. As she came forward, dressed in deep mourning, no one in the crowd cried, "Brava!" and no one asked for an autograph. They kissed her hands silently and touched the hem of her dress respectfully. Tebaldi had returned to the stage two months after the death of her mother.

During the terrible days in New York after her mother's death, Renata had confided her doubts about continuing her career to Cardinal Spellman. He wisely reminded her that a beautiful voice is a sacred gift and must be shared with others. There also had been rumors that Renata would enter a convent. But the path leading back to her career seemed marked for her.

The date of her debut in *Madama Butterfly* had been set for some time, and Tebaldi decided to keep that date for her return to the stage. She left Milan by train on January 16th. With her were Tina and Carmen Melis who, by accompanying her, hoped to ease the pain of her mother's absence. Renata

102

would never forget this grand gesture of friendship from her now elderly teacher. When Carmen Melis faced financial difficulties during the last years of her life, Renata did not hesitate to provide for her. After Melis's death, her only heir returned to Renata a gold locket which had been a present from her to her teacher. Carmen Melis had always worn it around her neck with Renata's photo in it.

The respectful and affectionate greeting after the first performance was followed by impassioned ovations at subsequent performances. At the Sunday matinee, the enthusiastic fans almost attacked the limousine that came for Tebaldi. The Italian chauffeur, somewhat alarmed, mixed Italian and Spanish nervously, shouting, "Tebaldi no está qui, está ahora in hotel." The police arrived to disperse the crowd. Then the fans rushed down the avenue and staged a joyful demonstration in front of her hotel as they waited for her.

Manuel R. De Llauder, in *El Noticiero Universal* of January 24st, 1958, wrote, "The audience was so moved that their overwhelming applause and shouts of 'Brava' obliged the celebrated singer to encore the aria, which she did, outdoing herself vocally and emotionally."

About the role of Butterfly, Renata had this to say: "It involved very painstaking preparation. The role had appealed to me for a long time, but I'd always felt that the time wasn't quite right. Butterfly is usually sung at the end of one's career because it may harm the voice. Waiting too long, however, may be risky because Butterfly requires a voice that is still truly responsive. Tenors, similarly, often wait to sing *Otello* at the end of their careers, and by that time their vocal means may be exhausted."

Tebaldi was too tall and majestic for the role of a petite Japanese. She prepared the role for her Metropolitan debut the following November with Yoshio Aoyama, the stage director. She went through a difficult training period of restraining not only her actions, but her emotions, too. Every gesture and expression had to be repressed. She had to learn to make herself appear smaller.

"I practiced long hours in my kimono, back and forth in my hotel room, trying to imitate their short steps. My skirt was tight and had a double fold which I continuously stumbled on. One foot would get in the other's way or trip the other, and I would look like a child wearing her shoes for the first time, toes pointing in, stumbling. I thought I'd never win the battle. I remember that, overcome by frustration, I cried several times.

"Puccini is one of my most preferred composers. I adore his music, what he does with it, the way he prepares the singing line; I'm particularly fond of the female roles. Puccini must have understood women deeply! I think it must have been impossible to resist the fascination of this man! The intimate empathy I feel for him, even if only through my interpretation of his music, makes his scores especially appealing to me. The role of Butterfly may present serious vocal problems, but, fortunately, I didn't encounter too many. Naturally, my Butterfly is *all'italiana* as Puccini wrote it even though the opera has a Japanese setting. And it must be sung that way, that is, as written...."

Jay Harrison of the *Herald Tribune* agreed with her in his review on November 10st, 1958. After beginning with, "Renata Tebaldi, in singing the role of Madame Butterfly for the first time at the Metropolitan on Saturday evening, has given what will be remembered as a historic performance," he continues, "The opera is as authentically Japanese as minestrone can be. In spite of the cherry blossoms, *Butterfly* is an Italian product and that is the way Miss Tebaldi sang it. She gave us the impression that she was in love with her role, singing it with the beauty and glory of the grand Italian style. The Japanese illusion was therefore of secondary importance, even though she was made up splendidly and had learned to make all those affected gestures and to bow deeply. But it was the voice that created the character of Butterfly...."

Tebaldi sang another memorable *Butterfly* that same year in Naples at the Arena Flegrea. In the cast were the renowned Giuseppe Valdengo as Sharpless and the young hopeful, Gianni Raimondi, as Pinkerton. Maestro Angelo Questa conducted. Senator Giovanni Leoni, Salvatore Gotta, and a large group of admirers from Milan led by Fosca Crespi were in the audience. Fosca Crespi, Puccini's adopted daughter, had been one of Maria Callas's most fervent supporters, but Callas's professional star had dimmed.

In January 1958, an unpleasant incident occurred in Rome when Callas walked out during her performance of Norma. In February her Metropolitan contract was cancelled because of her confrontation with Rudolf Bing, and she refused to sing in Chicago because of a financial dispute. In May she ended her relationship with La Scala, citing incompatability with the administration as the reason. In addition, after her return from a cruise on the *Christina* with Aristotle Onassis, she announced her separation from her husband, Giovanni Meneghini.

Tebaldi had patiently reorganized her plans so they would serve her in the long run; she knew how to wait, and now the day of her return to La Scala was approaching. Two meaningful events had already taken place. On April 28th, 1958, Renata sang a benefit concert, as she had done the previous year, at the Manzoni Theater. This time, Ghiringhelli, the administrator of La Scala, was in the audience with Wally Toscanini, the daughter of the great conductor, together with Fosca Crespi, and the stage director, Margherita Wallman. As Tebaldi made her stage entrance she was greeted by seemingly endless applause. She was warmed by a crescendo of enthusiasm as she sang her program and many encores. The concert ended with a tribute of flowers and an audience on its feet applauding, asking her to continue.

Contrary to her customary refusal, Renata was so moved

by the warmth and enthusiasm of the evening that she accepted an invitation to a party in her honor, a party where the segment of Milanese society that influenced decisions at La Scala would gather.

Soon after the concert, Ghiringhelli invited Tebaldi to perform with La Scala at the Expo in Brussels in June. Renata refused Ghiringhelli's invitation, but when the Ministry of the Arts invited her to represent Italy in a foreign country in such a distinguished event, she decided to accept. She was to sing *Tosca* with Giuseppe Di Stefano and Tito Gobbi, and Herbert Von Karajan was conducting. At the last moment Di Stefano was replaced by Giuseppe Zampieri.

"Pippo's" (Di Stefano's) appearances were always subject to unanticipated complications. In fact, he used to sign contracts "distractedly" and then forget all about them. Two months after a cancellation in Vienna, during the tour in Brussels, he failed to arrive at the theater for a dress rehearsal of *Tosca*. Everyone was on stage waiting in makeup and costume and Maestro Gavazzeni was on the podium. Someone finally suggested calling his hotel to see if anything had happened to him. Di Stefano was in the hotel. He was sleeping. Nothing was wrong. He had forgotten the dress rehearsal completely. When he arrived at the theater more than an hour late, he apologized, told some jokes, and that was the end of it. He sang in a black leather jacket because he had not had time to change into his costume.

"His personality worked for him...," recalls Renata. "It would have been impossible for me. I've always been too conscientious in my professional behavior, perhaps because what annoyed me most about my work was the inconvenience caused by negligence and superficiality. I always arranged everything in advance: makeup, costumes, all the details. I was in my dressing room two hours before a performance just in case something unexpected happened. In so doing, I was able to remain calm." Only once, at a perfor-

mance of *La Traviata* at La Fenice in 1949, was she heard
shouting at a beautician who had styled her hair in a way she
found horrible. Everybody tried to calm her down, but only
half-succeeded.

"Pippo was eccentric and temperamental but one was
inclined to forgive him anything. We often argued about professional ethics. He scolded me because I never put on airs.
He would say to me, 'With your famous name you should
arrive at the theater in a chauffeured limousine in eye-catch-
ing outfits; you have to be eccentric.' Evenings he was always eager for fun and he would tease me because I'd refuse
to go along with him. 'As always you'll be worrying about
your next performance. What kind of life is that? I want to
live and enjoy my years. *Mi sun minga matt!*[7] he would say
irresistibly in Milanese dialect with his Catanese inflection.
But I couldn't face having to explain to my audience that I
wasn't in good voice because I had been in a smoke-filled
night spot until three in the morning. He'd use that excuse,
but even if he didn't, he was often outlandish! But, that's
Pippo, and he's so lovable." One had to be prepared for anything with him. During a performance of *Forza del Destino*
with Di Stefano, in Palermo in 1956, Tebaldi encored "*Pace,
pace, mio Dio.*" Since that meant a long wait for him, he
grew impatient, went to his dressing room, changed and returned to his hotel leaving the others to do their best on stage
without him. Something close to a scandal followed.

---

[7] "I'm not crazy!"

❦18❧

1958: The Metropolitan's Diamond Jubilee

Tosca was Tebaldi's selection for the inauguration of the Metropolitan's 75th season on October 27, 1958. Mr. Bing was eager to please her since this was to be her opening night. (Callas had had one opening night with *Norma* and Zinka Milanov had had three.)

This was the fourth time in the history of the Metropolitan that *Tosca* opened the season. The first was in 1901 soon after its world premiere in Rome. On November 17, 1919, it returned on opening night with Geraldine Ferrar and Enrico Caruso and three years later on November 13, 1922, with Maria Jeritza, Giovanni Martinelli, and Antonio Scotti.

This 1958 opening night was memorable.

Curtain time was delayed seven minutes because of the throngs of people arriving and the pervading atmosphere of excitement. At last the orchestra started with the national anthem. Further delay followed to allow photographers time for pictures. This was followed by a roll of drums, and finally the gold curtain went up. Many of the 3,836 people in the audience had paid as much as $100.00 for a ticket. The proceeds at the box office were the highest ever recorded at the Met (some said the highest in the history of opera—

$1,500,000).

Press coverage of celebrities seated in the diamond horse-shoe, the jewelry, gowns, accessories, hairstyles, was copious and detailed. The diamond horseshoe got its name from the proverbial diamond jewelry worn by the ladies who sat in the boxes. The appearance of Mrs. Bradley Martin was legendary due to a diamond she wore that gossips said weighed more than her husband, or of Grace Vanderbilt, called the "queen mother of opera," who nonchalantly arrived at the theater wearing a million dollars worth of jewelry. Mrs. George Washington Kavanaugh, who died in 1954, refused to sit in the diamond horseshoe. Instead, she walked down the center aisle, and sat in the first row, always wearing her signature outfit: a grand ermine cape adorned with six orchids.

For the 1958 opening night of *Tosca*, the parure of diamonds and rubies worn by Mrs. Arpels caused a sensation. Ali Khan, for whom this opening night was a first, was a guest of Elsa Maxwell. Giovanni Martinelli, the Cavaradossi of the 1922 *Tosca*, was in the audience, as were numerous diplomats and other notables. Outside, around the opera house, the line of parked Cadillacs and Rolls Royces seemed to extend endlessly. On stage, two distinguished singers, Mario Del Monaco and George London, joined Renata Tebaldi under the baton of the celebrated Dimitri Mitropoulos.

A climate of excitement had prevailed during the rehearsals. There was even an unscheduled rehearsal for complete cast, orchestra, and conductor, requested by Mario Del Monaco, for which his wife was present with her tape recorder. After the rehearsal, without saying a word, Del Monaco left with his wife, walked across Times Square, his hand covering his mouth to keep out the cold, and visited his costume designer. As he entered, he was quickly surrounded by a half dozen people speaking six different languages, all translated into admiration for his physique. As he tried on the trousers of his costume he said gently, "The pants make me look shorter." The multilingual reply was "The pants are all wrong! We'll change them immediately!" He winked at his wife as he said, "Why should I say that the costume is fine and break their hearts? I have to be difficult. They expect it of me. Now they're happily trying to please me."

Tebaldi recalls that, "Mario was always worried about his height; he was afraid of being too short and would come into my dressing room to check on the heels I was wearing in order to determine the height of the heels he would wear."

A very beautiful wig had been prepared for her for this *Tosca*, but Mr. Bing found it too eccentric and decided she could not wear it. Renata cried with disappointment, but she didn't succeed in changing his mind.

Since her many commitments in Europe and Chicago had kept her away for a year, Tebaldi was returning to sing at the Metropolitan Opera for the first time following the death of her mother. The audience was aware of this and was as moved as she was. As she made her stage entrance after "Mario! Mario!" sung in the wings, she was greeted by overwhelming applause which repeatedly echoed through the house throughout the evening. Howard Taubman of *The New York Times* wrote on October 28th, "Miss Tebaldi is back in splendid form. Her voice remains one of the most exceptional instruments of our time. She has an extraordinary range, from rich chest tones to filigreed pianissimi, rich color, and an abundant reserve of power."

Tebaldi wore a red costume in Act I, but it was her second act costume, made for her Vienna debut, that caused a sensation. It was a gown of yellow satin beautifully adorned with fine stones, over which she draped a full-length black velvet cape with a train.

She posed for a series of photographs as Tosca, wearing a parure of diamonds and rubies on loan from Van Cleef, which at one time belonged to Josephine Beauharnais, the wife of

Napoleon. The photographs were taken under heavy police guard. The now-legendary photograph of Tebaldi as Tosca appeared on the cover of *Time* magazine. A lengthy biographical cover story accompanied the photograph.

Nini Castiglioni, unleashing personal couriers (including the collaboration of Alitalia pilots) across the Atlantic Ocean, managed to deliver a photo of Renata taken at the dress rehearsal in time for printing in Italian newspapers the very morning after the opening night performance. She had disobeyed Mr. Bing's order not to do this, but he was the first one to be pleased by the outcome of this heroic venture, since it brought him excellent publicity.

Tebaldi's busy Metropolitan schedule included five performances of *Tosca*, two of *Madama Butterfly*, five of *Otello*, three of *Manon Lescaut,* and one *Bohème* before the end of 1958. On Christmas eve Tebaldi sang her 269th *Tosca*.

By this time in her life, Tebaldi was emerging from her shell and speaking more freely about herself. Questions from the media, although still discreetly asked, now were directed towards her private life and not only her career.

Miss Tebaldi, are you tired of being single?

"I'm too busy to think about it."

Do you have other dreams besides your artistic aspirations?

"I'm too busy for dreams. I don't even have time for hobbies other than collecting works of art and ethnic dolls." (Years earlier, when asked that same question, she replied, "To be left in peace.")

Do you think that Callas's bizarre behavior takes the limelight away from you?

"Callas's whims don't take any more from me than they take from her."

Are you afraid of falling deeply in love?

"I'd rather wait the rest of my life than suffer disillusionment. There's nothing more beautiful than waiting for something wonderful that may happen any time, next year, tomorrow, now."

Years ago you were in love and almost married....

"Men, especially Italian men, are not fond of marrying a career. He loved children and we would have had ten, I'm sure. He had a big house in the country. I'd have lived a peaceful life...but, obviously, I didn't love him enough or it wouldn't have ended."

It was during this period that Renata's father, Teobaldo, in a statement to the press after many years of silence, expressed his desire to be reconciled with his daughter. After the death of Mamma Giuseppina, Teobaldo married Gisella Gasperini, the woman for whom he had left his family.

He had recently written Renata Tebaldi many letters hoping that a correspondence would begin. But if she could have forgiven him as a daughter, and perhaps she had already done so, Renata couldn't forget the pain that his actions had inflicted on her mother.

❧19❧

1959: Arturo Basile
Aida in Paris

1959 was a glorious, turbulent, exciting year for Renata Tebaldi.

It started at the Metropolitan with three performances of *La Bohème* and one of *Tosca*, followed by a series of recitals which took her to Washington D.C., Cleveland, Ann Arbor, Kalamazoo, Chicago, Montreal, Philadelphia, and Boston.

Until then, Tebaldi had given little thought to recitals, devoting her time almost exclusively to opera performances. "A recital is difficult because selections follow one another in sequence. In opera, the arias come at intervals throughout the action. Frequently, in recitals one is deprived of the release of tension from a high note since recital selections usually stress the middle register, exhausting it, and one runs the risk of becoming hoarse.

"In preparing a program for a recital, it's important to consider the selections, the sequence, and the overall effect, in order to create a meaningful musical experience...," but then Renata adds, "Certainly recitals are exciting. Almost more than opera. One is alone on stage and a grand piano replaces the orchestra. Making one's stage entrance wearing an elegant gown, the audience clearly in view, stirs an emotion that even now as I think of it, thrills me...."

In Toronto, Massey Hall was sold out. When Tebaldi entered the stage from the wings she was puzzled at the sight of 200 people sitting on stage—when she turned toward the auditorium where the other 2,800 were she understood that the overflow was sitting on stage. At Ann Arbor 5,000 spectators filled the theater to capacity.

After the recital in Philadelphia, a youth kneeled in front of Tebaldi and she caressed his head. A young girl, trembling with excitement, gave her a camellia which she pinned on her dress. In Kalamazoo a florist sent her 200 American Beauty roses which he renamed "Renata Roses."

During the last two weeks of March, Renata was involved with the opera season in Havana. Cuba was under the Castro regime and the era of jubilant festivities was only a memory. The country was overrun by squads of soldiers patrolling the streets as their dictator's voice could be heard through loudspeakers addressing the populace with comforting phrases and patriotic slogans.

Despite the austerity, there too, as in Barcelona, Naples, and Chicago, Tebaldi was successful in getting a new production of *Adriana Lecouvreur* and was more than ever determined to do so at the Metropolitan. She also sang *La Bohème* and *Manon Lescaut* before returning to Italy where for four performances of *La Bohème* in Naples, five performances of *Madama Butterfly* and a recital in Rome, before going on to Milan and Paris in June.

On her way up to Milan, Renata stopped in Florence to receive the San Luca Award from the Association of the Twelve Apostles, an award presented yearly to an artist.

Previously, awards had gone to Dimitri Mitropoulos for music, Orio Vergani for journalism, Vittorio De Sica for cinema, and Jean-Louis Barrault for the theater. Gino Bechi, the acclaimed baritone, had enthusiastically nominated Tebaldi for the award and, for this, he was delighted to have the pleasure of escorting her back to the hotel after the ceremony. The gourmet dinner at the famed Sabatini was shared in good spirits. Present at the dinner was Renato Mariani, the city comptroller, who spent a good part of the evening quipping about the cost of all the telegrams sent to Tebaldi to invite her, to determine that she would accept, and to explain to her the meaning of the award, "The Twelve Apostles," so that she wouldn't think that it was a religious sect inviting her.

A humorous malapropism occurred the previous evening when a young daughter of the sound director, Amerigo Gomez, who was orchestrating the affair, telephoned her grandmother saying, "Nonna, tonight I'm sleeping with you because Mommy is going to the station to meet Garibaldi"[8] instead of, "la Tebaldi." Judging from the festivities at the Florence train station for Tebaldi, the error wasn't so far-fetched.

On the 5th of June a grand *Aida* took place at the Paris Opera. Tebaldi had sung there last in 1949 with the San Carlo Opera Company. She arrived at the Gare de Lyon in Paris (accompanied by Tina, New, and a large number of suitcases) in the midst of a subway strike which snarled traffic terribly. After a tedious hour, she finally reached the Grand Hotel where she greeted the press with her usual radiant smile. Although she spoke little French, everyone there interviewed her. Some printed details were incorrect, as in *France Soir*: "Tebaldi was not born in Pesaro but in a small village called 'Pisaro.'" That was nothing compared to statements made after her first performance. Andre Malraux, minister and man of letters, rivalled Napoleon's enthusiasm at the foot of the Pyramids as he said, "Madame Tebaldi, I bring you the compliments of all of France!" Puzzling was the comment of the

---

[8] Giuseppe Garibaldi was the general who fought valiantly for the unification of Italy in 1860.

Minister of State, Jacquinot, who said, "Tebaldi is marvelous and, most important, she does not act like a clown," which gave rise to doubts concerning his knowledge of opera and *savoir faire*.

The press reported that Christian Dior's models, present at the performance as ushers, had rushed into Tebaldi's dressing room enthusiastically congratulating her for her beautiful figure. A reporter for *France Soir*, Marlyse Schaeffer, euphorically described the mountain of orchids, roses, and telegrams that decorated Tebaldi's dressing room, number 45, and then went on with a dazzling description: "Her alabaster skin, the gentle light from within, the captivating dimples, all reflected her serenity. We were seeing someone completely at peace with herself."

During supper at the Tour d'Argent after the performance, Tebaldi also received the enthusiastic congratulations of Josephine Baker who was singing at the Olympia in *Paris Mes Amours*.

The performance of *Aida*, televised from Paris, reached four million French viewers and 15 million Europeans as far away as Russia. Once again the headlines highlighted the Callas-Tebaldi rivalry and once again Tebaldi won. *Le Figaro* wrote, "Callas left us with the memory of an unforgettable presence, but Tebaldi has erased that memory," and "Tebaldi's is a voice without equal for its purity of timbre, extension, and depth." *France Soir*, June 8, 1959, wrote, "The celebrated Italian soprano, singing *Aida* at the Opéra, mesmerized the entire audience with her charm."

In truth, Callas, hindered by the stormy events of her private life, had not lived up to expectations created by her knack for attracting publicity.

While Tebaldi sang *Aida* in Paris, Gino Cervi, the Italian stage and film actor, was having great success at the Theater of the Nations in *The Merry Wives of Windsor*. An account of the meeting of the two stars appeared in the press stating that Tebaldi, disappointed that she hadn't been able to attend a performance by her Italian colleague, invited him to supper before she left Paris. It was said that the two ordered the celebrated escargots à la Bourgogne with Gino Cervi saying, "Allow me to offer you this famous dish in honor of your overwhelming success," and Renata accepted, replying, "This is the first time in my life that I have been offered a dish of escargots instead of a basket of orchids." This innocent essay by a reporter in search of a good story would have passed without comment except for the escargots. If there is one dish that Renata detests, it is, in fact, escargots!

After the two performances of *Aida*, Renata gathered up her photographs and amulets. They were always visible with fresh flowers near them, wherever she lodged. She packed her bags, made a visit to the Sacre Coeur to give thanks, and then left for Vienna.

Old friends went on this trip: Giulietta Simionato, Ettore Bastianini, Tito Gobbi, Eugenio Fernandi, and Maestro Antonino Votto. Nini Castiglioni also joined them. The atmosphere was festive. One evening Nini, always one to initiate, took "her" singers to a club in the old section of town, the Sieveringerstrasse, where Anton Karas could be heard playing the famous theme from the film, *The Third Man,* on the Viennese zither. In this "in club," between glasses of wine and Viennese-style breaded and fried chicken thighs, music was made on a zither and two accordians. That evening, singing was added to the music by a chorus of truly golden voices. However, their repertory was not opera. Deciding what was to be sung was Teddy Reno, the popular singer of Italian songs, also in Vienna for a show, who had joined the happy group. They had great fun singing the latest hits. Lively dancing followed. Renata, usually reluctant to dance, participated enthusiastically. ("I've had only a few occasions to dance, so I'm not very good at it.... Once, my dancing partner, Dr. Negri, the manager of the Regio di Parma, whose toes I must have

117

stepped on irreparably, commented in his Parmigiano dialect to our friends as he escorted me back to our table, '*La vol cmandèer lè, anca quand la bala!*'"[9]) In Vienna Renata radiated happiness, and one would have thought that dancing was her life's passion.

Tebaldi sang two performances each of *Tosca*, *Otello*, and *Aida*. After the *Aida* the *Neues Osterreich* of June 24, 1959 wrote of her marvelous, radiant soprano which rises effortlessly to the heights, is warm and full in the middle register, brilliant in "*Ritorna vincitor*" in the Nile scene aria, and in the marvelous final duet.

On July 2nd Tebaldi flew back to Milan where she was greeted at the airport by a group of photographers and reporters who asked, "Miss Tebaldi, is it true that you plan to be married?" and "Miss Tebaldi, is it true that you are in love? The name of an orchestra conductor is often mentioned...," or "Miss Tebaldi, it's been written that you'll marry Maestro Basile...." Renata's prompt reply was, "I haven't read the papers. I'll talk about it later. I'm tired from my trip," and with a winning smile she got into a waiting car with Tina and New, and they drove off to the apartment at Piazzetta Guastalla.

The man in question was Arturo Basile, an orchestra conductor born in Canicatti, Sicily, in 1914. After studying at the Conservatory in Torino, he entered a competition for young conductors at the Accademia di Santa Cecilia in Rome. Subsequently he became one of the principal conductors of the RAI Symphony Orchestra where he remained until 1953. He also had developed a respectable opera repertory.

He was *simpatico*, cordial, easy to know, down to earth and generous to a fault. He would "give you the shirt off his back" if you needed it. Linked to Nini Castiglioni's press office, he went to Nini for over a year asking her to intro-

---

[9] "She leads even when she dances!"

118

duce him to Renata Tebaldi. He went so far as to offer a pretext that he had often dreamed of Mamma Tebaldi. In the Autumn of 1958, during a visit to the observation deck of the Empire State Builiding, to his surprise he found Renata there with Nini, who jokingly said to her, "Renata, have pity on this poor fellow. He's been after me for a year to be introduced to you." And so the introduction took place.

Basile had been married for ten years, but his marriage deteriorated after long and frequent absences due to his career. For some years he had been involved with a voluptuous, young singer. After their meeting, Tebaldi and Basile were to see each other professionally on several occasions. Nothing happened that would give rise to rumors of marriage, and yet attractions can be felt. There was something in the air. And Renata, admitting nothing, perhaps not even to herself, gave herself away.

In September, returning again from Vienna, the new Tebaldi emerged. Her black hair, now auburn, had been cut. Once worn simply, restrained in a chignon, now it was short and loose, the color attractive and smart, almost a symbol of new freedom. As sometimes happens with women in love, she broke with the past, and one of her first actions was to create a new look for herself.

During an interview in Barcelona where she opened the 1959 opera season with *Manon Lescaut*, Renata was also less cautious in her replies.

Miss Tebaldi, what do you think of Callas's present situation?

"She's going through a crisis which I hope she'll overcome."

What do you think of her relationship with Onassis?

"I think it's publicity."

119

You're not fond of publicity?

"It's a double-edged sword when it's overdone."

Would you like to have a husband like Meneghini?

"*Pobrecito!*"

You've never thought of marriage?

"One day...perhaps, yes...."

If we print that, tomorrow you'll have a throng of admirers at your door.

"Fine! I'll finally meet my ideal. At any rate, I really don't want to marry a singer. Perhaps for a singer like me a conductor would be ideal...."

I'm so sorry that I don't conduct anything.

The reporter's concluding remark was gallant but he failed to read between the lines. Instead of focusing on Tebaldi's ideal, his article centered on the artist's charm and candor.

After her opening night performance she paid her usual visit to the Church of the Madonna delle Mercedes to offer the many flowers she had received the evening before from her admirers.

Publicity for the opening night of *Manon* was massive. The evening before, leaflets with Renata Tebaldi's picture were dropped on the city by plane. In addition, Generalissimo Franco's wife had arranged to have TV cameras installed in the theater so the performance could be seen all over Spain.

At the end of the Act III Tebaldi did not come forward for a curtain call and the audience feared that something was wrong. She later explained that since it was the "tenor's act" she wanted him to enjoy a solo curtain call. Her generosity, rare in the theater, was repaid during a subsequent performance when Renata had a moment of uncertainty in holding a high note and her partner cut his short immediately. Altruism like this quickly becomes part of opera lore since protocol strictly controls behavior on stage, and most artists tend to exploit whatever they can for themselves.

At the end of that 1959 opening night performance, which was also attended by Salvador Dali, the throngs of fans blocked Las Ramblas until two a.m. Among opera lovers who had climbed their way up to the family circle was a florid, robust young opera student who sang small roles and hoped one day to become a great singer. Her father always accompanied her to the opera house and then waited for her at the café in the square to take her home. In the family circle, performances were carefully followed by students with score in hand who, during intermissions, ate tortillas and fruit, and drank coffee they brought from home. The future primadonna never thought, as she sat there, that one day Renata Tebaldi would admire her artistry. "When I listen to birds singing with their incredible breath control, I always think of Montserrat Caballé...."

PART THREE

❧20❧

December 1959: Return to La Scala with *Tosca*

The day of Tebaldi's return to La Scala was drawing near. She had just returned from Barcelona where she sang *Manon Lescaut, Tosca,* and *La Bohème* and had agreed to one performance of *Adriana Lecouvreur* at the San Carlo Opera in Naples before going to La Scala for *Tosca.* Singing with her in Naples were Franco Corelli and Ettore Bastianini. After the dress rehearsal on November 26th, Tebaldi complained of a sore throat. The next day a medical bulletin defined it as "acute inflammation of the upper respiratory tract necessitating complete rest for five days." Magda Olivero was called in to cover the performance. Tebaldi barricaded herself in her room, number 327, at the Excelsior, for three days. On the morning of the 30th she left her hotel and attended a memorial mass at the Church of the Madonna del Carmine. It was the second anniversary of her mother's death.

The following day the diva was honored with the title of Commendatore della Republica by the Prefect of Naples. After the ceremony, she boarded the *Freccia del Sud* train to arrive a few hours later in Milan. Word spread that she was aboard, and her compartment became the site of a sort of pilgrimage with streams of people passing by and quietly greeting her. A shy youth looked in, extended his arm, dropped an orange into her hand and rushed away.

At stations along the route, small groups assembled to cheer the soprano whom they could see smiling as she looked out at them from behind the closed window of her compartment.

In Milan Renata went into seclusion. As the moment of the performance neared, the stress increased. Through the years La Scala had continuously attempted to engage her, but her reply had always been a firm, "I don't want to sing against anybody." Now that Callas had broken with La Scala, the road was clear. In fact, it was all hers.

This Tebaldi *Tosca* of December 9th, 1959, which included Di Stefano and Gobbi in the cast, was truly a second opening night of the season. Opening night had taken place two days earlier on the feast of St. Ambrose with a performance of *Otello* with Del Monaco, Leonie Rysanek, and Gobbi. The person most happy about Tebaldi's return to La Scala was Vittorio Grassi, the doorman at the stage entrance. He had first seen the young Tebaldi when she auditioned for Toscanini, and at that time he had been told by the seamstress, Novi Mengaroni, to "keep an eye on that girl because one day she'll walk through these doors in triumph." From that first day, Grassi's fondness for Tebaldi continued to grow, and he would joyfully greet her with a respectful bow every time he saw her. In 1949 when Tebaldi sang *Otello* at La Scala with Maestro De Sabata conducting, Grassi couldn't resist; he found someone to take his place at the stage door, and he slipped into the family circle during the dress rehearsal. At the end of the performance when Renata was leaving the theater, he impulsively said, "*Cara la mé tusa, come hai cantato bene!*"[10] His unusual behavior created a stir because Grassi was always so reserved with the artists and he never

---

[10] "My dear girl, how well you sang!"

took the liberty to judge a singer or to become familiar with one. In fact, that outburst was his one and only "indiscretion." But with every *Otello*, he continued to find a replacement for himself so he could run in to hear Tebaldi's *"Canzone del Salice"* and *"Ave Maria"* and then hurry back to his post.

The last performance Tebaldi had sung at La Scala was *La Forza del Destino* in May of 1955, but it seemed longer than four and a half years before because so much had happened. Two careers had taken shape: hers at the Metropolitan and Callas's at La Scala. Since Tebaldi's debut at La Scala thirteen years earlier, she had sung 199 performances there, and this *Tosca* was to be her 200th.

This was her favorite opera, the one in which she felt most at ease. It was as Tosca that she appeared on the cover of *Time* magazine and the role she sang at the Metropolitan's golden jubilee opening night performance. Floria Tosca, the artist, pious and jealous, was the heroine with whom Renata identified most. Yet, Renata Tebaldi was apprehensive. Those who were most able to reassure her—and this is meaningful—were the little people: Grassi, the doorman; Beretta, the prompter; Novi, the seamstress; Colli and Cibea, the inside doormen.

It was during this period that Callas was asked if she had any plans to return to La Scala soon, and her reply was, "At the moment there is much excitement over the long-awaited return of Tebaldi, and I think it's only right that the public's attention be focused on that important event without distractions of any kind. This year I've closed many chapters in my life, and I truly hope that this one, too, will be closed."

The excitement mounted.

A torrential rain fell on Milan on the morning of the first *Tosca*. At home, Tebaldi recited scores of *Ave Maria*s, then gathered her photographs and amulets and left for the opera house. She had done everything possible to protect herself from a recurrence of her Napoli laryngitis, even avoiding the final rehearsal. Since this was the same production as the Brussels *Tosca*, Renata was familiar with the staging, and Margherita Wallman was on hand to review it with her that evening, on stage before each act.

She defied superstition that evening. (She affirms that she is superstitious — among other things, every evening as she gets into bed, she places her slippers in such a way that the next morning, when she gets up, the right foot must go into its slipper first.) But that evening she dared to wear a violet costume in Act I![11]

As she made her stage entrance she was overwhelmed by more than four minutes of applause. She started to sing, and all her apprehension was over. Final curtain calls continued for forty minutes. Later, backstage in her dressing room, an endless parade of admirers greeted her, led by Begum Khan and the Prince of Polignac, the father of Ranier of Monaco. (A few years earlier, during a reception at the Waldorf Astoria celebrating Ranier's engagement to Grace Kelly, Tebaldi, a guest at the hotel, had waited in the lobby to catch a glimpse of the couple as they entered. She hadn't realized that she had only to announce her presence to have been the guest of honor.)

After the triumph of *Tosca*, if she had not still been in costume, one could have thought she was there to greet someone. In fact, it was after a performance that she was most happy, lighthearted, and so relaxed that she appeared almost unaffected. Once out of costume, she received the press. She was without makeup, in a brown cashmere sweater, with no jewelry except for a gold baptismal medal, her amber hair gently pulled back on the nape of her neck. She spoke openly about many things, "I think this was the most important evening of my life, as an artist and as a woman.... I don't think I've ever been so moved. I'd never imagined that after

---

[11] Tebaldi considered violet an unlucky color.

four years they were waiting for me with so much affection."

And the most beautiful moment?

"My entrance, after waiting in the wings, when I faced my audience—I was very moved—and heard the applause coming from the orchestra, the boxes, and the balconies, with such spontaneous and unanimous enthusiasm. That moment, even more than the triumphant finale of the opera, repaid me for the years that I spent far away." Then she added sadly, "If only Mamma were here. She would have been so happy...."

After singing six performances of *Tosca* at La Scala in December of 1959, Tebaldi remained in Milan in January for five performances of *Andrea Chénier*, with Del Monaco and Corelli, under the baton of Gianandrea Gavazzeni. Then she sailed to America on the *Cristoforo Colombo*.

During the crossing, a dog show was organized and Renata's poodle was led out onto the gangway by his very delighted mistress. New was very handsome in his home-styled clipping by Tina, but he lacked the professional touch needed to win. Perhaps too accustomed to the taste of success, Renata was so deeply disappointed that she went to her room and cried like a child. Word of her disappointment got around on board, the jury was reconvened and a new award was devised for New: The Congeniality Award.

❧21❧

1960: Reconciliation with Her Father
The Death of Leonard Warren on Stage
Paris and Vienna Again

In 1960, before leaving for the States, Tebaldi was reconciled with her father after nineteen years of silence between
them. Renata had avoided answering his many letters. She
had lived for too many years with the pain caused by her
father's abandonment in 1941, when he left his family to live
in Parma with the new woman in his life. Above all, Renata
couldn't forget the anguish she felt because of her mother's
unhappiness.

Now her father had sent word to her that he was in the
hospital suffering from a nasal hemorrhage and arrhythmia,
and that he continued to hope for a reconciliation with her.
It was on January 19, 1960, that Renata decided to go to
him. Fear of offending her mother no longer kept her away.
There was also something else now. A new happiness had
changed her life, and that, perhaps above everything else,
had convinced her to put an end to this sad and painful epi-
sode of her past. Because Renata was in love, she wanted to
rid her life of sadness. She understood now that love sometimes defies convention. After her father left the hospital,
Renata saw him twice. They lunched together; they strolled
through town. They never stopped talking, often saying, "We

have so much to catch up on," and Renata was as proud as she had been as a young girl, when she walked arm in arm with her father, and he wore his red, silver-braided uniform of a grenadier officer.

The tiring schedule and emotional drain of the past few months had exhausted Renata. She decided that she needed to rest for a while. Greatly disappointing Rudolf Bing and the public, she cancelled her January and February performances at the Metropolitan Opera. On March 4th she returned with *La Forza del Destino*. There was much anticipation of this new production of *Forza*, with the action set one century earlier. With Tebaldi, the cast included Richard Tucker, Leonard Warren, Cesare Siepi, and Jerome Hines. Thomas Schippers was conducting.

A thunderous ovation greeted Tebaldi, interrupting her singing for several minutes. The performance proceeded magnificently. The duet between Alvaro and Don Carlo in Act II was stupendous. After the duet, Alvaro (Tucker) was carried out on a stretcher, and Don Carlo (Warren) remained onstage for the celebrated *"Urna fatale."* Don Carlo seemed to have emerged from a Van Dyke portrait: a grand mustache, an aristocratic beard, a starched, laced collar, and a blue sash across his armor. Warren sang with extraordinary impetus. He was overwhelmed by applause. Only the furious invective, *"Gioia! Oh gioia! Egli è salvo!"* remained. He sang, *"Gioia!"* and collapsed face forward on the stage. Schippers stopped the music and the curtain came down.

The audience's first reaction was that Warren was simply indisposed, while other possibilities were discussed during intermission. In the meantime, a great deal was happening on stage. The Metropolitan's physician, Dr. Zargniotti, and Mrs. Warren and a family friend, Monsignor Broderick, had all rushed on stage. Rudolf Bing quickly had Mario Sereni called in to replace Warren, and then he, himself, appeared at the footlights to advise the public that Warren was ill and that Sereni would replace him. But at 10:30 p.m., after a long disquieting pause, Bing reappeared, this time his face ashen. "Ladies and gentlemen, this is the saddest evening in the history of the Metropolitan...," he started, his voice breaking. "I ask you to honor the memory of one of our greatest artists...."

Leonard Warren was dead at the age of 48 of a cerebral hemorrhage. During those dreadful moments on stage, a desperate attempt was made to administer mouth-to-mouth resuscitation until the arrival of an ambulance and oxygen. It soon became obvious that it was hopeless, and Monsignor Broderick administered extreme unction. By the time the ambulance arrived, Warren was no longer breathing. (His body was carried, still in costume, to his dressing room.) The other artists, who had been requested to remain in their dressing rooms until called, were informed of his death. Renata wept, deeply saddened.

Warren and Tebaldi had had similar artistic temperaments. Like her, his strength lay in the beauty of his voice and its incomparable power and expressiveness. He, too, was religious (born into the Jewish faith, he later converted to Catholicism); he lived a quiet life far from the social whirl, and he took good care of his voice. He was one of the pillars of the Metropolitan, so much so that, in order to remain faithful to that opera house, he continuously refused invitations from the other great opera houses of the world.

Frank Guarrera, the Italian-American baritone, was called in to replace Warren in the remaining performances of *Forza*. Later, to sing Warren's other roles, Mr. Bing engaged the Italian baritone, Anselmo Colzani.

Tebaldi continued through March and April with performances of *Simon Boccanegra*, *Andrea Chénier*, *Madama Butterfly*, and *Tosca* at the Metropolitan, plus two concerts, one at Carnegie Hall accompanied at the piano by Leonard Bernstein, and one at Dade Auditorium in Miami.

In 1960, for the 100th anniversary of the unification of Italy, Tebaldi was invited to sing at the White House with Franco Corelli. He described the scene. "When Renata entered, the entire audience, including President and Mrs. Kennedy gave her a standing ovation." A photograph of Tebaldi with President and Mrs. Kennedy at the White House is among her treasured memorabilia.

In May Renata was back in Europe for *Tosca* in Rome and a tour of concerts in Germany. After the tour, Tebaldi went on to Paris and then Vienna as she had done the previous year. *Tosca* was staged for her in Paris as she had requested the year before. The first performance was a gala evening at the Opera honoring the centennial celebration of the annexation of Savoy to France. The audience included five ministers, nine ambassadors, and seven academicians of France. Tickets at the box office were 12,000 francs; the black market price was 250,000 francs.

Philippe Bouvard's succinct review, rushed to the *Figaro* for its early edition, described "an exceptional evening, two brilliant intermissions, a splendid hall, and an enthusiastic ovation for Renata Tebaldi who was greatly applauded as Tosca."

Tebaldi admits that the applause after her "*Vissi d'arte*" was so prolonged that after awhile she became ill at ease. "I didn't know what else to do. I could neither start singing again nor thank the audience with a gesture or a smile out of context." Francis Poulenc, the French composer, declared, "Of all the singers in the world, Tebaldi is my favorite. Last winter I travelled to Milan to hear her in *Tosca* at La Scala. I admire her passionately." George Auric, composer of ballet and film music, commented, "Without hesitation I place Tebaldi in first place above all the singers of the world. And she's so charming offstage!"

The French actress, Edwige Feuillère said, "I have the greatest admiration for Tebaldi. She has a marvelous voice, admirable musicality, and she never looks for the easy effect." Andre Barsacq, the stage director of *Tosca* said, "It's a great pleasure for me to be associated with Tebaldi. She is so gracious and is such a great artist that nothing is difficult; everything happens spontaneously and with great ease." The general director of the Opera, Monsieur Julien, had this to say: "What an extraordinary voice and what graciousness!"

Declining an invitation to a banquet in her honor, Tebaldi returned to her hotel after the performance with a few intimate friends and together they celebrated her success. The next day, her photograph was on the front page of all the Paris newspapers. An inventive reporter described a perfected inhaler supposedly used by Tebaldi into which she added a secret mixture revealed to her by the widow of Enrico Caruso. That was, in fact, the first Renata had heard of such an elixir.

The Viennese heard Tebaldi in *Tosca* on June 20th and the 23rd with Herbert von Karajan conducting. For *Andrea Chénier* her partners were Franco Corelli on the 26th and Björling on the 29th, with Von Matacic conducting. Nikita Khrushchev was in Vienna and wanted very much to hear Tebaldi, but the dates of the *Tosca* performances conflicted with his commitments, and he categorically refused to see *Andrea Chénier* with its condemnation of tyranny. The director of the Staatsopera diplomatically settled the problem with a performance of *The Magic Flute*, an opera devoid of political criticism. Khrushchev saved face, but he lost his opportunity to see Tebaldi.

The Soviet leader had another favorite among western artists, the young Texan pianist, Van Cliburn, who was a great friend of Tebaldi. It was rumored that Khrushchev intended to invite them to the Soviet Union. Something Renata said seemed to support this possibility. She was asked if she would be willing to visit Russia and her reply was, "Certainly! A great deal of music goes on there. The Russian public's generous enthusiasm is very gratifying for an artist, but it is logistically difficult to bring over an entire opera company. Perhaps a tour of concerts would be simpler." Her idea would materialize, but not until fifteen years later.

While in Vienna, Renata found time to visit Sophia Loren on the set during filming of *Olympia*. The two women had remained friendly since their collaboration in the filming of *Aida*. "Sophia was very beautiful and unaffected, and at the time of the filming of the opera, unsophisticated. When I previewed the film for which I sang the title role, I was amazed at her ability. The voice dubbing was not noticeable even in the close-ups!"

Before returning to Italy, Tebaldi was asked by reporters what her future commitments were. Her radiant reply was that she was on her way to Rome to record for Decca, and then she would be vacationing as usual on the Adriatic before returning to the States. "Truthfully, a singer needs at least two months of complete relaxation before feeling the benefits. A shorter vacation is not enough to relieve the tensions constantly present in a career like ours." Then Renata added, "But I really wouldn't be upset if I had to give up my vacation." Everyone noted that she was radiant. She looked like a young girl (she was 38), and her elegance revealed a refinement of style. "Must be Paris," was one reporter's innocent assumption.

Soon after Renata returned to Italy, the news of Basile and his wife hit the press. On the 25th of June, Maestro Arturo Basile and his wife, Elisabetta Sangermano, were granted a legal separation, agreed upon by both. His wife had filed for the separation. No mention was made of any other woman, but soon, fanciful rumors were circulating of a Tebaldi-Basile wedding which would take place during a tour in the States (in Italy there was no divorce). The result of the gossip was Basile's cancellation of the tour. They did, however, record *La Wally* together in Rome as planned, and then had three days of relaxation together in the mountains. When he agreed to an interview with the weekly, *Gente,* he rather awkwardly and too heatedly insisted, "There is absolutely nothing between me and Renata Tebaldi."

In truth, Renata Tebaldi had, for the first time, met a man who could make her head spin. Once, speaking of Puccini, Renata affirmed that he was "a fascinating man, erotically exciting, with a thorough understanding of women. If I had lived when he did, I probably would have become his mistress! A man who never gives the slightest assurance, who keeps one guessing.... To be totally dependent on his whims." Arturo Basile was precisely that type of man.

That Renata Tebaldi had finally fallen in love was something that excited her fans. In their eyes she was now even more human, so very vulnerable, so feminine. However, just as the goldminers in *Fanciulla del West* found it difficult to accept Minnie's choice (Johnson, the bandit) Renata's choice of a man who was not free wasn't very pleasing. But her public forgave her. In fact, everyone felt that fate was hard on their darling who had already suffered so much, and it was feared that she would be facing further heartache. This fear united them in a fervent desire for her happiness.

How different the attitude of the world and the press was towards "the other one" who was facing similar heartache. Maria Callas had talked too much, made too many declarations, been too conspicuously self-assured to arouse much sympathy for her ambiguous love affair—a love affair which reeked of worldliness and millions. People weren't willing to accept it as the real thing. Ironically, these two women, Renata and Maria, so different in every way, were both badly treated by the men they loved most.

Renata was soon to realize that the "man who never gives assurances, who makes one suffer," in the long run destroys love because he not only refuses to give, but he also refuses to accept. Under those circumstances, loving becomes very very much like dying.

❦22❦

The Renata Tebaldi Music Club

During November and December of 1960, America had Renata on the move again, back on the merry-go-round: *Tosca*, *Fedora*, and *Simon Boccanegra* in Chicago and *Butterfly*, *Simon Boccanegra*, *Bohème*, and *Manon Lescaut* at the Metropolitan. Once again the sold-out performances, the applause, the fans.

In America the Renata Tebaldi fan clubs prospered. The RTMC (not a military organization, but the Renata Tebaldi Music Club) had its spontaneous beginning in 1955 in Jersey City. After seeing Renata off for Italy after her first season at the Met, a group of fans decided to prolong the magical feeling Renata had left them with by gathering at the home of one member of the group. The hostess, Maria, brought out Neapolitan-style *sfogliatelle* and vermouth and their American counterparts, whiskey and potato chips. Her daughters, Mary, a bookkeeper and violinist, and Josephine, a chemistry major and pianist, played Neapolitan songs and Renata Tebaldi recordings. The idea of an officially organized club was discussed, and $3.00 was decided upon as annual dues per person. Announcements were mailed, and hundreds of enthusiastic requests for membership arrived from as far away

137

as Texas and California. The necessary approval from Renata Tebaldi also arrived; "proud and happy," she accepted the position of honorary president of the club.

The activities of the RTMC were varied, but the most common was the trading of hundreds of photographs taken of the diva. An enjoyable fund-raising activity was a raffle at 10 cents a ticket, the prize being an autographed recording of Tebaldi. The person selling the most tickets received a special prize, an invitation to supper with Tebaldi at the La Scala restaurant, which, as the name indicates, was an opera-oriented place to eat.

The club published an annual magazine (with Tebaldi on the cover) which contained biographical notes about the soprano, performances and reviews gathered from publications during the year, her complete schedule for the following year, and news of its twin club, the RTMC in Italy, a club organized in Varese in 1954 after the performance of *La Forza del Destino* at La Scala.

The American club, despite its strength in numbers, was never granted any privileges at the Metropolitan, and its members spent long hours in line waiting to secure tickets, just as others did. But any inconvenience was more than repaid by the annual reunion dinner with their idol. The banquet with the diva present in all her splendor was the highlight of the club's activities.

The reunion was usually held at the New Yorker Hotel or Roosevelt Hotel where Renata would be greeted by hundreds of admirers filing past her, whispering their admiration, holding her hand, asking for her autograph, and, most often, hoping and asking to be photographed with her. Afterwards, everyone enjoyed a lavish dinner. Dancing sometimes followed, causing Renata some discomfort because everyone wanted to "dance with their diva." The highlight of the evening, however, came at the end when a drawing was held and the winner received a souvenir from Renata:

the handkerchief she used as Desdemona, the necklace worn as Aida, Adriana's earrings, Violetta's camellia. Renata was always very cordial and approachable, but the vibrant atmosphere of this affair remained dignified and *la divina,* although down-to-earth, remained the diva.

The club was like a large family which sometimes was touched by sadness, too. Michael, a photographer, one of many children of immigrant Italian parents, met Renata after a performance at the Metropolitan and became one of her most devoted admirers. Renata grew fond of this handsome fellow and even met his family. When Michael was transferred to Rome on business, he was always in the audience whenever she sang in Italy. A photograph he took of Renata was selected for the cover of one of her record albums. It was while in Rome that Michael discovered a tumor in his leg. He returned to New York immediately and entered Memorial Sloan-Kettering Hospital, but nothing could be done to save him. He suffered great pain. Renata visited him almost daily until the end, and for a long while after his death she helped his family.

In the 1960s, the Metropolitan was truly an international theater which included many Italians who sang and made their fortunes there. A sampling of the 1961 season with its international casts would include:

Feb.14 *La Bohème*—Tebaldi, Morell
    15 *Martha*—De los Angeles, Tucker
    16 *Tristan und Isolde*—Vinay, Nilsson
    17 *Rigoletto*—Merrill
    18 *Simon Boccanegra* (matinee)—Tebaldi, Guarrera, Tucker
    18 *Il Trovatore*—Corelli, Amara, Sereni
    20 *Aida*—Price, Fernandi, Merrill
    21 *Madama Butterfly*—Tebaldi, Gedda
    22 *Simon Boccanegra*—Milanov, Tucker, Colzani, Hines
    23 *Turandot*—Nilsson, Corelli, Moffo

Of these, Mario Del Monaco, Gianni Raimondi, Carlo Bergonzi, and Giulietta Simionato stayed at the Navarro at Central Park South for its proximity to Central Park and fantastic views it offered especially at night. Franco Corelli and his wife had rented an apartment on 57th Street. Corelli, to support his image, had acquired a stretch limousine and a miniature, silver-grey poodle which met with some disdain from "old guard" snobbery.

At the end of each day, with her many commitments attended to, Renata would return to her suite at the Murray, a quiet hotel on Park Avenue, where she felt at home. After many years at the Buckingham Hotel with Mamma Tebaldi, she now enjoyed the comfort of the Murray and its proximity to the opera house. The added advantage of storage space for costumes and clothing left behind for the following year lightened the burden of her many trips back and forth. Renata also enjoyed the warm, personal attention she received there.

❦ 23 ❦

Tebaldi and Basile
Many Commitments Abroad

After performances in New York, Philadelphia, and Miami, and a concert in Carnegie Hall, Tebaldi was on her way back to Italy in April of 1961. Her first performances were in Genoa where she arrived in her Lancia, with Tina behind the wheel defying pre-Easter traffic. She sang *Manon Lescaut* on April 6th and April 9th. She was "showered with flowers," wrote Carlo Rietman in *Secolo XIX*, "and the voice, this incomparable voice which emerges from a uniquely lyrical instrument to become the Tebaldi voice, shaped itself perfectly to the part, elegant in style, sustained in sound, rich in the understanding of human suffering." In Rome Tebaldi sang four performances of *Manon Lescaut* with Giuseppe Di Stefano. Arturo Basile conducted.

In May she flew to Germany for several concerts. Reporters waiting for Tebaldi at the Berlin airport speculated that she lived only for her career, got very little from life, shunned publicity, was reserved and secretive, and therefore sad. She arrived after a frightening flight, smiling, gracious, and elegant. She answered questions, signed autographs, and posed for photographs with endless patience. She didn't seem sad to anyone. On the contrary, she seemed lighthearted and

141

happy, as one who had everything she wanted in life. A reporter asked her who was the greatest singer of the century. She laughingly replied, "I am, naturally," leaving her interrogator shocked since he had just been hearing about the soprano's modesty. "I'm the greatest! I'm 5 feet 10 inches tall. Do you know anyone greater than I?"

In Berlin Tebaldi was greeted by the mayor, Willy Brandt, and at City Hall she added her name to the city's guest register. She and Brandt talked at length in English about their French poodles and how to care for them. New was photographed with a Tyrolean cap on his head, and the next day his picture appeared in all the papers.

In June Tebaldi returned to the Teatro Regio in Parma for a Verdi concert with Giuseppe Di Stefano and Aldo Protti, which Arturo Basile conducted. He also conducted in July as Tebaldi recorded *Fanciulla del West* with Daniele Barioni and Giangiacomo Guelfi for RAI in Rome.

At the Teatro dell'Aquila in Fermo where Tebaldi went in August for a performance of *Adriana Lecouvreur*, the sculptor, Alessandro Pisani was commissioned by the municipality to design a medallion, approximately 20 inches in diameter, with a likeness of Tebaldi. This was placed in the atrium of the Teatro Massimo in Aquila alongside those of Gigli, Giacomo Lauri-Volpi and Ermete Novelli, the noted Italian actor.

In the meantime, the Metropolitan Opera faced contract problems with the American Federation of Musicians. By the end of August, with no settlement in sight, Rudolf Bing cancelled the season. He notified his artists and released them from their contracts.

High level mediation followed, and a petition to President John F. Kennedy for assistance got him personally involved. The season was finally patched up only to be faced with new problems, however, since many artists had departed. It wasn't until the end of September that rehearsals began, and opening night was delayed until October 23rd.

Tebaldi, who was one of the first to leave after being released from her contract, had a second reason for going. She had insisted on *Adriana Lecouvreur* at the Metropolitan, but the new production scheduled for the following spring was one of the first to be eliminated. "Then I won't sing at all," was Renata's reply to Bing. "Agreed, stay at home then," Bing countered without batting an eyelash.

In September Tebaldi left for Tokyo. Emperor Hirohito was in the audience at her Japanese debut. She sang Maddalena to Mario Del Monaco's Andrea Chénier, and Basile conducted. Her Japanese fans learned of her passion for dolls, and they gave her a very valuable seventeenth century doll dressed in silk and gold.

"Japan is an orderly, serious, and gentle country. The public is disciplined even while enthusiastic. My most vivid recollection is of an enormous mass of people. I would look down from my suite on an upper floor of the hotel, and I would see what seemed to be an immense anthill. There are so, so many of them, and they are so very, very clean. There is no odor of crowds, of perspiration. They are all so fragrant...."

Unsure of Japanese cooking, Renata refused most invitations. She could not refuse one official invitation so she asked the Italian consul's cooperation and he gallantly functioned as food-taster, indicating which foods she should eat.

While in Japan, she was awarded that country's gold medal for highest achievement. In October, still in Tokyo, she sang *Tosca* and then repeated both operas in Osaka. Before she left Japan, the minister of culture of the Philippines invited her to visit Manila before returning to Europe. She agreed. She sang three concerts at the Araneta Coliseum and one at the Philamlife Auditorium. Arturo Basile conducted.

In December in Copenhagen, Tebaldi sang *La Bohème*, with Basile conducting, for the inauguration of the Italian

Festival of Opera in that city. On the 14th, 17th, and 19th of December, Tebaldi sang *Fedora* with Giuseppe Di Stefano in Naples at the Teatro San Carlo conducted by Basile. The audience was ecstatic. Alfredo Parente described it as a "triumph" in *Il Mattino* on the 15th of December.

If Renata's new production of *Adriana Lecouvreur* at the Metropolitan in the spring of 1962 was cancelled because of the strike, she still refused to consider the opera a dead issue. On the contrary, in April and May of 1962, she sang eight performances in Rome and Torino. Nino Piccinelli in *Momento Sera* on April 13, 1962, wrote that, "Tebaldi's voice dazzled with a thousand lights." In Torino one critic wrote, "One wonders why Tebaldi twists her hands, feigning tears— it is enough to hear her sing!"

She had a triumphant success with *Adriana* especially in Torino. She was returning there after an absence of ten years. The box-office remained open on the day of the performance only to inform everyone that tickets were sold out. During the performance, the composer's widow could be seen moved to tears.

When Renata Tebaldi's artistry is discussed, if reserve is mentioned, only her gestures or facial expressions come under question. It is in her voice primarily that Renata possesses great emotion. She realizes the entire human condition and manifests it in her singing. It was during a Barcelona performance of *Adriana* in 1958 that Giacinto Prandelli, listening in the wings to the tormented duet between the two women, commented aloud, "And some say Tebaldi is cold! I weep from the emotion!"

Tebaldi, in fact, had a reserve which she never completely abandoned and which kept her from fully "revealing" herself on stage. Emotion was revealed fully through her singing. "Tebaldi has everything in her voice," wrote Rodolfo Celletti, the Italian music critic, "a voice of supreme nobility achieved by its timbre, phrasing, phonation, and legato stlye."

Tebaldi's art of declaiming was exceptional, her pronunciation perfect, her emission pure. The volume of her voice was abundant and sumptuous. Her interpretations were grandly eloquent. Audiences were wildly captivated by Tebaldi's voice. There was no mystery, nothing to search for. It was the personification of beauty. And it was with this perfect instrument that she reached the intimacies of expression. Being attractive and statuesque, heroic roles were perfect for her. She refused to interpret roles, however, which called for cinema-style, intimate realism.

The beginning of 1962 had taken her to Parma for *La Bohème* at the Teatro Regio. The season, almost completely under the baton of Arturo Basile, had been subjected to whistles and bickering. Patrons in the balcony had become more menacing than ever. On opening night during *Don Carlo* the soprano, Giulia Barrera, was so whistled at that the scheduled teletaping of the performance was cancelled. The tenor in *La Traviata* fled in tears and was replaced by Alfredo Kraus. Basile had received such a share of insults that he decided to face the members of the balcony head on. The confrontation wasn't very cordial.

The meeting centered on the legitimacy of audience protest. Basile was asked his opinion of the whistling that greeted the start of his *Traviata* and his reply was, "I think it was healthy," which left everyone perplexed. Basile, however, went on to defend the tenor, Ruggero Bondino, saying, "He was applauded in the same opera in Lausanne and Brussels. He didn't deserve to be whistled at here. You buy a ticket and you think you have the right to ruin a performance that costs millions."

"Whistling is as spontaneous a reaction as applauding is. We can't control it. We who love Verdi find that a *Traviata* performed badly is a provocation. Even the preludes were unacceptable to our ears," was the reply that came from the opposition.

"But you attack everyone! You even protested Carlo Bergonzi in *Aida*!" "Yes! But we also carried him in triumph after *Un Ballo in Maschera* and *La Forza del Destino*. You can't sing *Aida* the way Luciano Tajoli sings love songs." (Bergonzi, who is a professional, held a press conference in which he demonstrated, with score in hand, that, precisely where they had attacked him, Verdi had marked "*ppp* [*pianississimo*]." The tenor emerged the victor but he never again sang in Parma.)

Basile's confrontation proceeded with hostility. "I'm not exactly an inexperienced conductor but I can assure you...," he tried to defend himself.

"You're not inexperienced? You even skipped over the high note in '*Don Fatale*' because the mezzo-soprano couldn't make it!"

"Stop talking nonsense! I take my job seriously. I want you to know that I turned down an important series of concerts...."

"You shouldn't have," was the reply.

It was this heated atmosphere that Tebaldi stepped into with her *Bohème*. Her performance reignited the audience with great enthusiasm. "Renata has saved the season in Parma!" were the front-page headlines.

Unfortunately, not everyone appreciated her rescue operation. Arturo Basile was consoling himself with a dancer, and Renata spent the night despairing over her loneliness. Since it was less painful to accept his excuses in order to go on loving him (and Basile was very persuasive) Renata forgave him and plunged right back into the affair.

On June 30th at the Maggio Musicale Fiorentino, while singing her third *Bohème* there, Tebaldi suddenly felt ill after the first act and was replaced by her standby, Alberta Pellegrini. It was the only time in her career that Tebaldi was forced to leave a performance in progress.

After a summer vacationing and recording the Puccini

146

Trittico for Decca, Renata sang *Otello* in Berlin at the Deutsche Oper. Then she was off to Spain for the month of September for *La Forza del Destino* and *Adriana Lecouvreur*. It was in Oviedo, Spain that she saw her first bull fight. Jaime Ostro dedicated his bull to her. Although Basile was with her, she was so unnerved by the spectacle that she smoked one cigarette after the other to calm herself. The Spaniards who had escorted them there were amazed. "You're so brave when you're on stage and face your audience...." "Singing and bullfighting may both be difficult, but the risks are so very different!" she replied. They told her that Maria Callas had watched the entire scene laughing. "She must be a lot braver than I," and she covered her eyes as she spoke to avoid a particularly distressing sight.

The tour had been a great success. It had been a month of triumphs and love. But it was not a happy love. She was losing control of her nerves. For the first time in her career singing was tiring her. Her voice seemed not to obey her anymore.

For more than a year Basile had been almost always at her side. He had emerged from a rather good, but routine career and entered the international music circuit through her. It gave her great pleasure to share her success with this man whom she loved. But she wanted more than that. Having accepted this relationship which only a few years before would have seemed impossible to her, she now wanted to live it completely and with full awareness. She had always been true to herself. She had lived without compromise, wisely and honestly, earning respect in her rapport with others. She had been a good daughter; she adored her mother. She had learned not to judge her father and was able to forgive him. Her whole existence had been devoted to her voice, which she considered sacred and for which she sacrificed fun, comfort, and almost all her freedom. Now Renata wanted to live her life fully.

Since she was religious, it had been very difficult to justify to herself an illicit love. Basile had been living away from his family since his legal separation from his wife in 1961. In Italy there was no divorce, so their relationship remained ambiguous. Despite this, Renata faced the situation and came to accept it completely. She had said that one day she would "love totally, depend totally," but paradoxically, in loving so submissively she needed total love in return. She became possessive, jealous, and uncompromising.

Basile was the exact opposite. He loved to have fun, he was noncommittal, and he loved women. Unfortunately, he also loved Renata. The situation was becoming very painful to her. It took her quite some time to fully understand the nature of this man, partly because she was too straightforward and partly because her pride kept her from believing the truth. Her friends would say to her, "Take him as he is, he needs his freedom." But Renata could accept nothing less than total commitment.

By the time she left for New York at the end of 1962, Renata had made her decision. *She didn't want to suffer anymore.*

❧ 24 ❧

1962: *Adriana Lecouvreur* at the Metropolitan
A Year's Absence from the Stage
Tebaldi's Second Career

After several performances of *Falstaff* and *La Bohème* at the San Carlo in Naples in December of 1962, Tebaldi was on her way to the States. Rudolf Bing had agreed to her persuasive requests for a new production of *Adriana Lecouvreur*, and Franco Corelli was to be her Maurizio. The opera had been missing from the Metropolitan for 55 years and had last been sung by Lina Cavalieri and Enrico Caruso. It was one of the rare times Caruso was whistled at in his entire career. In 1938, the great Rosa Ponselle requested that *Adriana* be included in the Metropolitan's repertory, and Edward Johnson refused her; she never set foot in the Metropolitan again.

In New York, in 1963, the reviews were not kind. The critics were not enthusiastic about the opera. Miles Kastendiek wrote, "Why this role attracts her so remains a mystery to me. She has to share the applause with at least three other singers at the footlights.... It seems that she considers this role ideal for her, but this first performance does not confirm her conviction."

Shortly after Renata's arrival in the States, an Italian weekly magazine printed a statement made by Arturo Basile:

"I'm going to America to marry Renata Tebaldi." Basile had, in fact, telephoned her from the office of the editor of the magazine to substantiate his declaration. This was a cruel and childish act. Hurt because he had been dropped by a girlfriend of many years, he opted for the old strategy: "You're leaving me? Well, I've got somebody more famous than you, and I'm going to marry her!" Renata's reaction to this unfair play was short and swift: she hung up the telephone receiver — forever. "I loved deeply, giving all that I had to give. I suffered. But I've never allowed anyone to upset my balance," Renata said later.

Then, to everyone's amazement, after the fourth performance of *Adriana Lecouvreur,* Tebaldi unexpectedly announced her decision to cancel her engagements for a prolonged period of rest. Although reworking the voice is frequently necessary at some point in a singer's career, it was difficult to believe that she, who was so tireless and indestructible, should feel the need to do so.

The remaining performances of *Adriana* were sung by Licia Albanese, and then this opera, which had been staged for Tebaldi, was removed from the repertory and from the Metropolitan's annual spring tour.

There were rumors about her future plans. During a TV interview with Franco Corelli, she confirmed her decision to leave the stage for a year and added, "I won't shut myself up in a convent, nor will I marry. I only need rest. I won't leave New York either, since among eleven million people I'm certain nobody will pay any attention to me."

In her year of absence, though, Renata did not just rest. She had been introduced the previous year to Maestro Ugo DeCaro by Arturo Basile, and she accepted his suggestion that he help her in reworking her voice. "I used to live in fear of catching colds, so I kept the heat up too high. I couldn't stand air conditioning. With Ugo's advice, my life became less complicated. My diet was healthy. I eliminated coffee, cheese, pasta, sweets, and alcohol. During my free time I rehearsed at the piano, and I went for long automobile rides, which I enjoyed. I regained control of my nervous system, a prerequisite for success on stage where one must be ready for anything."

So amidst work and relaxation, the year passed. At 42 years of age, her composure regained, radiant and self-confident, Tebaldi began a "second career." She sang *La Bohème* in Philadelphia on March 10, 1964. When she came on stage, the audience applauded for 18 minutes. She had won this battle, too. Perhaps it had been her most difficult battle since it had been waged against herself. She was being compared to the Tebaldi of the past. Four days later she was in New York at the Metropolitan, again singing *La Bohème*, again greeted triumphantly.

Several performances of *Tosca* and *Otello* followed through April and May, also at the Metropolitan. In the New York *Herald Tribune* of March 23, 1964, Alan Rich said in his review of *Tosca*, "Miss Tebaldi was stupendous.... Hers was an exciting interpretation, magnificently conceived...enveloped in dramatic singing of the highest quality." Harold Schonberg wrote in *The New York Times*, "What a joy it is to have the Tebaldi of the great years back again! When were we ever so privileged to hear a '*Vissi d'arte*' as we heard last evening? The audience was moved and the applause was tumultuous."

During a performance of *Tosca*, in Act II, a lighted candelabra was knocked over. Renata nonchalantly bent over, blew out the candles and replaced the candelabra on the table...all without missing a note. The echo of what happened, like everything else concerning Tebaldi, reached Parma. It was Aunt Marianna who dispatched all the news concerning her famous niece. The information was passed on to the Parma *Gazette* which printed events in bold titles. The editor was happy to highlight all events announcing Tebaldi's successes. It meant thousands of additional copies sold.

In the Autumn of 1964 she sang at the Lyric Opera of Chicago and then back to the Metropolitan for *Simon Boccanegra* and *Tosca*. She ended the year there with performances of *Otello*. Tebaldi's schedule was back to its former rapid succession of performances. In February and March of 1965 she sang concerts in Cleveland, Washington, D.C., Toronto and Montreal. She also appeared on "The Telephone Hour" and "The Ed Sullivan Show."

In Cleveland, after her concert at the Music Hall, Frank Hurby wrote, "One talks of the new Tebaldi, the changed Tebaldi, the Tebaldi of the past—which of the three sang for her audience last evening is not important. She left no doubt in anyone's mind. Today she is the same as always, the best. Too bad that she, too, has followed the latest trend and limited herself to so few pieces, only seven, and one encore. Too few in our opinion."

The Metropolitan tour in April and May proceeded successfully with alternating performances of *Tosca* and *Otello*. The result was glowing reviews. In the *Boston Traveler* on April 23, 1965, Alta Maloney's heading was "Tebaldi thrilling in *Otello*."

She completed her tour and agreed to a concert at Lewisohn Stadium where she had not sung since 1957. Renata's first reaction had been to decline. She tried to avoid singing outdoors, but she didn't succeed. She arrived on Bing's arm wearing a dazzling blue gown over which she draped a mink cape. Before the concert he good-naturedly stepped up to the microphone and addressed the audience saying, "I'm Rudolf Bing, and I work at the Met." For the occasion, Giancarlo Menotti composed the "Lewisohn Stadium Fanfare." Those fortunate enough to have been there will remember the magic of that evening—magical singing, a magical presence. The result was an ecstatic audience; someone was overheard saying, "She could be elected mayor this evening if she wanted...."

Her vacation, as always, was enjoyed in Italy, on the Adriatic. "I can't imagine vacationing away from the Adriatic; I've gone to Rimini for I don't know how many years. I used to return to the same suite at the Grand Hotel, number 307, which was reserved for me every year. The position of the hotel is stupendous; it has magnificent terraces and a huge private beach. Since the windows of my bedroom overlooked the sea, I often kept the shutters up all night to enjoy the moonlight in my room. In the morning I would awaken at dawn and watch the sun rise above the sea like a giant colored ball and slowly become a blinding light. And how can I ever forget the evenings when my friends and I stayed up all night after a concert waiting for the dawn, with the sun rising above the rocks of the jetty?"

At the beginning of September 1965, Tebaldi was back in the States for *Andrea Chénier* for opening night performances at the San Francisco Opera and the Los Angeles Music Center. In Chicago at the Lyric Opera Tebaldi sang several performances of *Mefistofele*, with Nicolai Ghiaurov, Alfredo Kraus, and Elena Souliotis, a young Greek-Argentinian, who was making her debut as Elena. A grand ball was held at the Hilton after the first performance and Renata, uncharacteristically, attended with friends. On opening night in Dallas, Tebaldi sang *Tosca* with a new Italian tenor, Franco Tagliavini. Two days later, on November 13th, a new Violetta made her debut, Montserrat Caballé, the girl from the family circle in Barcelona.

Tebaldi spent Christmas in New York after several performances of *La Bohème* and *Tosca* in December.

❧25❧

1966: Final Season at the Old Metropolitan
La Gioconda at the New Metropolitan

The final curtain had arrived for the old Metropolitan. It was time to replace the venerable theater and its echoes of past glories with a new Metropolitan at Lincoln Center. The decision to demolish the old opera house upset many artists, including Renata. "It's very painful for me," she declared, "even though I'm certain that at Lincoln Center a more modern and functional theater will be built. In many ways, for me, it's not the new stones that count, but what the old ones remember. What an uproar there would be in Milan if La Scala were threatened with demolition, even with the premise of a larger and more functional Scala to replace it."

A campaign similar to the one that saved Carnegie Hall was initiated, but it failed to save the old theater which fell under the attack of bulldozers and wreckers' balls in 1967. "I would prefer to have two Metropolitans and be embarrassed about choosing between the two rather than see the destruction of the present Metropolitan to which I am affectionately attached," was Tebaldi's reaction. But neither the petitions nor Licia Albanese's active attempt to arouse public sympathy by singing *Butterfly* in costume at the entrance of the old theater accomplished anything, and the beloved old Metropolitan went down.

Each artist who had ever sung there received a piece of the golden curtain as a remembrance. Renata had the privilege of receiving a piece of the gilded, braided cord. There was even a VIP who requested and received the toilet seat from the bathroom of the primadonnas' dressing room.

A gala farewell to the Metropolitan took place on April 16th, 1966, a colossal affair with most of the great artists of the past and the present taking part. Maestro Leopold Stokowski started the evening with the overture to *Tannhäuser*, which was followed by operatic selections sung by Robert Merrill, Leontyne Price, Cesare Siepi, Licia Albanese, Roberta Peters, Birgit Nilsson, Montserrat Caballé, Zinka Milanov, Richard Tucker, Nicolai Gedda, and many, many more. Alternating on the podium were Zubin Mehta, Francesco Molinari-Pradelli, Georges Prêtre, and Fausto Cleva. Renata Tebaldi and Franco Corelli sang the duet from *Manon Lescaut, "Vieni, con le tue braccia."*

Opening night at the new Metropolitan took place on September 21st, 1966 with Samuel Barber's *Anthony and Cleopatra*. On the 22nd of September, a magnificent new production of *La Gioconda*, brigantine and all, starring Tebaldi and Corelli was unveiled. On September 23rd, in the *Herald Tribune,* Alan Rich wrote of the "literally incredible performance of Renata Tebaldi in the role of the protagonist."

New York was enduring the final days of a particularly hot summer which had exhausted everyone. The new theater was in the throes of a breaking-in period. Since the air-conditioning system was still being adjusted, the temperature oscillated from freezing to hot from one day to another. The result was an epidemic of hoarseness, bronchitis, frogs in the throat, and other inconveniences which were detrimental for the *ugole d'oro*.[12] Nerves were on end, frequently approach-

---

[12] golden voices

ing crisis proportion.

Perhaps the biggest hurdle was the intricate floor plan of this gigantic building which had everyone losing his way in the labyrinth of corridors, tunnels, elevators, dressing rooms, and rehearsal rooms. Detailed maps had been distributed to facilitate internal traffic, but chaos reigned. Security guards were hired to help ward off other problems. The most serious misfiring occurred in the electronic command panel. This "room of buttons" seemed to rival Cape Canaveral. Only one technician with several weeks of intensive training understood the buttons, and if he was absent or failed to communicate his instructions quickly enough to other technicians, ludicrous things happened and sets were blocked for hours.

Despite these obstacles, *La Gioconda* was performed as scheduled, and even though the sets were modified here and there for simplification, it remained a stupendous spectacle. Tebaldi and Corelli received ovations. Renata revealed a dramatic drive that, some said, they had not seen in her before, not even as Tosca.

In the weekly Italian magazine, *Oggi,* an article appeared that created a stir. A caption identifying a photograph of Tebaldi read "Callas." Renata was angry enough to write from New York: "It's a pity that some donkey inserted Callas in the caption under my photograph. No excuse in the world can justify such a glaring error."

But hers was only professional resentment. Recently, the personal vicissitudes of the two women had, in a way, brought them closer. The compassion which would lead to their famous "reconciliation" two years later was growing. Several years earlier, in May of 1962, an attempt had been made to reunite the two great rivals during a rehearsal of *Les Huguenots* at La Scala. In the cast of this opera, one of the most sensational productions at that theater, were Joan Sutherland, Franco Corelli, Giulietta Simionato, Nicolai Ghiaurov and Fiorenza Cossotto. Maria Callas sat in the orchestra while

156

Tebaldi was in a box. During the intermissions, Maria was seen circulating in the corridors and dressing rooms. A futile attempt was made to extract Tebaldi from her box, but she remained anchored there tenaciously until the last few bars of the opera. Then she emerged and disappeared. The "grand occasion" had slipped by, not to occur again for several years.

Amidst the endless activity and thrilling successes of 1966, Tebaldi spent a jubilant afternoon in Philadelphia at Villanova University where she was awarded an honorary doctorate. She was only the sixth woman in 123 years to receive this award. Sold-out performances of *La Gioconda* brought 1966 to a close.

On January 1, 1967, a vast television audience across the country viewed "The Telephone Hour" and was thrilled when four superstar sopranos, Birgit Nilsson, Leontyne Price, Joan Sutherland, and Renata Tebaldi converged on the same stage to sing their arias. Tebaldi sang *"Voi lo sapete"* from *Cavalleria Rusticana* and *"Suicidio"* from *La Gioconda*. Each soprano was interviewed by Donald Vorhees, and the audience had the rare opportunity of feeling the charisma of these stars emanating from their television screens.

Performances of *Tosca*, *Otello*, and *La Bohème*, plus several concerts occupied Tebaldi through March, followed by a triumphant cross-country tour in *La Gioconda* with the Metropolitan Opera. In the *Minneapolis Star* on May 18, 1967, John K. Sherman wrote, "...the greatest thrill last evening was that of seeing and hearing the incomparable Renata Tebaldi in the role...."

Franco Corelli was in a particularly amiable mood during the tour. In Cleveland, he even agreed to cover Carlo Bergonzi, who was indisposed just before a performance. Actually, in order to get him to agree, Rudolf Bing and Bob Herman roguishly devised a plan to have Corelli find them kneeling in front of the door of his hotel room. Unfortunately, they placed themselves in front of the wrong hotel room. The result was a perplexed and frightened elderly woman, startled by two kneeling strangers as she exited her room. Trying to explain the embarrassing situation was great fun.

"Franco was known for being a temperamental artist," says Renata, "but it all stemmed from his fear of being sick. I used to tease him by saying that he earned his phenomenal fees if only for his efforts to overcome his agonizing fears. He'd forget his words, and I'd have to remember them for him because in his panic he'd even fail to hear the prompter...."

La Gioconda was back at the Metropolitan Opera in June. Kosygin's daughter, Ludmilla A. Gvishani, was in the audience during the performance. Her presence was made public only at the last minute. At the Russian Embassy her plans for the evening were not known until she was seen leaving at 7:30 p.m., accompanied by a member of the Embassy and two agents in street clothes. At the Opera she was ushered into a VIP box. At the end of the performance, Mrs. Gvishani visited Renata's dressing room. She greeted Tebaldi with "It's a pleasure to see you!" "Hello! It's my pleasure, and I hope to come to Russia to sing soon," Renata said happily. The dressing room filled with a phalanx of diplomats and photographers. The next day, a front page photo showed Mrs. Gvishani gazing up at Tebaldi with a look of admiration not uncommon among her admirers.

Renata, very much at ease in America, was enjoying a second artistic bloom. The Metropolitan audience adored her. Harold Schonberg commented one day in *The New York Times*, "Miss Tebaldi is your darling, my darling, everybody's darling...."

La Scala again sent overtures in her direction. In a letter written by Renata to a friend on November 20, 1966 she said, "Yesterday, Mr. Oldani, who was passing through New York, came to visit me. He came to say hello and to speak to me about my return to La Scala. But before I sing at La Scala, I want to sing in Naples and, perhaps, Rome." In Autumn 1967, the La Scala Opera company arrived in New York. In a letter dated October 26th Renata wrote, "I was at Carnegie Hall for the Verdi *Requiem* performed by the visiting company. It was a superb evening. I was especially impressed by the chorus—what stupendous singing I heard! I also had my share of success, even if I didn't sing. I was very happy to be there; everyone greeted me joyfully, especially the directors of the company. I even got the famous kiss on the forehead from Ghiringhelli! They're waiting for me at La Scala! But, at present I have no plans to accept." Elsewhere Renata said, "Ghiringhelli was very obsequious, but one can never tell what's really on his mind. It's never been possible to establish a sincere rapport with him."

Renata's life had assumed a certain rhythm: summers in Rimini and the rest of the year in the States. In 1967, after a brief vacation, she was back in Newport, Rhode Island for a memorable performance of *Otello* in concert form, with Jon Vickers and Peter Glossop, directed by Kurt Adler. At the Metropolitan in September, October, and November, Tebaldi sang eight performances of *La Gioconda* and five performances of *Manon Lescaut*. She returned to Philadelphia in early December for *Otello* amidst the excitement and preparations for her fast-approaching return to Naples to inaugurate the San Carlo opera season with *La Gioconda* on December 26th, 1967.

The last time Tebaldi sang in Naples was in 1962. Her long-awaited return to the San Carlo Opera brought together much of the musical elite of Italy. In *Il Mattino* on December 27, the morning after opening night, Alfredo Parente wrote, "Renata Tebaldi was awaited by everyone with the curiosity and perplexity of one who has passionately followed her ascent and remembers the grand, triumphant performances. Truthfully, one didn't expect that she would return, after so long an absence, with such an abundance of magnificent vocal means." Guido Pannain of *Il Tempo* on January 19, 1968, wrote of "a voice of indescribable sweetness, of colors which dissolved in invisible tears and inexplicable caresses, a voice that is ravishingly imbued with sensual melancholy."

Those who were listening to Tebaldi for the first time discovered a great voice, an exceptional voice, a voice that obeyed direction. Those who knew her voice from the past heard a different and amazing instrument. Besides the sound of pure gold that flowed as if by magic from the simple parting of her lips, now a new intensity, a new force was present.

But it was the new Tebaldi who really amazed everyone. She, who in her youth had been a vocal phenomenon for the ease and generosity of her incredible voice, had always been somewhat diffident and, as a result, cautious in her approach. Now she was sure of her voice and of herself, as if she had achieved everything for which she had prepared.

For the return of their darling, Naples prepared a triumphant welcome. Ribbons and banners of "Welcome Back Renata" were displayed in and outside the opera house, all four performances were sold out, and the opera house was beautifully adorned with an abundance of colorful floral arrangements. When Tebaldi arrived at the San Carlo for the first rehearsal, a delighted Pasquale Di Costanzo, the impresario, planted himself on stage, astride a chair, to enjoy her voice at close range.

❧26❧

1968: Historic Meeting with Maria Callas
Final Debut

In spite of negative reviews and Rudolf Bing's personal aversion to the opera back in 1962, the Metropolitan Opera, with a shrewd eye to the enthusiasm of the public, had decided that *Adriana Lecouvreur* should inaugurate the 1968 season. Before the event, Renata made sure that the news reached the Italian press. Remembering the last irritating error after her debut as Gioconda, she sent a cable to Nini Castiglioni cautioning, "Please check captions." Later in a letter she admonished, "With your connections with the press, be sure they don't make the same mistake with Adriana that they did with Gioconda, making it seem that the tenor is the protagonist."

Franco Corelli was again Maurizio. At a performance on the 28th of September he became ill and a young Spanish tenor, Placido Domingo, already well-known at the New York City Opera, was called in to replace him. In a letter Renata said, "The tenor, Placido Domingo, is doing well. He's been enthusiastically received by the public and the critics. I work with him with pleasure. The next performance on the 16th of October should also be his and those of the 29th and the 4th of November are Franco Corelli's."

161

On opening night an event occurred which would envelop *Adriana* in a whirl of international press coverage. The exciting and triumphant performance ended with an enthusiastic audience endlessly applauding in a standing ovation to the star and her tenor. Members of the audience, including this translator, happily noticed that Maria Callas had joined the standing ovation. The rejoicing over, Rudolf Bing entered Renata's dressing room to congratulate her. He seemed a bit hesitant until he finally came out with, "Renata, there is someone who would like to come to say hello to you...," then a pause, "a dear friend."

"Is it Zinka?"

"No, it's Maria."

After a brief silence she replied, "Of course! I'd be happy to see her!" Maria Callas was in Franco Corelli's dressing room awaiting Tebaldi's reply to the goodwill ambassador's query.

They met amidst a flurry of flashing bulbs and elated onlookers, including Rudolf Bing and Mayor Lindsay. The two women embraced. "I wish you a thousand of these successes and much happiness," Maria said to Renata. She had arrived in New York from Dallas two days earlier and had requested, through her recording house, two tickets for this opening-night performance. When Rudolf Bing learned of her request, he quickly offered her a box. He thought it wise to keep her from sitting in the orchestra where her entrance could cause a commotion. He took pains to ensure that all remained calm and that Tebaldi should know nothing before the performance. He didn't want Tebaldi to be upset by the news of Maria's presence. "My dear friend, Renata," Maria used to say to reporters years earlier, gritting her teeth as she spoke of Tebaldi to them.

"Truthfully, we were never friends. We never had the time or the opportunity," Renata would say smiling. That evening after the performance, however, they were like two friends who were meeting after a long time, and the shadow of the many bitter misunderstandings that had divided them now seemed instead to unite them. Those present at this historic embrace, preserved by the flashing of bulbs, had tears in their eyes.

A common destiny that went beyond the stage united these two great artists, one no longer singing, the other still at the height of her career. In August, Callas had been abandoned by Onassis who, two months later, married Jacqueline Kennedy. Five years later Onassis was dead.

In April, Tebaldi had learned of the death of Arturo Basile in an automobile accident on a rain-slick road near Vercelli, Italy. The memory of his much-publicized "Basile-Tebaldi wedding announcement" and their final telephone conversation had been very painful and had stained the memory of their love. Renata had strength to overcome her pain then. Now her life had assumed a tranquil rhythm; she was fulfilled both professionally and emotionally, and she had held on to her equilibrium. Maria Callas was involved in a tragic love story that she would not have the strength to endure.

"Maria was not a lucky woman. She suffered many terrible humiliations without having the strength to react to them," says Renata. "She was a great artist, and I admired her. Her voice was unique, and her success in creating a lower and middle octave, which nature had not given her, shows enormous willpower and intelligence."

Maria Callas left New York the day after Tebaldi's triumph in *Adriana*. Tebaldi tried to reach her by telephone at the Hotel Pierre, but she had already left. She wrote to Maria, and Maria's reply to Renata was *"di farsi viva"*[13] if she should ever be in Paris. They never met again.

The Hong Kong flu forced Renata to cancel the remainder of her performances in 1968. She returned to the Metro-

---

[13] "to get in touch"

politan in March of 1969 for several performances of *Tosca*, *Adriana*, and *Bohème*. On April 25th she was singing *Adriana Lecouvreur* at the Wade Memorial Auditorium as part of the Metropolitan Opera spring tour which also took her to Cleveland, Atlanta, Dallas, Minneapolis, and Detroit. She was back in New York for *Tosca* on June 2nd and *La Bohème* on June 7th, both with Franco Corelli. Then she happily prepared for her return to Italy and her vacation in Rimini.

The new season at the Metropolitan promised to be a difficult one. Tebaldi was scheduled to make her debut in *La Fanciulla del West* on opening night. To prepare for the role, she cut short her stay on the Adriatic and returned to the States at the beginning of August. The rest, although too short, had been good for her. On September 4, 1969, Renata wrote to a friend from New York, "This summer I had a wonderful vacation and I relaxed completely. I really needed it. I was so very tired when I got to Italy! My five weeks of complete rest by the sea brought me back to the world! As always, every time I leave Italy and arrive here, I feel terribly sad. I dislike everything around me. Then, slowly, everything returns to normal. Three days after I got here I started studying and now I'm completely immersed in *Fanciulla* which is a musically very difficult opera.... Things at the Metropolitan are not going well...." Preparation for *Fanciulla* had been a painstaking and scrupulous collaboration of many months with Maestro Ugo DeCaro. On the 12th of September she wrote again: "Things at the Metropolitan continue to go badly. Opening night has been delayed for another two weeks, bringing it to a total of four weeks so far. Yesterday Mr. Bing called me to personally inform me of the situation. I've heard of Domingo's great success and I'm very happy for him because he's such a fine fellow besides everything else...."[14]

---

[14] Tebaldi was referring to Placido Domingo's performances in *Turandot* and *Don Carlo* at the Arena di Verona.

164

The opening night, October 25th, 1969, passed, and the Metropolitan Opera House remained dark. On November 26th Renata again wrote, "The situation at the Metropolitan is not resolved. Still, no official announcement cancelling the season has been made."

On December 2nd, Renata went to Philadelphia to sing Mimi to Franco Corelli's Rodolfo at the Academy of Music. On December 13th she was in Cleveland for *Simon Boccanegra* in concert. Finally a short season was settled upon at the Metropolitan. For Renata, performances of *Tosca* began on New Year's Eve and continued into January, 1970, alternating with *La Bohème*. Her debut in *Fanciulla* took place on February 11, 1970.

As the evening of the debut performance approached, Tebaldi wrote to Nini Castiglioni asking her to prepare a statement for the Italian press. With humorous insight she added, "I'm fully aware that this event won't be all that interesting for the press because one must create scandals in order to be remembered!"

Sándor Kónya and Giangiacomo Guelfi (and later Anselmo Colzani) sang together with Tebaldi, and Fausto Cleva conducted. Her debut was a sensational event. Tebaldi was forty-eight years old. Youthful agility, good health, and exhilaration emanated from her person on stage. She wore the typical western outfit, the leather skirt and fringed vest and boots, while in the last act she wore pants for the first time on stage. (Tebaldi had lost weight; in fact, for the first time in her life she had the pleasant experience of shopping at Saks Fifth Avenue and choosing clothing which needed no alteration.)

Harold Schonberg of *The New York Times* wrote, "At the end of the opera the audience didn't want to let her go. New York had found a new *Fanciulla del West* to love. Not so much for her singing as for her acting.... She was the most perfect, tender, innocent incarnation of Minnie that the Met ever had. Temperament was there, too, but femininity and good manners prevailed, amdist great love and loyalty. Exactly what Puccini had in mind.... The striptease (which went as far as her drawers and corset) was enjoyed by everyone. Miss Tebaldi carried it off with a sort of modest urgency which was very exciting. But, that was nothing compared to the card game.... With what skill she hid the four aces in her garter! With what gesture of triumph she hurled the cards in the air as the defeated sheriff made his exit!" In this scene Tebaldi had become a cold-blooded, passionate woman fighting to protect her lover from death. Everyone in the audience was caught up in the emotion. Also applauding Tebaldi were many divas including Zinka Milanov, Birgit Nilsson, Leonie Rysanek, Christa Ludwig, Régine Crespin, Gabriella Tucci, and Raina Kabaivanska.

The exciting poker game was followed by tense moments in the last act: Tebaldi entered on horseback! (Tebaldi's phobia of horses which her mother had passed on to her was well-known).

Tebaldi sang five performances of *La Fanciulla del West* at the Metropolitan, followed by a concert with Franco Corelli in Miami, a *Bohème* in Boston, and nine performances of *Andrea Chénier* through December, 1970, at the Metropolitan.

❦ 27 ❦

Tranquil Fulfillment
Concerts in the Far East
La Scala: Two Grand Recitals

When Tebaldi left the stage for a year in 1963 to review her artistic and personal life, she lived on 54th Street in Manhattan. She soon moved to a larger, 18th-floor apartment on 55th Street off Sixth Avenue where she lived comfortably, surrounded by much that was dear to her.

These were years lived tranquilly. In Ugo DeCaro Renata had found a teacher and a companion. It was he who helped her regain her self-confidence as an artist and return to the stage. Connie DeCaro, Ugo's sister-in-law and one of her closest friends, who now flies to Italy each year to see Renata, says, "Renata has so enriched the lives of those who have had the good fortune to know her. Becoming a friend of such an extraordinary artist and human being was the turning point of my life. She has added insight and a wonderful glow to my perception of all things. She has an uncommon ability to observe, to listen, and to understand. When I'm with Renata or listening to her music, I am reassured; all that is good will remain."

Renata's life was well-organized between Italy and America during this period. Her very dear friends and relatives were—and still are—in Rimini and San Marino: her

167

cousin Lidia, married to a dentist; their three daughters, Christina, Gloria, and Isabella, who love music; her friends, Valentino and Mirella with their two children; and in Ancona, the children and grandchildren of her father's sister. These are the people with whom Renata is happy and feels at ease. Saying goodbye to them at the end of summer vacation was always painful.

Nostalgia is easily detected in her many letters. Something else becomes evident, too: even after all the years in America, Renata continued to rely on an Italian network of suppliers and shops. There wasn't a letter in which she didn't mention shoes, boots, dresses, jewelry, or medicine, and the name of a possible candidate soon arriving in the States who could personally hand-deliver the items. With her many colleagues crossing the Atlantic back and forth from Italy to the States, there was always someone to rely on, and Nini Castilglioni, her friend and agent, made all the necessary contacts.

"Mirella Freni will be arriving in October. Do you think she can manage to bring me an umbrella and a bracelet?... If you're coming over, I would have some things for you to bring me, if it's not too much trouble... I could use the two pairs of boots that are still at my shoemaker's... Please have Gianni Raimondi (the tenor) bring me two large jars of Nivea." "Please bring me 15 pairs of stockings, size 4, melon colored. You should also pick up the earrings that were not ready when I left, and two suits..." Once she sent a telegram in which she said, "Please bring me two cans of *caffè Hag*.[15] Thanks. Regards."

After the enormous success of *La Fanciulla del West*, Tebaldi started to lighten her professional commitments. In March, 1971, it was rumored in Italy that Tebaldi planned to sing *La Bohème* with Franco Corelli in Macerata, a sea-

---

[15] decaffeinated coffee

port on the Adriatic. Torino responded immediately by offering her any opera she wished to sing (the opera season there had opened with *I Vespri Siciliani* with which Maria Callas was making her directing debut with Di Stefano). Tebaldi turned down all offers for herself, but she did go to Macerata to hear her friend, Franco Corelli, who was to become her partner in the third and final phase of her career: recitals.

In 1971 Tebaldi sang *Otello* with Jon Vickers and Peter Glossop at the Academy of Music in Philadelphia. In 1972 there were several performances of *Falstaff* at the Metropolitan. Following that was a tour of concerts with Franco Corelli which took them to Memphis, New Orleans, San Antonio, Columbus, Washington, and Philadelphia. In January of 1973 Tebaldi sang her last three performances at the Metropolitan. The opera was *Otello*. James McCracken was Otello and Sherrill Milnes was Iago. James Levine conducted.

1973 was an exceptional year for Renata Tebaldi. At 51 years of age she embarked on a series of tours devoted solely to concerts which took her all over the globe. From February 13th through May 3rd she sang 14 recitals in 12 American cities, followed by Ottowa and Vancouver. In July she was joined by Franco Corelli for concerts in Cincinnati and at Temple University in Pennsylvania. After a brief vacation, on October 9th they were together in London for a concert at Albert Hall organized by Sandro Gorlinski, the legendary Russian manager. They were in Vienna at the Musikverein on October 14. With not too much time to spare, they were off to the Far East for three concerts in Manila, on the 23rd, 27th, and 31st of October. These were followed in November by two concerts in Tokyo, one each in Osaka, Seoul, Mito and Hong Kong. The Hong Kong concert on the 27th of November concluded their tour for 1973.

During their 1973 visit to Manila, the Italian artists were guests of the government. The group consisted of Tebaldi,

Franco Corelli and his wife, the journalist Bruno Tosi, and
Tina. They were lodged in a villa in the government palace
complex; they were served by President Marcos's personal
servant, a chef (Tina taught him some Italian specialties), a
nurse, and five bodyguards. Since Imelda, the president's wife,
recently had been the victim of an attack on her life, the
dictator's regime was taking every precaution for its official
guests, too. The concerts were held at the New Musical Center and at the Sports Palace. For the Italians, this three-week
stopover in Manila also served as a vacation. Fabulous parties and entertainment were organized in their honor. The
gardens around their villa were festively illuminated day and
night.

All the splendor, however, failed to ease some of the inconveniences. The humidity was so unbearable that air conditioning was necessary at all times, but the singers, fearing
for their voices, often requested that it be turned off, making
their lives less comfortable and disgruntling the personnel.
Then, during a reception, the walls of the building started to
quiver. Shifting objects created a stir of anxiety among the
guests as Renata eyed the reactions of the locals. To her
amazement she found no sign of alarm among them. Since
everyone remained calm, she regained her composure and
managed a smile. Later she was reassured that these telluric
shocks were common and that nobody worried about them
anymore.

Problems of language arose in Japan. In Mito the artists
were staying in a very new and comfortable hotel where,
however, only Japanese was spoken. It was pleasing to find a
beautiful kimono, a gift from the hotel, carefully laid out on
the bed, but it was disconcerting to pick up a menu written
in undecipherable little ideograms.

Tebaldi returned home with very tender memories of
Korea. The concert was held in an auditorium with perfect
acoustics. The audience consisted mostly of young people,

and she immediately felt their nearness and warmth. "They are like our people from the south of Italy, spontaneous and exuberant," recalls Renata. After the concert, with the applause over and the innumerable visits to her dressing room ended, she found on her person (in her pockets, bag, even in the sleeves of her cape), many, many little notes folded over and over again so as to look like confetti. The messages were written in English, such phrases as "Come back soon," "Thanks for everything," "We love you." The notes came from those admirers who had not had the courage or opportunity to express their enthusiasm directly, so they said their goodbyes through their messages of affection and admiration.

On September 7th, 1973, in Busseto, Verdi's birthplace, Renata Tebaldi was awarded the Verdi d'Oro. Mario Morini, the musicologist, presented the gold medal to Tebaldi saying, "Tebaldi's exquisitely refined technique is combined with an overwhelming, inspired musical interpretation." He concluded with, "It is with the greatest emotion that I present this second *Verdi D'Oro—Città di Busseto* to Renata Tebaldi, the soprano who, better than anyone else, has revived the best traditions of Italian bel canto."

With Christmas and New Year festivities over, Tebaldi and Corelli were back together, on the 12th of February, in Palm Beach, Florida, for their first concert of 1974. They were in New York at Brooklyn College on the 23rd of February, and together in Miami on the 26th of February.

Then Tebaldi embarked on a tour of recitals which took her from Post College in Long Island to Europe and Iceland: La Scala, Mantova, Como, Torino, Pavia, Reykjavik, Vienna, Rimini, Paris, Antwerp, Mannheim, Amsterdam, Barcelona, Madrid, and Valencia. On the 11th and the 14th of October, Paris had the pleasure of two recitals by Tebaldi at the Espace Cardin. The invitation had come from the celebrated designer, Pierre Cardin, asking her to sing in his theater.

Renata was very pleased to be at the Hotel Crillon for its elegance and for its proximity to the recital hall. Dominating the Place de la Concorde, the famous hotel was just a few steps from the Espace Cardin. Once again, in Paris, Tebaldi triumphed. Her audience wouldn't let her go. Chanting in unison, "Re-na-ta! Re-na-ta!" they were rewarded with six encores. Endless applause and countless flowers followed. Pierre Cardin was the perfect host after each recital, at the supper parties in honor of Renata, at two of the finest restaurants in Paris, the Chez Lamazaire and Le Coupe-Chou. The reviews of her recitals were many and enthusiastic: On October 16, 1974, the Paris *Le Monde* speaks of "a voice...of dreamy arabesques seeming to emerge from a perfect violin." From Barcelona on December 5th, in *El Noticiero Universal,* Juan Lluch writes, "She sang and there wasn't a sound. Seldom have I experienced anything quite so prodigious, a powerful permeation between singer and public. She revealed the mysteries of her great talent."

For Tebaldi, the event dominating 1974 was her return to La Scala on May 20th. It was preceded by a recital on the 15th of May at the Piccola Scala (a smaller theater adjacent to the venerable opera house); *"un po' per celia e un po' per non morire al primo incontro,"*[16] says Renata, "to soften the emotional impact of La Scala."

Fourteen years had elapsed since *Tosca* at La Scala, and Tebaldi was returning with a repertory of arias by Scarlatti, Paradisi, Pergolesi, Gluck, Bellini, Donizetti, Verdi, Puccini, and Zandonai. There were also Beethoven's *"Ah perfido!"* and Mascagni's *"Voi lo sapete"* from *Cavalleria Rusticana.* Six encores followed, by great demand. Once again, that characteristic rapport of love between her and her audience permeated the hall, that affinity which Renata Tebaldi con-

---

[16] "a bit playfully and so as not to die as we meet again," Act II, *Madama Butterfly.*

sidered a vital requisite to any performance, and one which she always succeeded in establishing. "If the audience doesn't love me, I can't sing." In *Corriere della Sera*, Milan, May 16, 1974, a critic wrote, "Recital at the Piccola Scala—Enthusiasm and Encores: After the concert, Tebaldi, overwhelmed by applause, gave in to encores.... The apotheosis lasted 45 minutes." In *Corriere della Sera*, May 18, 1974, Piermaria Paoletti writes, "The voice—vivid recollection of her legendary past...the velvet uniformity is intact; the voice emerges pure, from the first note of Scarlatti's lament to the pouring forth into those almost transparent sounds, the 'filati' spun off and concluding in barely a breath which her extraordinary technique has rendered incomparable." Paoletti summed up the recital at the Piccola Scala by saying, "Forty-five minutes of uninterrupted applause after the recital without a weakening of intensity is an unbelievably long time."

The overwhelming success of Renata Tebaldi's long-awaited recital at La Scala on May 20, 1974 was appropriately described in the Milan publication, *La Notte*, by Carlamaria Casanova: "At the end of the concert the audience gave not the slightest hint that they were aware that the recital was over. They all remained at their seats—if they did stand, it was only to better applaud.... Excitement, which had been growing continuously, exploded into a fifty minute ovation during which 'la Renata,' between handshakes, acknowledgement of floral tributes, smiles, emotion, and greetings, gifted her ecstatic audience with seven encores, beginning with '*Addio nostro picciol desco*' from *Manon*, '*Flammen perdonami*' from *Lodoletta*, and concluding with '*Non ti scordar di me*.' Then Renata Tebaldi, magnificent in her loosely draped rose-salmon gown, a bit short of breath, turned towards the ushers and said, 'Please darken the house—I can't go on....'"

In 1974, Tebaldi was honored with the impressive title of Grand Officer of the Order of Merit of the Republic of Italy.

As the award was presented, verses from Dante's *Divine Comedy* were read as an encomium to Tebaldi: "*Lo Raggio della Grazia/Onde si accende verace amore/Che poi cresce amando.*"[17] This title was the second prerequisite for the most prestigious—*Cavaliere della Gran Croce*—which she would receive in 1992. In 1970 Tebaldi had received the first of the three honors, the title of *Commendatore* of the Republic of Italy.

---

[17] The Aura of Grace/Where true Love glows/Which then loving, grows."

❧28❧

The Russian Tour

It was Paolo Grassi, Antonio Ghiringhelli's successor as director of La Scala, who willed Renata's return to La Scala, and it was he who promoted her tour to Russia. A few days after Renata's concert at La Scala in 1974, the opera company left for its second visit to the Bolshoi Theater. Both she and Paolo Grassi thought that this Italian-Russian cultural exchange could pave the way for a Tebaldi appearance in Russia, but neither had the time to speak of it. It was a common friend, Tilde Tenconi, whose timely inspiration set plans in motion. She sped to the airport to speak to Grassi who was leaving with the opera company for Moscow, but she was too late—he had already gone through customs. She was able, however, to get a note through to him, "See what you can arrange for Renata." The suggestion could not have been more propitiously timed.

While Paolo Grassi was in Moscow, Renata was on her way to an unusual destination: Reykjavik, Iceland where she was to sing on June 24th, 1974. Vladmir Ashkenazy, the pianist, who was making his conducting debut in that city, had requested that she honor him with her singing. In a letter to her friend, Connie DeCaro, Renata, with her usual keen perception, says, "The city is very characteristic with its houses painted in pastels, topped with roofs of bright yellow, red, green, and violet! From the airport to the city there's very little to see except lava from many eruptions. Our hotel is modern and comfortable. We have an apartment on the seventh floor with a wrap-around terrace and a stupendous view. It's always daylight...it really takes time to become accustomed. It's so strange to wake up at night and see the light of day...and what a sight on June 21st to see the sun go down at midnight!... Everybody here has an enormous affection for plants. It's the responsibility of the young to cultivate them, and they do so with enthusiasm, even the children: they weed, fertilize, hoe.... Fruits and vegetables are grown in huge hot-houses because weather conditions make outdoor cultivation difficult. There's no smog at all here. Houses are heated with natural hot springs, bath water too—all natural. Isn't it fantastic? One fills one's lungs with air that is so fresh that it seems scented! The hall where I'll sing is [of] the typical sports construction, but certainly better than many I've seen. Let's hope that the acoustics will still be good when the hall is crowded with people."

1975 started propitiously for Renata. At midnight on New Year's Eve she received the three telephone calls from male friends needed to bring in a good year!... a superstition in which Renata places much faith. In fact, each New Year's Eve her male friends are alert to their responsibility, and her female friends know enough to stay away from the telephone until January 1st to wish her a happy new year!

In October 1975, Tebaldi was on her way to Poland for the first of a tour of recitals which Paolo Grassi had arranged. Accompanying her were Tina, her friends Tilde and Giannino Tenconi, and Maestro Edoardo Müller and his wife. The first stop was Warsaw where at the airport an official delegation presented her with flowers. A press conference had been arranged which was followed by a reception at the embassy.

During the brief stopover in Poland, a visit was arranged to Chopin's home in Zelazowa Wola. For the occasion the house was closed to tourists, and a young pianist played Chopin preludes for the Italian guests, who were deeply moved by the experience.

Tebaldi's recital was held in the splendid hall of the Philharmonic which was so packed that the audience sat anywhere they could: in the orchestra, in the aisles, and on stage. At the end of the recital everyone converged to the stage applauding rhythmically.

The journey, as scheduled, would have taken the group to Kiev through Moscow, but it was decided to simplify matters by heading straight for the capital of the Ukraine. In Russia, the word "simplification," however, can have little success and unforeseen consequences. The arrival in Kiev before the scheduled date, in fact, had disastrous results. The small group arrived amidst the confusion of the Germany-USSR soccer competition, a game of historical importance since, during the war, Kiev had played against the same team and lost because of a political directive which ordered them to lose. There were no vacant rooms available in the hotel where they were to stay. Rooms were eventually found in a hotel that was still under construction and still overrun by painters. The embarrassed interpreter who had accompanied the group from the border finally brought the uncomfortable situation to an end. To make up for the discomfort, however, were a grand reception at the Film Palace and a chauffeured limousine. The chauffeur's wife, an obstetrician, later told Tebaldi that among the infants born in those few days in Kiev, an impressive number were named Renata or Renato.

Tebaldi's recital took place in front of 4000 enthusiastic music lovers at the Palace of Culture where ideal acoustics were achieved with an enormous wooden shell placed like a windscreen at the rear of the stage.

Their departure from Kiev to Moscow was made pleasant by a large group of fans who came to see Renata off. When Tebaldi and friends arrived in Moscow, although it was snowing and it was 7 a.m., they were greeted festively at the station by a group of artists from the Bolshoi Theater. This was the stop Renata was especially anticipating. For the first time the Bolshoi was to be used for a solo recital. It was a stupendous opportunity. "I certainly would have enjoyed singing an opera in a theater with such an illustrious tradition," Renata mused, "but when La Scala went to Moscow I had commitments at the Metropolitan." One problem did arise, however. The Bolshoi Theater was not large enough for half the number of tickets requested, and a second evening for a second recital was not available. It was decided to have the recital at the Congressional Palace at the Kremlin to accommodate everyone. Tebaldi was very much against the decision and even more so after her visit there to check the acoustics, which she felt were a catastrophe. Her voice did not bounce back to the stage of the great hall, TV cameras crowded the stage, and microphones placed behind each seat falsified the sound. Under those conditions she would not sing. The assurances of the technicians were useless. They worked diligently as she sat gloomily in one of the 6000 seats. Finally they asked her to sing again. She did, and to her amazement the problem was resolved; her voice "returned" and it reached every corner of the hall. It was then that one of the technicians made a surprising statement, "We told you not to worry. It's an ultra-perfected American system. It couldn't fail!"

N. Ciubenko said in the *Sovietskaja Kultura,* "This recital will long remain in the hearts of those fortunate enough to have heard it." When it was over, much of the huge audience overflowed the stage, crowding Renata, who was protected by four robust ushers. Following Russian custom, everyone had a small gift—from flowers to dolls, postcards of their city, chocolates, small souvenirs. They wanted to shake her hand and ask for a photograph. Tebaldi greeted her guests for an hour, and then she was the guest of honor at a reception offered by the artists of the Bolshoi Theater. The renowned Russian mezzo-soprano, Elena Obraztsova, who knows French, acted as hostess. The two women liked each other immediately. They were so different in temperament, yet they recognized that they stemmed from the same matrix. Tebaldi accepted Obraztsova's invitation to her performance of Carmen the next day at the Bolshoi replying, "I'll come to see you in your dressing room." Obraztsova quickly replied, "No, I'll come to honor you in your box." And so she did.

Paolo Grassi had arranged for a reception at the Italian Embassy in Moscow. According to Renata, it is one of the most beautiful embassies in the world along with the Italian Embassies in Paris and Lisbon. Present in the elegant 19th century salons of the embassy was the diplomatic corps, Italian journalists in service in Moscow, and many other distinguished guests. The next day Tebaldi had a guided tour of the Kremlin to visit the treasures of the Tsar. As a personal privilege, she was allowed to keep her fur on as she toured (regulation imposed removal of topcoats before visiting the treasures).

The last stop of the tour was Leningrad. The train accommodations and suite at the Europeskaia Hotel were regal. She visited the Hermitage and thoroughly enjoyed the picture galleries and treasures as well as the summer imperial palace, and the cemetery where Rimsky-Korsakov, Tchaikovsky, and Pushkin are buried. She innocently exclaimed to A. Petrovoretz, her interpreter, "I wish I had lived in the days of the Tsar!"—words he pretended not to hear.

The hotel was just a few feet away from the Philharmonic where the first recital was held and then repeated three days later. This most celebrated hall with its white columns, once

the assembly of the nobles, today the seat of the Philharmonic orchestra of Leningrad, has legendary acoustics. The
piano Tebaldi used to vocalize in her dressing room had belonged to Rachmaninoff.

As in Moscow, the audience here was perfectly acquainted
with the program. The spectators spoke of Pergolesi and
Paradisi with the same ease with which they spoke of Puccini
and Verdi. On the final evening, the time to say goodbye,
many were deeply moved. One young man succeeded in
reaching Tebaldi through the crowd and with a trembling
voice said, "I want to thank you for what you have given me
this evening; the memory of your voice will sustain me when
I reach my final hour." It was such an emotionally charged
moment of farewell that Renata, too, was moved to tears,
and she cried so much that she lost one of her false eyelashes.

A thick crowd lined the street to the hotel and there, again,
was a continuous presentation of gifts. The morning after,
many came to see her off at the train. A young woman asked
for a sort of impromptu breathing lesson, "Where do we
draw the breath? From the diaphragm? Lower?" and while
the train pulled away, Tebaldi continued to demonstrate from
behind the window of her train compartment as the the young
woman ran along the station platform. The woman finally
pointed to her stomach to demonstrate that she had understood.

❧ 29 ❧

1976: Carnegie Hall Farewell
La Scala: Farewell Recital

In 1974 Tebaldi decided to live in Milan and close her apartment in New York. She and Tina painstakingly packed her belongings: her crystal and china, her paintings and photographs, her costumes, and her clothing. She left many of her favorite art objects with her friends. When she closed the door to her apartment for the last time, she cried.

With her Russian tour over in October, 1975, Tebaldi returned to Naples, a city very dear to her, for a recital in November at the San Carlo. Then, during Christmas festivities, she prepared for her return to New York for recitals in January.

On January 16, Carnegie Hall was sold out. The hall seemed to mirror the delight and enthusiasm of an audience eager to hear Tebaldi sing again. She was beautiful as she faced her public, who stood spontaneously as soon as she appeared. She started to sing and quickly realized that her voice was not responding. After the first aria she returned to the wings. A disconcertingly lengthy pause ended with her return, and as she approached the footlights she announced that she could not continue. "I'll come back," was her reply to an audience asking that she sing anything as long as she sang. She said, "I can't sing tonight; forgive me. But I'll be back." A cold had seemed less severe to her than it proved to be that evening. A large part of the audience remained behind in the hall talking about their concern for Tebaldi and their unhappiness over the unfortunate turn of events.

Tebaldi kept her promise and returned to Carnegie Hall on February 19th. "When I returned, a joyful pandemonium occurred in the hall as the rhythmic chanting of my name was added to the applause. They were all there. They had returned for me. The hall was packed. I was so moved I was afraid that I wouldn't be able to sing. Then I regained my self-control and the evening was a triumph in every way!"

There was electricity in the air. Just returning from a very wonderful and emotional experience in Russia, Renata was overwhelmed by an irrepressible affection emanating from her soul to her audience. Her friend, Connie DeCaro, describes the scene: "Renata approached the footlights and her adoring public, and, as soon as the ovation following Gluck's 'Divinità infernal' quieted, said, 'You know something? I love you very much!' Her audience again expressed its love and admiration with an emotional and ringing ovation.

"Bringing to a close a recital that was filled with magic from the first to the last note, Renata sang her seventh encore, 'Addio senza rancor.' As she sang, she controlled every corner of the grand hall, reaching each spectator individually, singing to each one, bringing to each, once again, the realities transcended.... Then the entire audience rose, moved towards the stage to be closer to their Renata, to give her a flower, to clasp her hand, to express their love for her, to hold on because they knew she would leave them sooner or later."

That evening, without realizing it, Renata Tebaldi sang her farewell to her American public.

She returned to Italy.

On March 27th she sang a recital at the Teatro Grande in

Brescia, one of the theaters where she debuted at the beginning of her career. It was there that Giacinto Prandelli gave her the exciting news, "Toscanini is waiting for you at La Scala."

Tebaldi sang a benefit recital at La Scala on May 23rd. The proceeds went to aid the victims of the catastrophic earthquake that hit the Friuli section of Italy. She wore a flowing royal blue gown; her beauty and the splendor of her voice belied the passing of time. Her program, which concluded with "*Voi lo sapete o Mamma*" and "*Musetta's Waltz*," was followed by seven encores; the last, "*Tu che m'hai preso il cuor.*" Renata sang as though she were the heart of La Scala. She was showered with hundreds of white and rose carnations. From the family circle a young man cried, "You are a revelation!" She replied with kisses and a tear or two. Before she disappeared behind the curtain, Renata raised her arm high in her characteristic gesture of farewell.

Her smile was as radiant as ever.

The audience wanted to take something of the miracle of that inimitable voice with it, and everyone lingered, hesitating to leave the hall. No one thought that this would be the last time.

May 23rd: the anniversary of her debut in Rovigo, thirty-two years later.

❧ 30 ❧

Renata Tebaldi: Now

As her busy schedule permits, Tebaldi divides her time between Milan and San Marino where she vacations. From her
terrace in San Marino she delights in the breathtaking view
of the valley and "her" Adriatic. As she vacations, she enjoys
the company of her dear friends of many years, Mirella and
Valentino, who share so many wonderful memories with her,
and of her cousin, Lydia, who would be very happy if Renata
accepted all of her invitations to the dinners which she prepares so expertly. Renata receives so many invitations from
her many friends that it's sometimes difficult for her to please
everyone. Tactful solutions are necessary to rescue her.

She walks as often as possible when at home in Milan,
and in nearby Rimini during her visits to San Marino. With
an expert eye, Renata enjoys studying window displays in
elegant shops along her route. She knows where to shop for
a special pair of shoes or a bag, clothing, jewelry, or a gift.
She is an excellent source of information for friends who are
not quite as adept as she is.

Although she no longer indulges her weakness for desserts and chocolate and carefully controls her diet, she often
dines with friends in one of several restaurants she prefers.

The Gran San Bernardo in Milan has delicious sautéed *risotto al salto*, the Novecento in Rimini serves excellent *passatelli in brodo,* and Zaghini's in Sant'Arcangelo offers *tagliatelle* with fresh tomato sauce, all of which Renata eats with pleasure. The restaurant in Sant'Arcangelo, a town near Rimini, is adjacent to a piazza reminiscent of the last century. Renata enjoys strolling through the piazza after supper as she comments on the peace, beauty, and old-world atmosphere which she likes so much.

Frequently, friends travel from foreign countries and within Italy to see her. They find a more mature Renata, always beautiful and elegant, who continues to delight them, particularly when her eyes reflect the happiness of a shared moment, or her smile flashes that spontaneous, radiant smile they remember so well. Together they relive the memories of the past while they accumulate new memories for the future.

In the past, replying to the frequently asked question, "Have you ever thought of teaching voice?" Renata would say, "No, not as a way of life. I become too involved with the subject, and then, patience is not my strength." As it turned out, however, after her retirement she did teach master classes in Busseto collaborating with Carlo Bergonzi and The Chicago Bel Canto Foundation, and at the Mozarteum in Salzburg. Through the years she coached selected artists who came to her for advice, including Aprile Millo.

Those fortunate enough to observe Tebaldi as she taught saw her thoroughly absorbed in imparting invaluable musical insights to students with whom a strong bonding had developed. With the patience she said she lacked, she worked with a color, a phrase, an attack, and above all, with the attainment of musical and dramatic truth. On rare occasions Tebaldi would sing the first note of an aria in *sotto voce* to illustrate that a note must be prepared, it must be there before it emerges, and when it is sung, the attack must be pure and perfectly placed. One was in awe of this artist with such a glorious past who so generously shared her precious knowledge.

In answer to the question, "What does Renata Tebaldi do these days," she candidly replies, "I receive honors."

Besides the many testimonials Tebaldi has received through the years, in 1992 and 1994 Italy and France, respectively, honored her again. At the Quirinale Palace in Rome, the president of Italy, Oscar Scalfaro presented her with the most prestigious title in Italy, *Cavaliere della Gran Croce.* The French have announced that her name is being added to the illustrious list of revered members of the *Légion d'Honneur.*

Interviews for French, German, and Italian television have turned her elegant home in Milan into a studio of bright lights for the occasion, and Italian journalists photograph and interview her frequently for their cover stories.

All this activity is coordinated with her frequent trips within Italy and abroad. In London Tebaldi was thrilled to learn that young people, who had discovered her voice through CDs, were there to applaud her together with her admirers from the past. Testimonial dinners and concerts in her honor take her to many cities and towns throughout Italy. Her schedule is sometimes so hectic that her friends teasingly say that she returns home to unpack and leave again.

In Paris, at the Palais Royal, in February, 1987, together with Luciano Pavarotti, Tebaldi received *La Cravatte De Commandeur Des Arts Et Lettres,* a very distinguished award. Amidst the splendor of the palace, with its brightly lit chandeliers, floral tributes, an elegant audience, and expressive commendations, the two superluminaries of opera received the *Cravatte* from the minister of culture, Francois Leotard. During this period, Pavarotti was singing Nemorino in *Elisir d'Amore* at the Paris Opera, and Renata attended one of the performances. Her escort for the evening, Valentino Bertinotti, her fraternal friend from Rimini, describes what happened.

1—Giuseppina Barbieri, Tebaldi's mother, as a Red Cross nurse during World War I.

2—The Barbieri home in Langhirano.

3—Kindergarten class in Langhirano, 1927. Tebaldi is the sixth student from the left in the second row from the top.

4—With Mamma Tebaldi in Langhirano, 1929.

5—First Communion
with parents.

6—Published in an
Italian magazine, after
Tebaldi had been ill, as
an advertisement for a
nutritional supplement.

7—Carmen Melis, Tebaldi's voice teacher and mentor.

8—*Faust,* debut in the role of
Margherita, Arena, Verona, 1947.

9—At the home of a friend, 1950.

10—*La Traviata*, 1948.

11—Official portrait of the prima donna, ca. 1950.

12—From the cast of *Otello* at La Scala—Ramon Vinay and his wife, 1951.

13—On board the *Giulio Cesare* en route to Rio de Janeiro with Carlo Tagliabue, Giacinto Prandelli, and Ugo Savarese, 1952.

14—*Eugene Onegin,* as Tatiana, La Scala, Milan, 1953.

15—Before a performance of *La Wally*, La Scala, Milan, 1953.

16—After a performance of *Tosca* with Vittorio De Sabata and Giuseppe Di Stefano (on the right), La Scala, Milan, 1953.

17—On the *S. S. Augustus* with Mamma Tebaldi.

18—After a performance of *Lohengrin* with Guilio Neri, Elena Nicolai, conductor Gabriele Santini, and Gino Penni, Teatro San Carlo, Naples, 1954.

19—As Elsa in *Lohengrin*, Teatro San Carlo, Naples, 1954.

20—With Marian Anderson, Leonard Warren, Impresario Sol Hurok, and Jan Peerce at the piano, 1955.

21—With Rudolf Bing at the Metropolitan, 1955.

22—With Salvador Dalí, 1955

RENATA TEBALDI
in «Aida»

23—*Aida*, ca. 1955.

24—With Mario Lanza, 1955.

25—Debut at the Metropolitan, New York, as Desdemona in *Otello*, 1955.

26—*Otello* with Mario Del Monaco, Metropolitan, 1955.

27—*La Forza del Destino*, Metropolitan, 1956.

28—With Mamma Tebaldi.

29—"NBC Festival of Music," *La Bohème*, with Jussi Björling, 1956.

30—With Elsa Maxwell, 1956.

31—On tour greeting fans, ca. 1957.

32—On the set of *La Traviata* with Charles Anthony and photographer
Louis Mélançon, Metropolitan, 1957.

33—*La Traviata*, Metropolitan, New York, 1957.

34—With Rolf Gérard, chief costumer for the Metropolitan, New York, ca. 1957.

35—*La Bohème*, Metropolitan, New York, 1957.

36—With Director Carol Fox (center), Chicago, 1957.

37—*Otello*, in the role of Desdemona, ca. 1958.

38—With Giacinto Prandelli in Barcelona, 1958 (debut in *Madama Butterfly*).

39—Barcelona, 1958.

40—*Tosca*, La Scala, Milan, 1958.

41—Cover of *Time* magazine, 1958.

42—Studio portrait, Vienna, ca. 1958.

43—*Madama Butterfly*, Arena Flegrea, Naples, 1968.

44—*Falstaff*
with Cornell MacNeil,
Anna Maria Canali, and
Giulietta Simionato,
Chicago Lyric Opera,
1958.

45—*Madama Butterfly* with Giuseppe Di Stefano, Chicago Lyric Opera, 1958.

46—*Tosca*, Metropolitan, New York, 1958.

47—*Tosca*, Metropolitan, New York, 1958.

48—*Tosca* with
Mario Del Monaco,
Metropolitan, New York,
1958.

49—After a performance
of *Tosca* with Mario Del
Monaco, Rudolf Bing, and
conductor Dimitri
Mitropoulos.

50—*Madama Butterfly*, Metropolitan, New York, 1958.

51—*Madama Butterfly*, Act II, with
Mildred Miller as Suzuki,
Metropolitan, New York, 1958.

52—*Aida*, State Opera, Vienna,
1959.

53—*Tosca*, State Opera, Vienna, 1959.

54—*Simon Boccanegra*, Metropolitan,
New York, 1960.

55—*La Bohème* with Giuseppe
Gismondo, Teatro San Carlo, Naples,
1959.

56—*Simon Boccanegra*, Metropolitan, New York, 1960.

57—With Franco Corelli, ca. 1960.

58—With Gianni Rivera, soccer superstar who wanted to meet her and was invited to dinner, Milan, 1960.

59—Backstage with Roddy McDowall, ca. 1961.

60—With her father, 1961.

61—With Arturo Basile at the airport in Manila, 1961.

62—*Fedora*, Teatro San Carlo, Naples, 1961.

63—*Falstaff* with Tito Gobbi, Teatro San Carlo, Naples, 1962.

64—*Adriana Lecouvreur* with Franco Corelli, Metropolitan, New York, 1963.

65—*Adriana Lecouvreur*, Metropolitan, New York, 1963.

66—*Adriana Lecouvreur* with Irene Dalis, Metropolitan, New York, 1963.

67—In costume for *La Gioconda* with Rock Hudson, 1966.

68—*Mefistofele*,
Chicago Lyric Opera, with
Alfredo Kraus, 1965.

69—Debut in *La Gioconda*, Metropolitan, New York, 1966.

70—*La Gioconda*, Metropolitan, 1966.

71—*La Gioconda*, Act I, Metropolitan, 1966.

72—Backstage with Barbra Streisand after *Tosca*, Metropolitan, 1966.

73—Pianist Van Cliburn pays
Tebaldi a surprise visit at her
apartment, New York, 1966.

74—*La Bohème* with Placido Domingo, Boston Lyric Opera, 1966.

75—Aria "Suicidio," "Telephone Hour," New York, 1967.

76—With Rosa Ponselle after a concert, Baltimore, 1966.

77—*Manon Lescaut* , Act I, with Richard Tucker, Metropolitan, New York, 1967.

78—*Manon Lescaut*, Act II, Metropolitan, New York, 1967.

79—With Helen Hayes after a performance of *Manon Lescaut*.

80—*Otello*, Academy of
Music, Philadelphia, 1967.

81—*La Gioconda* with
Margherita Rochow,
Teatro San Carlo, Naples,
1968.

82—*La Gioconda* with Franca Mattiucci, Lamberto Gardelli and Gianfranco Cecchele, Teatro San Carlo, Naples, 1968.

83—After a performance of *La Gioconda*, Teatro San Carlo, Naples, 1968.

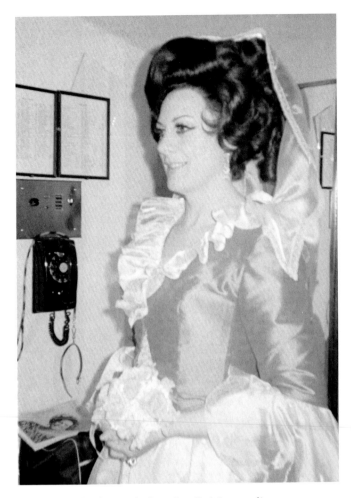

84—*Tosca*, backstage before Act II, Metropolitan,
New York, 1968.

85—*Tosca* with Franco
Corelli, Metropolitan,
New York, 1968.

86—*Manon Lescaut*
with Placido Domingo,
Bushnell Memorial,
Hartford, 1968.

87—During rehearsal for *Adriana Lecouvreur* with Anselmo Colzani,
Metropolitan, New York, 1968.

88—*Adriana Lecouvreur* with Placido Domingo, Metropolitan, New York, 1968.

89—*Adriana Lecouvreur,* opening night with Rudolf Bing and Maria Callas, Metropolitan, New York, 1968.

90—*Adriana Lecouvreur,* 1969.

91—*Fanciulla del West*, debut in role of Minnie with Sandor Konya, Metropolitan, New York, 1970.

92—*Andrea Chénier*, Act II, with Placido Domingo, Metropolitan, New York, 1970.

93—With the Director of the Regio di Parma, ca. 1970.

94—Receiving "Premio Alle Carriere"(career awards) with Lidia Alfonsi and Anna Moffo, at Savioni's, Riccione, ca. 1970.

95—At the Grand Hotel, Rimini, ca. 1970.

96—With Valentino and Mirella Bertinotti, Franco and Loretta Corelli, Grand Hotel, Rimini, ca. 1970.

97—Grand Hotel, Rimini, ca. 1970.

98—*Falstaff*, Metropolitan, New York, 1972.

99—Concert with Franco Corelli, Manila, 1973.

100—Concert with pianist Martin Katz, La Scala, Milan, 1974.

101—With Montserrat Caballé after a performance of *Norma*, La Scala, Milan, 1974.

102—At a fashion show with friends, Rimini, ca. 1975.

103—Concert, Teatro San
Carlo, Naples, 1975.

104—At a reception honoring Paolo Grassi, Director of La Scala, with Mirella and Valentino Bertinotti and Carlo Bergonzi.

105—At her home in Milan with Connie and Aristide DeCaro, 1980.

106—At a celebration in her honor, Milan, 1982.

107—Teatrino Busseto master class with Carlo Bergonzi (standing), Busseto, 1985.

108—Teatrino Busseto master class with Carlo Bergonzi (standing), Busseto, 1985.

109—With Luciano Pavarotti after they received *La Cravatte de Commandeur des Arts et Lettres*, Palais Royal, Paris, 1987.

110—With
Georges Delbard
who created the
Tebaldi Rose, 1987.

111—70th birthday celebration, La Scala, 1992.

"When it was time for us to enter our box, Renata asked me to wait with her until the House was darkened. She was afraid that if the public saw her it would cause such a commotion that it would diminish Pavarotti's well-deserved tribute. And so we waited. By the end of the first act her presence had become known and the House exploded in enthusiastic applause. The director of the Opera, unable to signal the start of the second act because of the incessant applause, came to her box and asked her permission to announce to the audience that the opera house would be opened the following afternoon to enable her to greet her admirers. Despite a heavy snow, the foyer was packed as everyone waited his turn to approach Renata, speak with her and ask for an autograph. Again Renata was happy to see that so many of those who had come to honor her were very young adults. They had learned to love her through her recordings, and now they rushed to meet her."

In 1987 Renata also visited Villa Grimaldi in Nervi, the Royal Palace in Monza, and the monument to Giuseppe Verdi in Busseto, for the ceremonial planting of the Tebaldi Rose in the rose gardens of these prestigious sites. The year before, in June of 1986, the Tebaldi Rose, created by the renowned horticulturist, Mr. Georges Delbard, was "baptized" in Paris, in the Jardin de Bagatelle. As Renata describes it in a letter to a friend, "It was a period of extreme heat and horrible traffic in Paris, and I did not have time to visit even one boutique.... My days were filled from 11 a.m. to 8 p.m., and only then would I return to my hotel, pull off my shoes, and eat something in my room!" She described the day of the "baptism" enthusiastically, "Everything was marvelous! The sun and the blue sky were beautiful. As I removed the white tulle veil protecting the roses (which are a stupendous salmon—coral color, about three feet tall, with a delicate and elegant fragrance and an impressive personality) to everyone's pleasure, "*Madre pietosa Vergine*" from *Forza del Destino* was played and everyone was moved! Madam Nebout, the Vice Mayor of Paris, and I uncorked a bottle of champagne and sprayed the roses!"

Later that evening at the Chateau Bagatelle, Madame Chirac, wife of the mayor of Paris, awarded her the Grande Plaque Vermeille of the City of Paris. Renata described Madam Chirac as "very pleasant, an elegant lady." The award presentation was followed by refreshments, many more photographs and interviews. "All this was also very moving! Unable to attend the various ceremonies, Mr. Chirac gallantly filled my room in the hotel with stupendous roses everyday (but not as beautiful as the Tebaldi Rose!)" Once again, Tebaldi was happy to see that many admirers who came to greet her were young adults, too young to have heard her except on recordings. An elegant reception was held for Renata at the Italian Embassy in Paris hosted by Ambassador Gardini and Mrs. Gardini, whom Renata found very amiable and cordial. The following day she left Paris for Malincome, the hometown of Mr. Delbard.

"After five hours in the car, we arrived in Malincome at an old castle, now a hotel (eight rooms)!...The next morning at 9 a.m. we visited Mr. Delbard's gardens—more photographs, TV cameras and interviews—and at 11 a.m. we entered the church. I walked down the aisle alone as '*Adeste Fideles*' was played—followed by Gounod's '*Ave Maria*' during the preface of the Mass, '*Panis Angelicus*' during Communion, and concluding with '*O Divine Redeemer*,' all from my Christmas Festival. The church was decorated with roses which formed the colors of our flag. In front of the altar, in the center, an enormous composition of my roses had been placed. The religious baptism of the Tebaldi Rose was very touching. At a certain point, a swallow entered the church, flew around the cupola above the altar, and then rested on a cornice near me. I was greatly moved because I immediately thought of Mamma who used to call me '*cara la mia rondinella*'![18] I felt that she had sent it to me or that it was she! This will be another precious memory!"

On April 18, 1994, in Trieste, the *Assicurazioni Generali*[19] organized an evening of celebration to honor the 50th anniversary of Tebaldi's debut in that city, as Desdemona in *Otello*. The presence of an adoring public thrilled by rare, previously never seen videocassettes, added to the excitement of the evening. Again many ovations, encomiums by musicologists and music critics, made it a very moving experience for Renata and everyone present.

During one of the countless testimonial dinners honoring her, Tebaldi was asked, "What did Renata Tebaldi feel as she sang those ecstatic phrases, arias, concertati, for which she will be long remembered?" Her reply was, "I was overwhelmed by a beautiful sensation.... I felt almost that it was not I who was singing; it was as though Someone far superior to all of us was using my voice as the instrument for His singing.

"I felt carried away into a world of dreams and wished that the enchantment would never end because it was so very beautiful! It's so difficult to explain. I can only say it was the complete sublimation of all that emanates from the soul; I no longer existed; my singing was as free as a songbird's and it carried me into an enchanted celestial world; my feet no longer touched the ground. I was somewhere near the source of my great gift and I felt so much joy....

"I remember those moments so well. They were extraordinary and absolutely unforgettable. I would listen to this voice emanating from my throat and I was overwhelmed by the marvelous sound which the Lord so generously wished me to have. It brought me great happiness.

"What I did was so completely sincere that I succeeded

---

[18] "My precious little swallow"

[19] An Italian insurance giant.

in transmitting my feelings to my public. I immediately felt that they understood what I meant. It was as though I had a mission; 'I had to' with my voice bring happiness to all those who were listening to me while also expressing with every word precisely what the composer intended.

"It was a very beautiful experience! I felt that I was speaking with each person present in the theater; I felt that I was able to give comfort to all those who at that moment were sad, and I felt certain that they understood.

"I know that my voice has entered into the hearts of many people and has caused beautiful reactions. Some, hearing me sing, have become more religious; some who were ill felt joy; friends, while in hospital, played my tapes whenever they felt ill; they all said that my voice gave them the strength needed to stand the pain.

"Therefore, how can I *not* be thankful for this great gift?"

❧Testimonials❧

1957: Grand Cross of the Order of the Dames of the Holy
       Sepulcher presented by Cardinal Spellman
1961: Highest Achievement Medal presented by the Japanese
       government
1966: Honorary Doctorate Degree presented by Villanova
       University in Philadelphia (Tebaldi was the 6th woman
       in 123 years to receive the award.)
1970: *Commendatore della Repubblica Italiana*
1973: *Verdi d'Oro—Citta' di Busseto*
1974: *Grand' Ufficialato dell'Ordine della Repubblica
       Italiana*
1975: *Cavaliere Grand' Ufficiale dell'Ordine Equestre di S.
       Agata* presented by the Republic of San Marino
1980: *Una Vita per La Lirica* presented in Milan
1986: *Il Premio Caruso* (Tebaldi was the first woman to
       receive this award.)
1986: Grande Plaque Vermeille presented by the mayor of
       Paris at the Chateau Bagatelle
The Tebaldi Rose created by noted horticulturist Monsieur
       Georges Delbard (Ceremonial planting took place in
       the Jarden de Bagatelle, Paris.)
1987: *La Cravatte de Commandeur des Arts et Lettres*
       presented by the French minister of culture at the
       Royal Palace
1992: *Cavaliere della Gran Croce* presented by the President
       of Italy, Oscar Scalfaro at the Quirinale Palace in
       Rome
1994: *Légion d'Honneur* presented by the French government

✣Epilogue✣

SINGING TECHNIQUE

What modifications occurred in your singing technique, if any, during your career?

"My singing technique remained the same, as singing techniques should. What I learned at the beginning of my career served the needs of my unique vocal characteristics. Through the years, I tried to avoid chest voice, which would occasionally occur spontaneously, for fear of vocal damage. Later on, for Gioconda and Fanciulla my chest voice developed as the roles demanded. As I matured, my roles became more and more a part of me, resulting in more subtle and profound interpretations. In 1963 in New York, when I stopped singing for a year, my voice teacher helped me to regain confidence and the courage to continue, but I could not alter my technique because it was part of me."

What are the "constants" imposed by tradition?

"Tradition cannot 'impose.' However, one can respect an established tradition. Tradition teaches us to learn the bel canto technique in which one 'sings on the breath.' The young singer learns to sing legato with a *fiato lungo*.[20] Mozart,

---

[20] sustained breath

192

Bellini, and Donizetti teach us to 'sing on the breath,' to spend and save in order to reach the end of a phrase, much as a violin does with an up and downward stroke of the bow. A singer must not break a musical phrase for more breath. Singing in a bel canto style, with 'on the breath' at the base, with *legato, pianissimo,* and *note pulite,*[21] may be considered a technique which tradition has 'imposed.' Tradition allows us some freedom when *oppure* (*opr*) appears in the score, indicating a singer's preference in a cadenza or high note. This was usually established when the composer was alive and approved of the variation."

Was there a change in your breathing technique?

"During my career I changed neither my breathing nor my support techniques. The male singer should breathe through the diaphragm only or harmful tensions can occur, but the female voice uses additional support which varies with each singer. I used diaphragmatic support, and I also expanded my breathing deeply so that I felt it in my back. It is most important to avoid any tightening of the shoulder muscles. The voice must float on the breath. A young singer must understand that the voice and breathing are like a glass containing a drop of oil floating on water. The oil does not drop into the water, it remains floating. The voice must remain floating or supported above the breath. Perhaps some changes can be made towards the end of one's career to make it possible to sing a bit longer. The use of chest voice can help certain difficult passage notes, such as the E, F, F#, G."

Do you hear the sound in your head? In the mask? Elsewhere?

---

[21] clean notes

"If the voice is properly placed, the sound will automatically go into the mask. The breath sustains the voice *in maschera* and then B flat, B, and C are sung in head voice. One must be secure in the vocal register break, which keeps the A in line. Above all, one must think, not feel, that the sound is in the mask."

What physical discipline did you impose on your body? Posture? Thorax? Neck? Position of the head?

"A cardinal rule of singing is an erect posture without rigidity for maximum use of the diaphragm. Above all, one must be relaxed. The throat must be free; the sound should resonate in the cheeks, not the nose; one should have the sensation that the sound is rising to the very top of the head."

Were you already recognized as a lirico spinto *in your very early career, or did you achieve this goal by developing your unique vocal gifts? Which roles did you sing in the early years that helped to develop those qualities and which, later, when your voice had reached maturity?*

"I started to sing as a lyric soprano. Then, as the years passed, my voice matured and assumed a darker color. Not more volume; I've always had that. It was the darker color which made it possible for me to sing a more dramatic repertory, although I've never truly been a dramatic soprano. I sang many dramatic roles with a dark color, but not as dark as was expected of dramatic sopranos of the past. When I was reluctant to sing my first *Aida*, Maestro Toscanini advised me 'cantare sulla parola'—to sing on the words. The Maestro explained that I had to search for the expression of each word. That would help me find the proper accent and would resolve some difficult parts of the role which is not, in my opinion, among the most dramatic of Verdi's operas. To understand *each* word, thus to sing the words, facilitates expression and the singing is easier and fulfillment becomes greater. In the beginning I sang only lyric roles which would not hurt my voice, but naturally, being young and desirous of fame, I did accept *Tosca*. After singing the role several times, however, and especially when I could afford, artistically, to say no, I returned to *La Bohème, Faust, Otello*, and *Chénier* and left *Tosca* for later in my career. I did not sing *Chénier* often, and when I did, I sang using my true color without forcing or overdoing, for fear of damaging my voice. However, I never tried to save my voice by holding back at a given time because a difficult phrase or high note was approaching. I always sang with great sincerity. I gave all that I had to give, note by note. It goes without saying that I never sang an opera if I was not convinced of being able to sing it well."

Which persons have given you maximum support? Mother? Family?

"I've often said that my mother held me back and did not encourage me. She hoped that I would become a pianist, or rather, a fine piano teacher. She was afraid that a career as a singer would bring me bitterness and very little pleasure, but when accolades continued, she became convinced. From that moment she devoted her life to my career. Although I lived with my father only a short time, he did help me with my piano studies. My grandfather helped to pay for my early lessons."

Were your experiences with vocal teachers always beneficial?

"My teacher, Carmen Melis, became my mentor. My very

first teacher was Campogalliani and I must give him credit for not ruining my voice, which sometimes happens when one first starts to study. However, the magic touch was given to me by Carmen Melis. In that first, brief period, only 15 days, in Pesaro, when I worked on some scores with her, she changed my singing so that those who had previously heard me no longer recognized my voice. That is, she improved my voice without changing it. If I were to try to explain how her way of working affected my singing so enormously, I would have to say, by adding legato and interpretation. She had such a way of communicating her ideas that I instinctively understood, and I treasured all that she told me. I studied with her for three years in Pesaro until World War II forced us to stop the lessons. As soon as the war ended she moved to Como, and I went to her for advice as often as I could. If I had a new score to prepare, I would study it first with Maestro Pais, who was a fabulous coach. Then, before my debut, I would sing the role for Carmen Melis who would help me avoid problems before they became difficult habits to correct. Her death was a painful shock for me. I lost the person to whom I went for professional advice and guidance."

How do you advise a student who must find himself a good vocal teacher? Should one's own instincts be followed or should one place himself completely in the hands of a vocal teacher?

"I believe that the relationship between student and teacher must be spontaneous and sincere. A teacher should feel the responsibility of telling his student, after a reasonable amount of time, if he feels that no further progress is possible, or if another teacher would be more helpful. Sometimes the lack of progress can be attributed to physical, artistic, or musical incompatibility between student and teacher, as sometimes is the case between doctor and patient. One must be able to communicate freely and openly. Even if the teacher has, in the past, been a great singer, he must not impose his technique on the student. The teacher must only advise, suggest, and then allow the student to apply his words to his own voice. The teacher must teach the basics of singing: breathing and emission—the basic preparation—without imposing a comprehensive technique, since each voice is unique. At most, a good teacher will try to suggest the best way to reach a certain goal, or several ways, depending on the student's vocal possibilities. Finally, I would like to emphasize how important it is to teach a young singer the correct way to breathe even before he is taught to sing. So many singers do not know how to breathe."

How did you keep your nerves under control during the preparation of a new opera? How did you relax? What did you think about while on stage?

"Preparation of a new role is very difficult, and can be damaging if it is not sung into one's voice properly. To begin with, I would read the score, become aware of the words and dynamics, visualizing the score with my mind, and I would join the words to the music. Music and words are of equal importance because the words help to learn the music and the music helps one to understand and feel the development of the role. The score would soon become second nature to me, and I would begin to nurture it. (I have always compared the learning of a role to the creation of any work of art—an artist germinates the piece before working on it and when he is ready he begins his creation, be it a painting, a sculpture, or a literary work. Or better, preparing a new role is like an expectant mother carrying her baby in her womb, creating it and introducing it to the world. So, a role matures within us and when it is time we bring it to the world.)

"During preparation of the score, care must be taken to

197

stop when necessary, analyze the problems, and make corrections. My best time during this period of preparation was at bedtime. With silence and darkness all around me as I lay in bed, I thought through the score and sang my role silently, sometimes going through the entire role. That was the most relaxing time for me, and I was very happy! I would awaken with a deeper understanding of the role. If I felt unsure about anything, I would check the score right away. As one's self-assurance is reinforced by the absence of vocal or musical preoccupations, one is less tense and is free to enter into and interpret the person of the role to be sung. Spontaneity is lost if tension exists over a difficult passage, and the audience senses it immediately. One must be like a good driver who is so sure of himself that he can engage in conversation, admire the panorama, and at the same time be ready to slam on the brakes or turn the wheel to avoid a problem instantly. In order to become totally immersed in a new role I also found it helpful to read about the historical background of the character and the period involved."

Did you find it necessary to modify your singing technique during recording sessions?

"No, I didn't. The lack of stage and action caused some difficulties, and scheduling breaks interrupted the creation of dramatic tension. To overcome this, I always attempted to create my own atmosphere around me as I recorded. In every opera house it is important to hear one's voice come back, even outdoors where the sound is partially lost. The sound of the voice must travel through the entire hall and then return to you; only then do you know that all of the audience can hear you. There are 'deaf theaters,' as we say in theatrical vernacular. In that case, singers may make the very natural but serious mistake of producing a louder sound. It's wrong to modify a singing technique to try to accommodate the acoustics of a particular theater. The acoustical problem is not the singer's concern during a recording. It is the responsibility of the technicians involved. They know their job. The most they ever advised me to do was to step away from the microphone when I sang a high note, or to turn my head to the left or right in order to avoid distortions."

At what age do you think one should approach the dramatic repertory? Does it depend on age or a singer's talent?

"To attempt the dramatic repertory at the beginning of one's career is always dangerous. Early in one's career, an intelligent singer will avoid those operas which can damage the voice. Nonetheless, one cannot wait too long. I sang *Gioconda* and *Fanciulla* during the last years of my career but I still had enough voice to do them properly. The intelligent singer must decide whether it is wise and when it is time to use chest voice, which everyone knows can be harmful and cause deterioration of the voice. Age isn't the determining factor; it is timing, when one feels that the risk of damage to the voice has been minimized. My advice to a young singer is to avoid singing *Tabarro, Cavalleria, Fanciulla,* or even *Butterfly* at the beginning of her career. These roles may do great harm to the voice."

How did you warm up your voice? How long did you vocalize each day? How frequently on the day of the performance? How did you manage when you were not in voice?

"I warmed up my voice by vocalizing the usual way, but done letter-perfectly. Otherwise there would be no voice left for the performance and one might just as well stay home! Vocalizing makes one aware of what condition the voice is in. Some singers have little tricks or habits to help them determine the condition of their voices; it's enough for them to produce a trumpet-like sound to know if they are in voice or not. I've never done that. I believe it depends on one's individual makeup. Some of my colleagues know as soon as they get up in the morning if their voice is all right. Of course, one must always vocalize before any lessons or rehearsals. Singers must massage their muscles just as pianists and ballerinas do. It is well known that many great pianists exercise their fingers on mock keyboards; so it is for singers who must exercise their vocal chords, which are muscles, to prepare them for the moment of attack.

"Vocalizing is a must before a performance. When? That depends. My time for vocalizing was a half hour before leaving the hotel, not continuously, and then at the theatre for about 20 minutes, also intermittently. As I applied my makeup I would continue to check my voice. There would be no vocalizing on the morning of a performance, but I could tell if my voice was all right. I found that if I vocalized in the morning and then not at all later it was as though I had not vocalized at all. A single rule doesn't exist. It's a subjective matter. It's important that the *passaggio* (vocal register break) be free. If, by vocalizing, one feels that the voice "passes," then, even if other problems are present, the voice can be brought into line through further vocalizing. If the voice does not "pass," it's wise to stop because the voice can be damaged by continued vocalizing. On those evenings when, already in my dressing room, I became aware that my voice did not respond or "pass," as it had earlier, and it was too late to cancel, I had to concentrate all my attention on the creation of the sound, sacrificing, if necessary, color and expression."

It is often said that yours is the most beautiful natural voice of your era. Is the voice everything in opera?

"In truth, I was blessed by God with a voice of exceptional

beauty. I'm more and more convinced that to sing really well, one must have a special voice even if a technique is then adapted to it. I disagree with theatergoers who are satisfied that "she does not have a beautiful voice, but she is a great actress." Of course, it is important to be a good actress, to make everything more realistic for the audience, but, above all, I go to the opera to hear people who sing. Therefore, if there is a beautiful voice and a great interpretation I return home perfectly happy and satisfied. But, if I must choose between a great actress with a so-so voice and a great singer who interprets adequately, I select the one with the great voice. If I want a great actress, I'll go to see a play."

Did you find inspiration from any earlier celebrated singers?

"I never wanted to follow a 'model' from the past. Each voice is unique. A singer must allow his own personality to emerge instinctively. Each voice has its own characteristics and the singer's overall persona depends on the characteristics of that voice. Upon hearing a voice one can determine the sensitivity or temperament of a singer. I used to like Toti dal Monte, whose voice had nothing in common with mine since she was a coloratura soprano. I've always derived pleasure from the *virtuosismi* of the light soprano voice which sound to me like little birds singing. For example, Joan (Sutherland) is an acrobatic phenomenon!"

Are the spinto *voices and the big voices scarce today? Is repertory essential to the development of the voice?*

"Yes, today, great voices are rare, but I'm convinced that the fault lies in the intonation of the orchestra. It is the diapason which creates the upset. We are witnessing the phenomenon that nothing is sung in the original key any longer. Orchestras today are tuned to such a high tonality that the tone no longer corresponds to the original score. In the last century the diapason was between 333 and 334. When I started to sing it was at 440. Since Von Karajan, orchestras have been tuned to 443 and 444. So, now it's said that there are no more true contralti, mezzosoprani, baritones, or basses. The last true mezzosoprani in Italy were Fedora Barbieri and Fiorenza Cossotto. These were the true mezzo voices; the others are halfway between soprano and mezzosoprano. These true voices cannot disappear so quickly without reason. I am convinced that if we allowed the voices today to sing in the original key of the composer, all those voices which seem to have disappeared would emerge again. Singing in a higher intonation causes the voice to be 'strangled' because the throat closes as one forces to produce a higher note. On the other hand, the more open the throat remains, the more freely the sound emerges.

"'Is repertory essential to the development of the voice?' Certainly! As long as it is the right repertory. Singing incorrect repertory can drastically shorten one's career. Roles must be suitable for the individual voice. It seems that it is fashionable today to show that one can sing everything! That can be very harmful to the voice."

Did you have any colleagues with a great deal of talent who did not succeed in their careers?

"No. It is my experience that those gifted with a great talent have succeeded in having great careers. Some, perhaps, with delays, but if a great talent truly exists, sooner or later it is discovered."

Is there one composer who has inspired you more than others? What has your relationship with contemporary music been?
"Puccini. He is my great favorite. My voice and my temperament were perfectly attuned to his music and his heroines,

for whom I felt a particular affinity. Of course, Rossini, Bellini, Donizetti, and Verdi wrote masterpieces, always respecting the voice, even when they composed difficult passages.

"I cannot even evaluate contemporary opera from a vocal point of view. Voices are treated very badly and sometimes very unpleasantly. One is no longer dealing with bel canto or dramatic singing. It's music that is so different."

Would you suggest any technical books? Which have you read? To which other art forms have you been attracted? Painting? Literature? What part has religion played in your art?

"Garcia has certainly written the most educational texts on the technique of singing. However helpful these texts may be, it's still necessary to work with a teacher who hears you, advises you, and evaluates your progress. I did not look for instruction from textbooks because mine was a voice of natural beauty, a gift from God, and my efforts were concentrated solely on eliminating a few defects in my singing.

"I learned something new about my technique with each performance. Even more than classical ballet I am attracted to modern dance, especially that of Luciana Savignano who worked with the French choreographer, Béjart. Modern painting disturbs me. I admire the works of Renoir, Degas, Monet, early De Chirico and Picasso's Blue Period.

"Modern authors are too brutal. I prefer romantic writers. I devoted most of my reading to the background of operas. Other composers? Tchaikovsky, Mahler, Scriabin. I adore melodic music and the cello, the instrument which is closest to the human voice, the most expressive, especially the enormous phrases.

"Religion in my art? I have always felt that it was my soul which was singing and as I sang, the joy of my soul transported me to heaven. My happiest moments came when

I sang without restraint or apprehension and released my soul to sing freely and interpret with transcendent truth. I felt transported, almost in a dream. Then I would be overcome with the joy of singing."

While you were singing did you follow a diet? Is it advisable for singers to follow one? When and what did you eat on the day of a performance?

"Singers must control not only what they eat, but when they eat. Once I tried eating a steak at five in the afternoon (I had a rehearsal at nine in the evening), because a colleague suggested that it would give me extra energy. I wasn't able to sing. If it had been a performance, I would have had to cancel. I digest very slowly so I had to eat six hours before a performance — at one or two o'clock. My meal consisted of a filet of beef and rice, then nothing until after the performance. I would sometimes drink coffee or apple juice. This varies from person to person. Some of my colleagues had to eat early to have strong support for the diaphragm, others would dine in their dressing rooms during an intermission. If my stomach was full, I no longer had breath; my respiration was so deep that it involved both the thorax and diaphragm, so it was essential that my stomach be empty to ensure completely free breathing.

"There was a period when I had a problem with my weight so I went on a diet, but a limited one because I did not want to harm the voice. It's best to stay away from too many sweets, fats, and alcohol. It was a great struggle for me to eliminate sweets, because I always had such a sweet tooth!"

From the economical standpoint, should a singer have a manager?

"It's smart to have a manager during one's career as a safeguard and also to avoid direct contact with an employer. Even when one sings, as I did, for the joy of it, financial agreements had to be reached, and I always found them embarrassing. My manager, who knew my terms, arranged everything for me and left only the signing to me. It seemed undignfied for me to bargain with my voice as one would with any kind of merchandise.

"A good manager will protect and defend you in case of contractual difficulties. It's best to place yourself in the hands of an internationally-known manager, because you will be better represented, better protected, and better respected by theater administrations."

It is often said that artists are superstitious. Do you agree?

"The theatrical environment makes one superstitious even if one isn't otherwise. It is often said that only unintelligent people are superstitious. I think not. Even Napoleon was superstitious. My stuffed animals brought me luck because my dearest friends gave them to me. I always had them with me when I travelled. It was more important for me to have my bag with all my mascots than even my bag with all my shoes. What a disaster for me if I had lost them! The theater perpetuates certain fears. It is 'known' that *Forza* brings bad luck. When we consider that we lost Leonard Warren during a performance of *Forza*.... Another admonition is that one must enter the stage with the right foot first. I must place my feet in my slippers the same way each morning as I get up from bed."

What factors led to your early retirement from the stage?

"I might have continued to sing, not operatic repertoire but concerts, which I enjoyed very much, if physical problems had not appeared. I so enjoyed singing art songs—instantly

205

feeling their drama—each one turning out differently. I knew that, sooner or later, I would have to decide and I thought, 'Better now, at the right time, and not later at the wrong time.' It seems to me that my decision was right. Of course, God gave me the enormous strength needed to overcome the great pain of my decision. I was never very ambitious. I was concerned with my audience and their approval. When I stopped singing I felt that the 'singing being' that existed within me had gone away."

Have you ever thought of devoting yourself to teaching?

"In the past I never considered teaching, even though I received many requests. However, when the Belcanto Foundation in Chicago sent 18 students to Busseto to study with Carlo Bergonzi a few years ago, I was invited to collaborate with him. Since we have been good friends for many years, and I knew it would please him, I agreed. I also wanted to learn for myself what it meant to teach. I found the experience exciting and moving. I became totally involved in transmitting my thoughts and emotions to my students. I did not sing for them. Instead, I advised them. I asked them to sing for me and then evaluated what they were doing.

"I would not feel at ease if I had to teach beginners with no training at all. I was somewhat obsessed by the fear of ruining a student if I didn't understand a voice and consequently channelled it incorrectly. I did enjoy the Busseto seminar. After a period of relaxation after all the years of sacrifice, I agreed to teach master classes in Salzburg at the Accademia Mozartiana for three weeks. The students should have been selected carefully, but they were not sufficiently trained. I found it very tiring and distressing since it took so much energy to make any progress. I gave one-hour lessons with twelve students in a class. I alternated the classes so the students could experience singing at different hours of the day.

Being in Salzburg was an exhilarating experience with music permeating every corner of the city!

"I gladly listen to singers who come to me for advice during the preparation of a new role. I have taught a young singer who is now singing in Europe. I become affectionately involved in the problems of my students. Ties are formed which are close and sometimes draining."

TEBALDI'S LEADING MEN

You sang with some of the greatest tenors of the age. How would you describe them?

"I had many wonderful partners. Mario Del Monaco was my recording and stage partner through most of my career. He had unquestionable bravura. When we were in costume for *Chénier* where we both wore white wigs, we were taken for siblings because of the similarity of our profiles. He did make a point of informing you of his lifestyle—his houses, his cars, his triumphs, and he was easily upset by others' successes. He was fun to be with and *molto simpatico.*

"Francesco Merli was the most attentive and obliging of all my colleagues. When I was preparing for my Trieste debut as Desdemona with him as my Otello, he gave me drama lessons while we were still in Milan. We would work together in the home of Contessa Scalvini who was a patron of the arts and entertained many artists.

"Franco Corelli was a nervous colleague. He suffered throughout his entire career. In the wings he would always unload his fears on me by telling me he was not in good voice and that he would not make it through the performance. I tried to minimize his fears, but I didn't allow him to unsettle me. He was something on stage, a *numero,* tall, handsome, elegant. It was worth the price of a ticket just to see him make his entrance! He was always courteous and kind but he suffered too much.

"Placido Domingo is an artist who has always been very involved in the drama of opera. He was a sweet, superb partner, very handsome on stage. Together we made 'electricity.' We were an interesting couple, transmitting so much emotion. He was a wonderful partner with whom to develop an interpretation. It was an inspiration to sing with him. During a memorable non-subscription performance of *Tosca* at the Metropolitan conducted by Zubin Mehta we were the perfect trio. It was as if we had performed it many times but actually we had had only one piano rehearsal. The public went wild! All Placido's interpretations are so fine. Ten years after his first Otello at La Scala, the same cast was assembled, including Mirella Freni as Desdemona. His Otello had matured magnificently. He had added many remarkable subtleties, making it a monumental performance."

❧Repertory☙

Opera

BOITO	*Mefistofele* (2 roles)
CASAVOLA	*Salammbò*
CATALANI	*La Wally*
CILEA	*Adriana Lecouvreur*
GIORDANO	*Andrea Chénier, Fedora*
GOUNOD	*Faust*
HANDEL	*Giulio Cesare*
MASCAGNI	*L'Amico Fritz*
MOZART	*Don Giovanni, Le Nozze di Figaro (The Marriage of Figaro)*
PONCHIELLI	*La Gioconda*
PUCCINI	*La Bohème, La Fanciulla del West, Madama Butterfly, Manon Lescaut, Tosca*
REFICE	*Cecilia*
ROSSINI	*L'Assedio di Corinto (The Siege of Corinth), Guglielmo Tell (William Tell)*
SPONTINI	*Fernando Cortez, Olympia*
TCHAIKOVSKY	*Evgeny Onegin (Eugene Onegin)*
VERDI	*Aida, Falstaff, La Forza del Destino, Giovanna d'Arco (Joan of Arc), Otello, Simon Boccanegra, La Traviata*
WAGNER	*Lohengrin, Die Meistersinger, Tannhäuser*

Oratorio

J. S. BACH	*St. Matthew's Passion*
MOZART	*Requiem*
ROSSINI	*Stabat Mater*
VERDI	*Requiem, Te Deum*

❧Repertory in Order of Performance❧

1944   *Mefistofele* (2 roles) by Boito: Elena (Rovigo, Teatro Sociale)

1945   *La Bohème* by Puccini (Parma, Teatro Ducale)
L'Amico Fritz by Mascagni (Parma, Teatro Verdi)
Andrea Chénier by Giordano (Parma, Teatro Verdi)
Otello by Verdi (Trieste, Teatro Verdi)

1946   *Lohengrin* by Wagner (Parma, Teatro Regio)
Te Deum by Verdi (Milan, La Scala)
Mefistofele by Boito: Margherita (Milan, Palazzo dello Sport)
Tosca by Puccini (Catinia, Teatro Bellini)

1947   *Die Meistersinger (I Maestri Cantori)* by Wagner (Milan, La Scala)
Faust by Gounod (Verona, Arena)
La Traviata by Verdi (Catania, Teatro Bellini)

1948   *Tannhäuser* by Wagner (Naples, Teatro San Carlo)
Salammbò by Casavola (Rome, Teatro dell'Opera)

1949   *Don Giovanni* by Mozart (Lisbon, Teatro Sao Carlos)
Falstaff by Verdi (Lisbon, Teatro Sao Carlos)
L'Assedio di Corinto (The Siege of Corinth) by Rossini (Florence, Teatro Comunale)

1950   *Aida* by Verdi (Milan, La Scala)
Stabat Mater by Rossini (Lisbon, Teatro Sao Carlos)
Olympia by Spontini (Florence, Teatro Comunale)
St. Matthew's Passion by J. S. Bach (Milan, La Scala)
Requiem by Mozart (Milan, La Scala)
Requiem by Verdi (Milan, La Scala)
Giulio Cesare by Handel (Pompeii, Teatro Grande)

1951   *Giovanna D'Arco (Joan of Arc)* by Verdi (Naples, Teatro San Carlo)
Fernando Cortez by Spontini (Naples, Teatro San Carlo)

1952   *Le Nozze di Figaro (The Marriage of Figaro)* by Mozart (Rome, Teatro dell'Opera)
Guglielmo Tell (William Tell) by Rossini (Florence, Teatro Comunale)
Adriana Lecouvreur by Cilea (Naples, Teatro San Carlo)

1953   *Cecilia* by Refice (Naples, Teatro San Carlo)
La Forza del Destino by Verdi (Florence, Teatro Comunale)
La Wally by Catalani (Milan, La Scala)

Repertory

1954   *Evgeny Onegin (Eugene Onegin)* by Tchaikovsky (Milan, La Scala)

1956   *Simon Boccanegra* by Verdi (San Francisco Opera)

1957   *Manon Lescaut* by Puccini (Chicago Lyric Opera)

1958   *Madama Butterfly* by Puccini (Barcelona, Teatro Liceo)

1960   *Fedora* by Giordano (Chicago Lyric Opera)

1966   *La Gioconda* by Ponchielli (New York, Metropolitan)

1970   *La Fanciulla del West* by Puccini (New York, Metropolitan*)

*In 1961, in Rome, RAI Studios.

❧Chronology❧

1944

May 23, 25, 27	Rovigo Teatro Sociale	*Mefistofele* by Boito (debut in the role of Elena) Onelia Fineschi, Renzo Pigni, Tancredi Pasero Conductor: Giuseppe Del Campo

1945

January 20, 21	Parma Teatro Ducale	*La Bohème* by Puccini (debut in the role of Mimi) Wilma Colla, Virginio Assandri, Antonio Salsedo,Giuseppe Campanini, Renzo Fornaciari Conductor: Renzo Martini
February 27	Parma Teatro Verdi*	*La Bohème* Emma Tegani, Antonio Annaloro, Scipio Colombo, Giorgio Ruffo, Deo Terzi Conductor: Giuseppe Podestà
April 1, 2	Parma Teatro Verdi*	*L'Amico Fritz* by Mascagni (debut in the role of Suzel) Maria Forcato, Luigi Infantino, Scipio Colombo. Conductor: Renzo Martini
April 10	Parma Teatro Verdi*	*Andrea Chénier* by Giordano (debut in the role of Maddalena) Leonida Bellori, Scipio Colombo Conductor: Renzo Martini
July 26, 27	Langhirano	Concert (benefit for war veterans) with Virginio Assandri (with pianist Guiseppina Passani)
December 30 January 1, 3, 6 (1946)	Trieste Teatro Verdi	*Otello* (debut in the role of Desdemona) Francesco Merli, Piero Biasini Conductor: Edmondo De Vecchi

1946

January 10, 13	Trieste Teatro Verdi	*Andrea Chénier* Mario Del Monaco, Cesare Bardelli Conductor: Argeo Quadri
January 17, 19, 20	Parma Teatro Regio	*Lohengrin* by Wagner (debut in the role of Elsa) Elena Nicolai, Giacinto Prandelli, Otello Borgonovo, Ottavio Serpo, Andrea Mongelli Conductor: Giuseppe Podestà
February 21, 24 March 2	Genoa Teatro Grattacielo	*Andrea Chénier* Giuseppe Momo, Gino Bechi Conductor: Gianandrea Gavazzeni

*As the Teatro Regio was called from December 1943 to April 1945

212

April 28 May 3	Brescia Teatro Grande	*L'Amico Fritz* Wanda Madonna, Giacinto Prandelli, Scipio Colombo. Conductor: Giuseppe Podestà
May 11, 14	Milan La Scala	Concert celebrating the inauguration of the new La Scala (Selections performed: Prayer of *Moses* by Rossini, with Jolanda Gardino, Giovanni Malipiero and Tancredi Pasero, and *Te Deum* by Verdi). Conductor: Arturo Toscanini
May 23, 25	Milan Teatro Lirico	*Andrea Chénier* Giuseppe Momo, Ugo Savarese Conductor: Umberto Berrettoni
July 27, 31	Milan Palazzo dello Sport	*Mefistofele* (in the role of Elena) Onelia Fineschi, Mario Binci, Tancredi Pasero Conductor: Franco Ghione
August 3, 10	Milan Palazzo dello Sport	*Mefistofele* (debut in the role of Margherita) Fornarina Vieri, Mario Binci, Tancredi Pasero Conductor: Franco Ghione
September 18	Milan Palazzo dello Sport	*Lohengrin* Elena Nicolai, Renzo Pigni, Giovanni Inghilleri, Enrico Campi, Tancredi Pasero Conductor: Sergio Failoni
October 17, 20, 27	Catania Teatro Bellini	*Tosca* (debut in the title role) Mario Filippeschi, Mario Basiola Conductor: Guiseppe Pais
November 5, 7, 10, 13	Bologna Teatro Comunale	*Lohengrin* Cloe Elmo, Max Lorenz, Ettore Nava, Anselmo Colzani, Andrea Mongelli Conductor: Franco Ghione
December 20	Milan La Scala	Concert (with Giovanni Malipiero, Cesare Siepi) Conductor: Tullio Serafin

1947

January 8, 11	Bologna Teatro Duse	*Otello* Francesco Merli, Piero Guelfi Conductor: Guiseppe Podestà
January 18, 21, 23, 26, 29	Trieste Teatro Verdi	*Lohengrin* Elena Nicolai, Giovanni Voyer, Ettore Nava, Anselmo Colzani, Duilio Baronti Conductor: Franco Ghione
February 14, 16, 18	Venice Teatro La Fenice	*Otello* Francesco Battaglia, Giovanni Inghilleri Conductor: Mario Rossi/Ettore Gracis

213

Renata Tebaldi

March 26, 29 April 1	Catania Teatro Bellini	*Andrea Chénier* Rafael Lagares, Ugo Savarese Conductor: Umberto Berrettoni
May 2, 5, 8	Milan La Scala	*Die Meistersinger (I Maestri Cantori)* (debut in the role of Eva) Angelica Cravcenco, Mario Binci, Gino Del Signore, Antenore Reali/Sandor Sved, Carmelo Maugeri, Cesare Siepi Conductor: Tullio Serafin
May 4, 7	Milan La Scala	*La Bohème* Ornella Rovero, Mario Binci, Carlo Tagliabue, Michele Cazzato, Cesare Siepi Conductor: Sergio Failoni
June 1, 3, 5, 8	Venice Teatro La Venice	*Tosca* Arrigo Pola, Sandor Sved Conductor: Franco Capuana
June 24, 26	Milan La Scala	*La Bohème* Ornella Rovero, Mario Binci, Carlo Tagliabue, Michele Cazzato, Cesare Siepi Conductor: Franco Capuana
July 13	Langhirano	Benefit Conert with Wilma Colla (with pianist Guiseppina Passani)
August 3, 7, 9, 15	Verona Arena	*Faust* (debut in the role of Margherita) Anna Maria Canali, Giovanni Malipiero, Danilo Checchi, Nicola Rossi-Lemeni Conductor: Tullio Serafin
October 4, 5	Pesaro Teatro Rossini	*Tosca* Gianni Poggi, Antonio Salsedo Conductor: Giuseppe Podestà
November 11, 13, 16, 20	Catania Teatro Bellini	*La Bohème* Leila Mastrocola, Arrigo Pola, Maria Borriello, Carlo Bergonzi, Luciano Neroni Conductor: Antonio Narducci
November 22, 26, 30 December 4	Catania Teatro Bellini	*La Traviata* (debut in the role of Violetta) Ugo De Rita, Ugo Savarese Conductor: Alfredo Strano
December 6, 9, 14, 17, 21	Rome Teatro dell'Opera	*Otello* Francesco Merli, Gino Bechi/Tito Gobbi Conductor: Gabriele Santini
December 26, 29, 31	Parma Teatro Regio	*La Traviata* Arrigo Pola, Arnaldo Voltolini, Otello Bersellini/ Enzo Mascherini. Conductor: Nino Marenzi

Chronology

1948

January 7, 10, 13, 15	Venice Teatro La Fenice	*La Traviata* Vasco Campagnano, Mario Basiola Conductor: Tullio Serafin
January 19, 21	Bologna Teatro Duse	*La Traviata* Arrigo Pola, Mario Basiola Conductor: Nino Marenzi
January 29, 31	Ravenna Teatro Alighieri	*La Traviata* Arrigo Pola, Amilcare Blaffard, Edgardo De Alnaide. Conductor: Ino Savini
February 8, 10, 12	Parma Teatro Regio	*Mefistofele* Anna Di Giorgio, Mario Binci, Andrea Mongelli Conductor: Oliviero De Fabritiis
February 21, 26, 29 March 4	Naples Teatro San Carlo	*La Traviata* Bruno Landi, Ugo Savarese/Francesco Nascimbene/ Vito Vittorio. Conductor: Giuseppe Baroni
April 3, 6, 9, 11	Naples Teatro San Carlo	*Tannhäuser* by Wagner (debut in the role of Elisabetta) Livia Pery, Max Lorenz/Giovanni Voyer, Raimondo Torres, Nicola Rossi-Lemeni Conductor: Karl Böhm
April 14, 17, 22 May 5	Rome Teatro dell'Opera	*La Traviata* Giacinto Prandelli, Carlo Tagliabue/Mario Basiola. Conductor: Vincenzo Bellezza
April 27, 30 May 3	Rome Teatro dell'Opera	*Salammbò* by Casavola (lead role) Giovanni Voyer, Armando Dadò, Giuseppe Flamini, Giulio Tomei. Conductor: Gabriele Santini
May 13, 16, 23	Florence Teatro Comunale	*Lohengrin* Elisabeth Höngen, Giovanni Voyer, Ettore Nava, Lido Pettini, Boris Christoff Conductor: Jascha Horenstein
June 1, 3, 6	Turin Teatro Lirico	*La Bohème* Bruna Fabrini, Mario Filippeschi, Piero Guelfi, Pierluigi Latinucci, Ettore Bastianini Conductor: Francesco Molinari-Pradelli
July 22, 25, 31 August 3	Verona Arena	*Otello* Ramon Vinay, Carlo Tagliabue Conductor: Antonino Votto
August 12, 16, 19	Rome Terme di Caracalla	*Otello* Francesco Merli, Tito Gobbi Conductor: Umberto Berrettoni

215

August 22, 26, 29	Rome Terme di Caracalla	*Mefistofele* Maria Minetto, Mario Filippeschi, Nicola Rossi-Lemeni. Conductor: Oliviero De Fabritiis
September 21, 23, 26 October 5	Milan La Scala	*Andrea Chénier* Mirto Picchi, Enzo Mascherini/Giuseppe Taddei Conductor: Angelo Questa
October 22, 24	Rovigo Teatro Sociale	*Andrea Chénier* Mario Del Monaco, Raimondo Torres Conductor: Umberto Berrettoni
October 29, 31	Cesena Teatro Bonci	*Otello* Emilio Marinesco, Piero Guelfi Conductor: Francesco Molinari-Pradelli
November (4 performances)	Trieste Teatro Verdi	*Tannhäuser* Giovanni Voyer, Carlo Tagliabue, Livia Pery Conductor: Herbert Albert
November 18, 21, 24, 30	Catania Teatro Bellini	*Faust* Aida Londei, Giacinto Prandelli, Ugo Savarese, Giulio Neri/Luciano Neroni Conductor: Oliviero De Fabritiis
December 13	Turin RAI Studios	Martini & Rossi Concert with Giacinto Prandelli Conductor: Alfredo Simonetto
December 19, 22	Pesaro Teatro Rossini	*Andrea Chénier* Antonio Annaloro, Carlos Guichandut Conductor: Riccardo Santarelli
December 30 January 4, 11, 25, 30 (1949)	Milan La Scala	*Faust* Silvana Zanolli, Francesco Albanese/Giacinto Prandelli/Arrigo Pola, Enzo Mascherini/Paolo Silveri, Cesare Siepi. Conductor: Antonino Votto

1949

January 21, 23	Parma Teatro Regio	*Andrea Chénier* Vasco Campagnano, Carlos Guichandut Conductor: Antonio Narducci
January 27, 29	Modena Teatro Comunale	*Andrea Chénier* Vasco Campagnano, Vincenzo Guicciardi Conductor: Emidio Tieri
February 5, 8, 10, 13, 16, 20	Milan La Scala	*Otello* Ramon Vinay, Gino Bechi/Paolo Silveri Conductor: Victor De Sabata
February 18, 22, 27	Brescia Teatro Grande	*Andrea Chénier* Antonio Vela, Giuseppe Taddei Conductor: Alberto Erede

Chronology

March 6, 8	Milan Teatro aila Scala	*Andrea Chénier* Mario Del Monaco, Paolo Silveri Conductor: Victor De Sabata
March	Lisbon Teatro S. Carlos	*Don Giovanni* by Mozart (debut in the role of Donna Elvira) Jolanda Magnoni, Elena Rizzieri, Luigi Infantino, Gino Bechi, Tancredi Pasero, Rolando Panerai Conductor: Pedro De Freitas Branco
April 10, 12	Lisbon Teatro S. Carlos	*Falstaff* (debut in the role of Alice) Elena Rizzieri, Ebe Stignani, Myriam Pirazzini, Luigi Infantino, Gino Bechi, Rolando Panerai, Giulio Neri. Conductor: Antonino Votto
June 4, 8, 12	Florence Teatro Comunale Maggio Musicale Fiorentino	*L'Assedio di Corinto* by Rossini (debut in the role of Pamira) Myriam Pirazzini; Mirto Picchi, Raimondo Torres, Giulio Neri Conductor: Gabriele Santini
June 15, 19, 21	Genoa Teatro Carlo Felice	*Andrea Chénier* Antonio Annaloro, Carlo Tagliabue, Giuseppe Taddei. Conductor: Angelo Questa
July 2, 5, 10	Rome Terme di Caracalla	*Lohengrin* Maria Benedetti, Renzo Pigni, Benvenuto Franci, Rodolfo Azzolini, Giulio Neri Conductor: Gabriele Santini
July 21, 24, 28, 30	Verona Arena	*Lohengrin* Elena Nicolai, Irma Colasanti, Anny Konetzni, Gianni Poggi, Raimondo Torres, Enrico Campi, Boris Christoff. Conductor: Herbert Albert
October 1, 5, 9	Turin Teatro Nuovo	*Andrea Chénier* Antonio Annaloro, Ugo Savarese Conductor: Guiseppe Baroni
October 30	Turin RAI Studios	*La Bohème* Dora Gatta, Alfredo Vernetti, Rolando Panerai, Pierluigi Latinucci, Luciano Neroni Conductor: Antonio Guarnieri
November 20	Rome RAI Studios	*Tannhäuser* Mirella Freni, Giovanni Ugolotti, Carlo Tagliabue, Luciano Neroni. Conductor: Herbert Albert
December 2, 4, 7, 11	Bologna Teatro Comunale	*La Bohème* Lydia Melisci, Giacinto Prandelli, Luigi Borgonovo, Michele Cazzato, Cesare Siepi Conductor: Oliviero De Fabritiis

217

1950

January 6, 10, 15, 18, 22	Milan La Scala	*Falstaff* Alda Noni, Fedora Barbieri, Jolanda Gardino, Francesco Albanese, Mariano Stabile, Paolo Silveri, Cesare Siepi. Conductor: Victor De Sabata
January 24, 27	Brescia Teatro Grande	*La Bohème* Franca Marcenato, Alfredo Vernetti, Pietro Biasini, Alberto Albertini, Gianfelice De Manuelli Conductor: Fulvio Vernizzi
February 12, 15, 18, 21, 23, 26 April 22	Milan La Scala	*Aida* by Verdi (debut in the lead role) Fedora Barbieri, Mario Del Monaco, Raffaele De Falchi/Aldo Protti, Cesare Siepi Conductor: Antonino Votto
March 12, 14, 16	Naples Teatro San Carlo	*Tannhäuser* Livia Pery, Hans Beirer, Carlo Tagliabue, Boris Christoff. Conductor: Karl Böhm
March 19	Naples Teatro San Carlo	*La Bohème* Lydia Melisci, Galliano Masini, Saturno Meletti, Gerardo Gaudioso, Igino Riccò Conductor: Franco Patanè
March 31 April 3	Lisbon Teatro Sao Carlos	*Faust* Anna Maria Canali, Gianni Poggi, Enzo Mascherini, Giulio Neri. Conductor: Antonino Votto
April 6	Lisbon Teatro Sao Carlos	*Stabat Mater* by Rossini (debut in the lead role) Ebe Stignani, Gianni Poggi, Luciano Neroni Conductor: Antonino Votto
April 8, 11	Lisbon Teatro Sao Carlos	*Falstaff* Fiorella Carmen Forti, Ebe Stignani, Anna Maria Canali, Guilhermo Kyölner, Gino Bechi, Afro Poli, Giulio Neri. Conductor: Antonino Votto
April	Lisbon Teatro Sao Carlos	*La Traviata* Gianni Poggi, Enzo Mascherini Conductor: Antonino Votto
May 14, 17, 21	Florence Teatro Comunale Maggio Musicale Fiorentino	*Olimpia* by Spontini (debut in the lead role) Elena Nicolai, Giorgio Kokolios, Giacomo Vaghi, Mario Petri. Conductor: Tullio Serafin
June 9, 10	Milan La Scala	*St. Matthew's Passion* by J. S. Bach (debut in the lead role) Cloe Elmo, Giacinto Prandelli, Petre Munteanu, Boris Christoff, Cesare Siepi Conductor: Issay Dobrowen
June 19, 20	Milan La Scala	*Requiem* by Mozart (debut in the lead role) Marijana Radev, Giacinto Prandelli, Cesare Siepi Conductor: Guido Cantelli

Chronology

June 26, 27	Milan La Scala	*Requiem* by Verdi (debut in the lead role) Cloe Elmo, Giacinto Prandelli, Cesare Siepi Conductor: Arturo Toscanini
July 6, 8, 9	Pompeii Teatro Grande	*Giulio Cesare* by Handel (debut in the role of Cleopatra) Elena Nicolai, Gino Sinimberghi, Cesare Siepi, Antonio Cassinelli, Fernando Piccinni. Conductor: Herbert Albert
July 16, 20, 22, 27	Verona Arena	*Mefistofele* Franca Sacchi, Giacinto Prandelli, Andrea Mongelli. Conductor: Angelo Questa
July 30 August 1	Naples Villa Floridaina	*Faust* Aida Londei, Alfredo Vernetti, Ugo Savarese, Italo Tajo. Conductor: Franco Ghione
September 4, 9	Edinburgh Usher Hall	*Requiem* by Verdi Fedora Barbieri, Giacinto Prandelli, Cesare Siepi Conductor: Victor De Sabata
September 8	Edinburgh Usher Hall	*Requiem* by Mozart Fedora Barbieri, Giacinto Prandelli, Cesare Siepi Conductor: Guido Cantelli
September 12, 14, 16	London Covent Garden	*Otello* Ramon Vinay, Gino Bechi. Conductor: Victor De Sabata
September 17, 19	London Covent Garden	*Requiem* by Verdi Fedora Barbieri, Giacinto Prandelli, Cesare Siepi Conductor: Victor de Sabata
September 26	San Francisco Opera	*Aida* Elena Nikolaidi, Mario Del Monaco, Robert Weede, Italo Tajo. Conductor: Fausto Cleva
October 10, 19	San Francisco Opera	*Otello* Ramon Vinay, Giuseppe Valdengo Conductor: Fausto Cleva
December 6	Naples Teatro San Carlo	*Requiem* by Verdi Ebe Stignani, Gianni Poggi, Nicola Rossi-Lemeni Conductor: Tullio Serafin
December 7	Naples Basilica di S. Francesco di Paola	*Requiem* by Verdi Ebe Stignani, Gianni Poggi, Nicola Rossi-Lemeni Conductor: Tullio Serafin
December 26, 28 January 1, 3 (1951)	Milan La Scala	*Otello* Ramon Vinay, Gino Bechi Conductor: Victor De Sabata

219

1951

January 10, 13	Naples Teatro San Carlo	*La Bohème* Elda Ribetti, Giacomo Lauri Volpi/Alfredo Vernetti, Tito Gobbi, Saturno Meletti, Giulio Neri. Conductor: Gabriele Santini
January 18, 20	Naples Teatro San Carlo	*Andre Chénier* Mario Filippeschi, Carlo Tagliabue Conductor: Gabriele Santini
January 27	Milan La Scala	*Requiem* by Verdi Nell Rankin, Giacinto Prandelli, Nicola Rossi-Lemeni. Conductor: Victor De Sabata
February 3	Milan La Scala	*La Traviata* Giacinto Prandelli, Giuseppe Taddei Conductor: Victor De Sabata
March 15, 18, 20	Naples Teatro San Carlo	*Giovanna D'Arco* by Verdi (debut in the lead role) Gino Penno, Ugo Savarese Conductor: Gabriele Santini
March 30 April 1, 3, 6, 8, 12, 15, 17, 21	Naples Teatro San Carlo	*La Traviata* Giacinto Prandelli/Alfredo Vernetti, Carlo Tagliabue/Rolando Panerai Conductor: Gabriele Santini
April 4	Naples	Concert (with Mario Petri and pianist Gabriele Santini)
April 23	Naples	Concert (with pianist Franco Patanè)
April 26, 28	Naples Teatro San Carlo	*Faust* Fernanda Cadoni, Mario Filippeschi, Rolando Panerai, Italo Tajo. Conductor: Franco Patanè
May 5, 9, 11, 13	Rome Teatro dell'Opera	*L'Assedio di Corinto (The Siege of Corinth)* Myriam Pirazzini, Mirto Picchi, Andrea Mongelli, Giulio Neri. Conductor: Gabriele Santini
May 26	Milan RAI Studios	*Giovanna d'Arco* Carlo Bergonzi, Rolando Panerai Conductor: Alfredo Simonetto
June 5, 7	Milan La Scala	*Falstaff* Alda Noni, Cloe Elmo, Anna Maria Canali, Cesare Valletti, Mariano Stabile, Paolo Silveri, Silvio Maionica. Conductor: Victor De Sabata
June	Strasbourg	Concert (with Rosanna Carteri, Miti Truccato Pace). Conductor: Carlo Maria Giulini
June 30 July 3	Paris Opéra	*Giovanna d'Arco* Gino Penno, Ugo Savarese Conductor: Gabriele Santini

Chronology

July 5	Paris Église de la Madeleine	*Requiem* by Verdi Ebe Stignani, Mirto Picchi, Italo Tajo Conductor: Gabriele Santini
August 24, 26 September 1	Rio de Janeiro Teatro Municipal	*La Traviata* Guiseppe Campora, Paolo Silveri, Antonio Salsedo. Conductor: Antonino Votto
August 28 September 8	Rio De Janeiro Teatro Municipal	*La Bohème* Diva Pieranti, Giuseppe Di Stefano/Giuseppe Campora, Paolo Silveri, Guilhermo Damiano, Antonio Lembo, Giuseppe Modesti Conductor: Nino Sanzogno/Antonino Votto
September 2, 4	S. Paolo, Brazil Teatro Municipal	*La Traviata* Giuseppe Di Stefano, Tito Gobbi Conductor: Tullio Serafin
September 14	Rio De Janeiro Teatro Municipal	Concert (with Maria Callas, Disma De Cecco, Cristina Carrol, Elena Nicolai, Anna Maria Canali, Giuseppe Campora, Salvatore Puma, Enzo Mascherini, Paolo Silveri, Antonio Salsedo, Boris Christoff, and pianists Nino Gaioni and Enrico Sivieri)
September 19, 22	Rio De Janeiro Teatro Municipal	*Aida* Elena Nicolai, Mario Filippeschi, Paolo Silveri, Antonio Salsedo, Giulio Neri Conductor: Antonino Votto
September 29	S. Paolo, Brazil Teatro Municipal	*Andrea Chénier* Beniamino Gigli, Gino Bechi Conductor: Edoardo De Guarnieri
September 30	S. Paolo, Brazil Teatro Municipal	Concert (with pianist Armando Belardi)
October 1	S. Paolo, Brazil Teatro Municipal	*Requiem* by Verdi Fedora Barbieri, Beniamino Gigli, Giulio Neri Conductor: Tullio Serafin
October 3	Rio De Janeiro Teatro Municipal	*Tosca* Gianni Poggi, Paolo Silveri Conductor: Antonino Votto
October 18, 21	Bergamo Teatro Donizetti	*La Traviata* Giacinto Prandelli, Giovanni Fabbri Conductor: Carlo Maria Giulini
October 25, 27	Parma Teatro Regio	*Falstaff* Elda Ribetti, Cloe Elmo, Vittoria Palombini, Agostino Lazzari, Mariano Stabile, Walter Monachesi, Marco Stefanoni Conductor: Antonino Votto

221

November 3	Catania Cattedrale	*Requiem* by Verdi Ebe Stignani, Mirto Picchi, Italo Tajo Conductor: Gabriele Santini
November 26	Turin Conservatorio G. Verdi	Martini & Rossi Concert Paolo Silveri. Conductor: Carlo Maria Giulini
November 27, 30 December 2	Florence Teatro Comunale	*Aida* Fedora Barbieri, Giacomo Lauri Volpi/Giuseppe Vertechi, Raffaele De Falchi, Giulio Neri Conductor: Gabriele Santini
December 15, 19, 23	Naples Teatro San Carlo	*Fernando Cortez* by Spontini (lead role: Amazily) Gino Penno, Aldo Protti, Afro Poli, Italo Tajo, Antonio Cassinelli. Conductor: Gabriele Santini

1952

January 2, 6, 10	Naples Teatro San Carlo	*L'Assedio di Corinto (The Siege of Corinth)* Myriam Pirazzini, Mirto Picchi, Mario Petri, Raffaele Ariè. Conductor: Gabriele Santini
January 17, 20, 24, 26, 30 February 3, 5	Naples Teatro San Carlo	*La Traviata* Giuseppe Campora, Giuseppe Taddei/Raimondo Torres. Conductor: Gabriele Santini
February 14, 17, 20, 23	Rome Teatro dell'Opéra	*Le Nozze di Figaro (The Marriage of Figaro)* by Mozart (debut in the role of Contessa) Elena Rizzieri, Giulietta Simionato, Giuseppe Taddei, Mario Petri, Vito De Taranto, Gino Sinimberghi. Conductor: Vittorio Gui
March 22	Genoa Teatro Carlo Felice	*La Traviata* Agostino Lazzari, Enzo Mascherini Conductor: Franco Capuana
April 12, 16, 18, 20, 29 May 5, 11	Milan La Scala	*Mefistofele* Carla Martinis/Disma De Cecco, Ferruccio Tagliavini/Giacinto Prandelli, Nicola Rossi-Lemeni. Conductor: Victor De Sabata
May 15, 18	Bari Teatro Petruzzelli	*La Traviata* Gianni Raimondi, Giovanni Fabbri Conductor: Vincenzo Bellezza
May 26, 29 June 16	Milan La Scala	*Falstaff* Rosanna Carteri/Rosetta Noli, Cloe Elmo, Anna Maria Canali, Cesare Valletti/ Giacinto Prandelli, Mariano Stabile, Paolo Silveri/ Renato Capecchi, Italo Tajo Conductor: Victor De Sabata
May 28	Milan RAI Studios	*La Traviata* Giacinto Prandelli, Gino Orlandini Conductor: Carlo Maria Giulini

Chronology

June 8, 10, 12, 14	Florence Teatro Comunale Maggio Musicale Fiorentino	*Guglielmo Tell (William Tell)* by Rossini (debut in the role of Mathilde) Kurt Baum, Nicola Rossi-Lemeni, Mario Petri. Conductor: Tullio Serafin
June 29	Florence Piazza SS. Annunziata	*Stabat Mater* by Rossini Nan Merriman, Gianni Poggi, Italo Tajo Conductor: Antonino Votto
August 15, 23, 31	Rio De Janeiro Teatro Municipal	*La Traviata* Alvino Misciano, Ugo Savarese/Carlo Tagliabue Conductor: Oliviero De Fabritiis
September 3, 13	Rio De Janeiro Teatro Municipal	*Andrea Chénier* Roberto Turrini, Carlo Tagliabue/Ugo Savarese Conductor: Olivieri De Fabritiis
September 23	Rio De Janeiro Teatro Municipal	*Tosca* Gianni Poggi, Silvio Vieira Conductor: Umberto Vedovelli
October 30 November 1, 4	Turin Teatro Nuovo	*Tosca* Gianni Poggi, Paolo Silveri Conductor: Gianandrea Gavazzeni
November 20, 23, 26, 30	Trieste Teatro Verdi	*La Traviata* Francesco Albanese, Gino Bechi Conductor: Antonino Votto
December 13, 16, 18, 21	Naples Teatro San Carlo	*Otello* Ramon Vinay, Gino Bechi. Conductor: Gabriele Santini
December 26, 28, 31 January 4 (1953)	Naples Teatro San Carlo	*Adriana Lecouvreur* by Cilea (debut in the lead) Maria Benedetti, Gianni Poggi, Giuseppe Campora, Giuseppe Taddei, Augusto Romani Conductor: Gabriele Santini

1953

January 10, 14,18	Naples Teatro San Carlo	*Cecilia* by Refice (debut in the lead) Alvinio Misciano, Saturno Meletti, Rolando Panerai, Giulio Neri Conductor: Licinio Refice
January 27, 30	Palermo Teatro Massimo	*Mefistofele* Disma De Cecco, Gianni Poggi, Giulio Neri Conductor: Franco Capuana
February 6, 8	Reggio Emilia Teatro Municipale	*Tosca* Pier Miranda Ferraro, Victor Damiani Conductor: Antonio Narducci
February 15	Brescia Teatro Grande	*Tosca* Giuseppe Savio, Renato Cesari Conductor: Glauco Curiel

April 7, 10, 12,15, 17	Naples Teatro San Carlo	*Aida* Ebe Stignani, Gino Penno, Ugo Savarese, Giulio Seri. Conductor: Gabriele Santini
April	Monte Carlo Grand-Théâtre	*La Traviata* Gianni Raimondi, Aldo Protti
April 12, 15, 18, 20, 23, 29, May 3, June 2	Milan La Scala	*Tosca* Ferruccio Tagliavini, Giuseppe Di Stefano, Paolo Silveri. Conductor: Victor De Sabata
May 7, 9, 12, 21, 24	Milan La Scala	*Adriana Lecouvreur* Oralia Dominguez, Giuseppe Campora, Afro Poli, Silvio Maionica Conductor: Carlo Maria Giulini
June 14, 16, 18, 21, 23	Florence Teatro Comunale Maggio Musicale Fiorentino	*La Forza del Destino* by Verdi (debut in the role of Leonora) Fedora Barbieri, Mario Del Monaco, Aldo Protti, Renato Capecchi, Cesare Siepi Conductor: Dimitri Mitropoulos
July 24, 29 August 2	Buenos Aires Teatro Colon	*Aida* Ebe Stignani/Tota de Igarzabal, Carlo Bergonzi, Renato Cesari, Juan Zanin/Pindaro Hounau Conductor: Alberto Erede
August 7, 9, 12, 15, 25	Buenos Aires Teatro Colon	*Tosca* Carlo Bergonzi/Marcos Cubas, Giuseppe Taddei Conductor: Juan Emilio Martini
September 4, 6, 17	Rio De Janeiro Teatro Municipal	*Tosca* Ferruccio Tagliavini, Paolo Silveri Conductor: Ferruccio Calusio
September 10, 13, 19	Rio De Janeiro Teatro Municipal	*Otello* Ramon Vinay, Paolo Silveri Conductor: Ferruccio Calusio
September 15, 20, 26	Rio De Janeiro Teatro Municipal	*La Bohème* Diva Pieranti/Clara Marise, Gianni Poggi, Paolo Silveri, Renato Cesari, Giuseppe Modesti Conductor: Albert Wolff
October 2, 6	Rio De Janeiro Teatro Municipal	*Adriana Lecouvreur* Maria Henriques/Fedora Barbieri, Gianni Poggi, Renato Cesari/Paulo Fortes, Guilhermo Damiano Conductor: Nino Stinco
November 4	Barcelona Teatro Liceo	*La Traviata* Francesco Albanese, Enzo Mascherini Conductor: Angelo Questa
November 12, 17, 22, 24	Barcelona Teatro Liceo	*Tosca* Gianni Poggi, Giuseppe Taddei Conductor: Angelo Questa

Chronology

November 30	Milan RAI Studios	Concert: Martini & Rossi Conductor: Nino Sanzogno
December 7, 11, 13, 17, 20, 23	Milan La Scala	*La Wally* by Catalani (debut in the lead) Renata Scotto, Jolanda Gardino, Mario Del Monaco, Mario Ortica, Giangiacomo Guelfi, Giorgio Tozzi. Conductor: Carlo Maria Giulini

1954

January 7, 10	Milan La Scala	*Otello* Mario Del Monaco, Leonard Warren Conductor: Antonino Votto
January 16, 20, 23, 26, 31 February 20	Naples Teatro San Carlo	*La Forza del Destino* Myriam Pirazzini, Gino Penno/Roberto Turrini/ Primo Zambruno, Antonio Mancaserra/Carlo Tagliabue, Saturno Meletti, Giulio Neri/ Plinio Clabassi. Conductor: Gabriele Santini
February 7, 10, 14	Naples Teatro San Carlo	*La Wally* Mafalda Micheluzzi, Amalia Pini, Roberto Turrini, Carlo Tagliabue, Antonio Cassinelli Conductor: Gabriele Santini
February 24, 26, 28	Naples Teatro San Carlo	*Le Nozze di Figaro (The Marriage of Figaro)* Alda Noni, Giulietta Simionato, Italo Tajo, Scipio Colombo, Endré Von Koreh, Piero De Palma. Conductor: Jonel Perlea
March 11, 14, 17, 20	Rome Teatro dell'Opera	*Andrea Chénier* Mario Del Monaco/Antonio Galiè, Paolo Silveri Conductor: Angelo Questa
March 25, 28, 31 April 3, 6	Rome Teatro dell'Opera	*Otello* Mario Del Monaco, Tito Gobbi Conductor: Franco Capuana
April 14, 19, 21, 24, May 2, 23, 30 June 9, 13	Milan La Scala	*Tosca* Giuseppe Di Stefano/Mario Ortica, Paolo Silveri/ Rodolfo Azzolini. Conductor: Antonino Votto
May 10, 13, 15, 18	Milan La Scala	*Evgeny Onegin (Eugene Onegin)* by Tchaikovsky (debut in the role of Tatiana) Ira Malaniuk, Cloe Elmo, Giuseppe Di Stefano, Ettore Bastianini, Raffaele Ariè. Conductor: Arthur Rodzinski
May	Monte Carlo	*Tosca* Giacinto Prandelli, Giuseppe Taddei
July 3, 6, 10, 15, 18	Naples Arena Flegrea	*La Traviata* Ferruccio Tagliavini/Giacinto Prandelli, Carlo Tagliabue. Conductor: Tullio Serafin

225

July 25, 28	Rome Terme di Caracalla	*Tosca* Mario Del Monaco, Giangiacomo Guelfi Conductor: Ottavio Ziino
September 2, 5, 11	Rio De Janeiro Teatro Municipal	*La Forza del Destino* Giulietta Simionato, Gino Penno/José Soler, Paolo Silveri, Guilhermo Damiano, Giulio Neri Conductor: Oliviero De Fabritiis
September 17, 19	Rio De Janeiro Teatro Municipal	*Cecilia* José Soler, Paulo Fortes, Lourival Braga, Giuseppe Modesti. Conductor: Oliviero De Fabritiis
September 21 October 2	Rio De Janeiro Teatro Municipal	*Tosca* Giuseppe Di Stefano, Giuseppe Taddei Conductor: Oliviero De Fabritiis/Edoardo De Guarnieri
October 5	Rio De Janeiro Teatro Municipal	*Otello* Mario Del Monaco, Giuseppe Taddei Conductor: Edoardo De Guarnieri
November 4, 7, 13	Barcelona Teatro Liceo	*La Forza del Destino* Jolanda Gardino, Gino Penno, Giuseppe Taddei, Saturno Meletti, Giulio Neri Conductor: Armando La Rosa-Parodi
November 11, 16, 20	Barcelona Teatro Liceo	*La Bohème* Ornella Rovero, Gianni Poggi, Manuel Ausensi, Alberto Albertini, Giulio Neri Conductor: Ugo Rapalo
November 29	Rome Auditorium RAI	Concert (with Giuseppe Di Stefano, Giuseppe Taddei). Conductor: Alberto Paoletti
December 6, 9, 12, 15, 18, 21	Rome Teatro dell'Opera	*La Forza del Destino* Giulietta Simionato, Gino Penno/Roberto Turrini, Aldo Protti/Antonio Mancaserra, Renato Capecchi, Giulio Neri Conductor: Gabriele Santini
December 26, 29 January 2 (1955)	Naples Teatro San Carlo	*Lohengrin* Elena Nicolai, Gino Penno, Giangiacomo Guelfi, Enzo Viaro, Giulio Neri Conductor: Gabriele Santini

1955

January 31 February 11 March 1, 5, 12	New York Metropolitan	*Otello* Mario Del Monaco, Leonard Warren Conductor: Fritz Stiedry
February 7	New York NBC-TV	Concert ("Telephone Hour")

Chronology

February 9	New York Metropolitan	*La Bohème* Jean Fenn, Giuseppe Campora, Ettore Bastianini, George Cehanovsky, Norman Scott Conductor: Fausto Cleva
February 23	New York Metropolitan	*Andrea Chénier* Mario Del Monaco, Ettore Bastianini Conductor: Fausto Cleva
February 27	New York	Concert (with Mario Del Monaco and Ettore Bastianini). Conductor: Fausto Cleva
March 8	New York Metropolitan	*Tosca* Giuseppe Campora, Walter Cassel Conductor: Fausto Cleva
April 26, 28, 30 May 3, 5	Milan La Scala	*La Forza del Destino* Marta Perez, Giuseppe Di Stefano, Aldo Protti, Renato Capecchi, Giuseppe Modesti Conductor: Antonino Votto
May 19 June 11, 18, 21	Florence Teatro Comunale Maggio Musicale Fiorentino	*Otello* Ramon Vinay/Ralph Lambert/Mario Del Monaco, Tito Gobbi. Conductor: Gabriele Santini
June 16, 19	Florence Teatro Comunale	*Falstaff* Aureliana Beltrami, Fedora Barbieri, Myriam Pirazzini, Giuseppe Campora, Tito Gobbi, Mariano Stabile, Renato Capecchi, Giulio Neri Conductor: Antonino Votto
June 28 July 2, 4, 8	London Covent Garden	*Tosca* Ferruccio Tagliavini, Tito Gobbi Conductor: Francesco Molinari-Pradelli
September 5	New York	Televised Concert ("Telephone Hour")
September 15, 22 October 16	San Francisco Opera	*Aida* Claramae Turner/Nell Rankin, Roberto Turrini, Leonard Warren, Giorgio Tozzi Conductor: Fausto Cleva
September 28	San Francisco Opera	Concert (with Elisabeth Schwarzkopf)
October 4, 8	San Francisco Opera	*Andrea Chénier* Richard Tucker, Leonard Warren Conductor: Fausto Cleva
October 19	San Francisco Opera	*Tosca* Richard Tucker, Robert Weede Conductor: Glauco Curiel

227

October 21	Los Angeles Shrine Auditorium	*Andrea Chénier* Richard Tucker, Leonard Warren Conductor: Fausto Cleva
October 26	Los Angeles Shrine Auditorium	*Aida* Nell Rankin, Roberto Turrini, Leonard Warren, Giorgio Tozzi. Conductor: Fausto Cleva
November 1, 4	Chicago Lyric Opera	*Aida* Astrid Varnay, Doro Antonioli, Tito Gobbi, William Wildermann. Conductor: Tullio Serafin
November 7, 9	Chicago Lyric Opera	*La Bohème* Gloria Lind, Giuseppe Di Stefano, Tito Gobbi, Richard Torigi, Nicola Rossi-Lemeni Conductor: Tullio Serafin
November 19, 24 December 10	New York Metropolitan	*Aida* Blanche Thebom, Elena Nikolaidi, Mario Ortica, Ettore Bastianini, Giorgio Tozzi/Norman Scott/ Nicola Moscona. Conductor: Fausto Cleva
November 22	Philadelphia Academy of Music	*Aida* Elena Nikolaidi, Mario Ortica, Ettore Bastianini, Nicola Moscona. Conductor: Fausto Cleva
December 8, 13, 30 January 7, 18 (1956)	New York Metropolitan	*Tosca* Richard Tucker/Giuseppe Campora, Leonard Warren/Tito Gobbi Conductor: Dimitri Mitropoulos
December 12	New York NBC-TV	Concert ("Telephone Hour")
December 18	New York Carnegie Hall	Concert (with pianist Martin Rich)
December 20	New York Carnegie Hall	Concert (with Jussi Björling and pianist Leonard Bernstein)
December 23	New York	Televised Concert ("Telephone Hour")
December 31	New York Metropolitan	Performance of the aria from Act I of *Adriana Lecouvreur* during the performance of *Die Fledermaus* of Strauss (Act II)

1956

January 2, 14	New York Metropolitan	*Andrea Chénier* Richard Tucker/Mario Ortica, Leonard Warren Conductor: Fausto Cleva

228

Chronology

January 5	New York Town Hall	Concert (with Regina Resnik, Mario Ortica, Jerome Hines)
January 10, 21	New York Metropolitan	*La Forza del Destino* Margaret Roggero/Rosalind Elias, Richard Tucker, Josef Metternich/Leonard Warren, Fernando Corena, Jerome Hines/Giorgio Tozzi Conductor: Pietro Cimara
January 24	Philadelphia Academy of Musica	*Tosca* Giuseppe Di Stefano, Paul Schöffler Conductor: Dimitri Mitropoulos
January 27	Toronto Massey Hall	Concert
January 29	Newark Auditorium	Concert (with Giuseppe Campora and pianist Martin Rich)
January 30	New York NBC-TV	Televised Concert ("Producers' Showcase" with Jussi Björling)
February 1	Boston War Memorial Auditorium	Concert (with pianist Martin Rich)
February 4	Washington Constitution Hall	Concert (with pianist Martin Rich)
February 6	Hartford Bushnell Memorial	*La Forza del Destino* Marta Perez, Kurt Baum, Francesco Valentino, Nicola Moscona. Conductor: Pietro Cimara
February 8	Englewood	Concert (with Marshall and J. Harms Chorus)
February 10	New York Carnegie Hall	Concert
March 7, 10, 13	Palermo Teatro Massimo	*Tosca* Gianni Poggi, Mariano Stabile Conductor: Franco Ghione
March 26, 28, 31 April 2	Palermo Teatro Massimo	*La Forza del Destino* Jolanda Gardino, Giuseppe Di Stefano, Giuseppe Vertechi, Enzo Mascherini, Enrico Campi, Giuseppe Modesti. Conductor: Tullio Serafin
April 11, 13, 15	Napoli Teatro San Carlo	*Guglielmo Tell (William Tell)* Mario Filippeschi, Rolando Panerai, Giuseppe Modesti. Conductor: Tullio Serafin
April 19, 22, 26	Rome Teatro dell'Opera	*Tosca* Ferruccio Tagliavini/Giacinto Prandelli, Giangiacomo Guelfi. Conductor: Ottavio Ziino

229

RENATA TEBALDI

May 6, 10, 13, 26, 31 June 5, 17	Florence Teatro Comunale Maggio Musical Fiorentino	*La Traviata* Nicola Filacuridi, Ugo Savarese/Dino Dondi/ Ettore Bastianini. Conductor: Tullio Serafin
May 17, 20	Rome Teatro dell'Opera	*Andrea Chénier* Umberto Borsò, Giuseppe Taddei Conductor: Gabriele Santini
June 8, 10, 13	Florence Teatro Comunale Maggio Musicale Fiorentino	*La Forza del Destino* Fedora Barbieri, Giuseppe Di Stefano/Flaviano Labò, Giangiacomo Guelfi, Melchiorre Luise, Giulio Neri. Conductor: Gabriele Santini
August 30	Los Angeles	Concert Conductor: Kurt Adler
September 9	San Francisco Opera	Concert (with Giorgio Tozzi, pianist Glauco Curiel)
September 15, 23	San Francisco Opera	*Tosca* Richard Martell/Jussi Björling, Leonard Warren/ Anselmo Colzani. Conductor: Glauco Curiel
September 16	San Francisco Golden Gate Park	Concert
October 3	San Francisco Opera	Concert (with Elisabeth Schwarzkopf)
October 9, 13	San Francisco Opera	*Simon Boccanegra* by Verdi (debut in the role of Maria) Roberto Turrini, Leonard Warren, Heinz Blankenburg, Boris Christoff Conductor: Oliviero De Fabritiis
October 20	Los Angeles Shrine Auditorium	*Simon Boccanegra* Roberto Turini, Leonard Warren, Heinz Blankenburg, Boris Christoff Conductor: Oliviero De Fabritiis
October 30, November 2, 5	Chicago Lyric Opera	*Tosca* Jussi Björling, Tito Gobbi Conductor: Bruno Bartoletti/Leo Kopp
November 8, 12	Chicago Lyric Opera	*La Forza del Destino* Giulietta Simionato, Richard Tucker, Ettore Bastianini, Carlo Badioli, Nicola Rossi-Lemeni Conductor: Georg Solti
November 10	Chicago Lyric Opera	Concert (with Giulietta Simionato and Ettore Bastianini). Conductor: Georg Solti
November 14, 16	Chicago Lyric Opera	*La Bohème* Dolores Wilson, Jussi Björling/Barry Morell, Ettore Bastianini, Henri Noel, Miroslav Cangalovic. Conductor: Bruno Bartoletti

Chronology

December 5, 8, 11	Barcelona Teatro Liceo	*Tosca* Flaviano Labò, Mario Zanasi Conductor: Angelo Questa
December 14, 16, 20	Barcelona Teatro Liceo	*Aida* Dora Minarchi, Umberto Borsò, Mario Zanasi, Giuseppe Modesti. Conductor: Angelo Questa
December 20	Barcelona Teatro Liceo	Concert

1957

January 3	Milan Teatro Manzoni	Concert (with pianist Giorgio Favaretto)
January 7	Milan RAI Studios	Martini & Rossi Concert (with Ettore Bastianini.) Conductor: Oliviero De Fabritiis
January 13	Parma Teatro Regio	*Andrea Chénier* Carlo Guichandut, Aldo Protti Conductor: Angelo Questa
February 8 March 13	New York Metropolitan	*La Bohème* Heidi Krall, Richard Tucker, Ettore Bastianini/ Frank Guarrera, Clifford Harvuot/George Cehanovsky, Giorgio Tozzi Conductor: Thomas Schippers/Tibor Kozma
February 10	New York Carnegie Hall	Concert (with pianist Martin Rich)
February 21 March 2, 6, 12, 15, 21, 23 April 6, 17	New York Metropolitan	*La Traviata* Giuseppe Campora/Gianni Poggi/Daniele Barioni, Leonard Warren/Robert Merrill/ Frank Guarrera/Ettore Bastianini Conductor: Fausto Cleva
February 27 April 20	New York Metropolitan	*Tosca* Jussi Björling/Daniele Barioni, Leonard Warren/ George London. Conductor: Dimitri Mitropoulos/Kurt Adler
March 10	New York	Televised Concert ("Ed Sullivan Show" with Richard Tucker)
March 18	New York NBC-TV	Televised Concert ("Telephone Hour")
March 28	Pittsburg Syrian Mosque	Concert

231

Renata Tebaldi

April 1	Baltimore Lyric Theatre	La Traviata Giuseppe Campora, Ettore Bastianini Conductor: Fausto Cleva
April 3	New York Carnegie Hall	Concert Conductor: Dimitri Mitropoulos
April 10	Brooklyn Academy of Music	Concert
April 23	Cleveland Public Auditorium	La Traviata Gianni Poggi, Leonard Warren Conductor: Fausto Cleva
April 27	Cleveland Public Auditorium	Tosca Gianni Poggi, Leonard Warren Conductor: Kurt Adler
April 30	Richmond City Auditorium	La Traviata Giuseppe Campora, Ettore Bastianini Conductor: Fausto Cleva
May	Atlanta Civic Center	La Traviata
May 8	Memphis Municipal Auditorium	La Traviata Giuseppe Campora, Frank Guarrera Conductor: Fausto Cleva
May 11	Dallas State Fair Music Hall	La Traviata Giuseppe Campora, Ettore Bastianini Conductor: Fausto Cleva
May 14	Houston Music Hall	Tosca Giuseppe Campora, George London Conductor: Dimitri Mitropoulos
May 18	Minneapolis Northrop Auditorium	La Traviata Giuseppe Campora, Robert Merrill Conductor: Fausto Cleva
May 21	Bloomington	La Traviata Giuseppe Campora, Leonard Warren Conductor: Fausto Cleva
May 25	Chicago Lyric Opera	La Traviata Giuseppe Campora, Robert Merrill Conductor: Fausto Cleva
May 28	Toronto Massey Hall	La Traviata Giuseppe Campora, Robert Merrill Conductor: Fausto Cleva
May 31	Toronto Massey Hall	Tosca Daniele Barioni, George London Conductor: Dimitri Mitropoulos

Chronology

June 3	Montreal Forum	*La Traviata* Giuseppe Campora, Robert Merrill Conductor: Fausto Cleva
June 13, 16	Havana Auditorium	*La Traviata* Brian Sullivan, Walter Cassel Conductor: Alberto Erede
June 21	Havana Auditorium	*Tosca* Mario Ortica, Walter Cassel Conductor: Fausto Cleva
June 24	Havana Auditorium	*Aida* Nell Rankin, Mario Ortica, Robert Merrill, Norman Treigle. Conductor: Fausto Cleva
June 27	New York Manhattan Stadium	Concert Conductor: Julius Rudel
August 20	Verona Arena	*La Bohème* Silvana Zanolli, Gianni Poggi, Ettore Bastianini, Giorgio Giorgetti, Ivo Vinco Conductor: Francesco Molinari-Pradelli
August 24	Verona Piazza San Zeno	Concert
October 11, 18	Chicago Lyric Opera	*Otello* Mario Del Monaco, Tito Gobbi Conductor: Tullio Serafin
October 21, 25 November 9	Chicago Lyric Opera	*Manon Lescaut* by Puccini (debut in the lead) Jussi Björling, Cornell MacNeil, Carlo Badioli Conductor: Tullio Serafin
October 30 November 2	Chicago Lyric Opera	*Andrea Chénier* Mario Del Monaco, Tito Gobbi Conductor: Gianandrea Gavazzeni
November 13, 16	Chicago Lyric Opera	*Adriana Lecouvreur* Giulietta Simionato, Giuseppe Di Stefano, Tito Gobbi, Carlo Badioli. Conductor: Tullio Serafin

1958

January 23, 26 February 6, 11	Barcelona Teatro Liceo	*Madama Butterfly* by Puccini (debut in the lead) Giacinto Prandelli, Otello Borgonovo, Rina Corsi Conductor: Carlo Felice Cillario
January 31 February 2, 4	Barcelona Teatro Liceo	*La Bohème* Eugenio Fernandi, Manuel Ausensi, Silvana Zanolli, Luis Andreu Conductor: Carlo Felice Cillario

233

February 9, 13	Barcelona Teatro Liceo	*Adriana Lecouvreur* Adriana Lazzarini, Giacinto Prandelli, Manuel Ausensi. Conductor: Angelo Questa
February 22, 26 March 2	Naples Teatro San Carlo	*Adriana Lecouvreur* Myriam Pirazzini/Adriana Lazzarini, Nicola Filacuridi, Renato Capecchi, Antonio Sacchetti Conductor: Francesco Molinari-Pradelli
March 6, 9, 23	Naples Teatro San Carlo	*Tosca* Franco Corelli, Giuseppe Gismondo, Tito Gobbi/ Ettore Bastianini. Conductor: Ugo Rapalo
March 15, 18, 20	Naples Teatro San Carlo	*La Forza del Destino* Oralia Dominguez, Franco Corelli, Ettore Bastianini, Renato Capecchi, Boris Christoff Conductor: Francesco Molinari-Pradelli
April 3, 6, 12, 16, 19, 22	Vienna State Opera	*Tosca* Giuseppe Zampieri, Tito Gobbi/Walter Berry Conductor: Herbert von Karajan
April 9	Vienna State Opera	*Otello* Carlo Guichandut, Tito Gobbi Conductor: Herbert von Karajan
April 28	Milan Teatro Manzoni	Concert (with pianist Giorgio Favaretto)
April 30	Genoa Teatro Carlo Felice	Concert (with pianist Giorgio Favaretto)
May 13	Florence Palazzo Vecchio	Concert (with pianist Giorgio Favaretto)
May 31	Milan RAI Studios	*Manon Lescaut* Eugenio Fernandi, Guido Mazzani, Franco Calabrese. Conductor: Nino Sanzogno
June 5	Zurich Tonhalle	Concert (with pianist Giorgio Favaretto)
June 12, 15	Venice Teatro La Fenice	*La Forza del Destino* Giulietta Simionato, Giuseppe Savio, Giangiacomo Guelfi, Guido Mazzini, Raffaele Arie. Conductor: Oliviero De Fabritiis
June 20	Brussels Auditorium	*Tosca* Giuseppe Di Stefano, Ettore Bastianini Conductor: Gianandrea Gavazzeni
August 9, 13, 17, 20, 24	Naples Arena Flegrea	*Madama Butterfly* Gianni Raimondi, Giuseppe Valdengo Conductor: Angelo Questa

Chronology

October 10, 17	Chicago Lyric Opera	*Falstaff* Anna Moffo, Giulietta Simionato, Anna Maria Canali, Alvinio Misciano, Tito Gobbi, Cornell MacNeil, Kenneth Smith Conductor: Tullio Serafin
October 13, 15	Chicago Opera	*Madama Butterfly* Giuseppe Di Stefano, Cornell MacNeil Conductor: Kyrill Kondrascin
October 27 November 1, 4 December 6, 25	New York Metropolitan	*Tosca* Mario Del Monaco/Giuseppe Campora/Eugenio Fernandi, George London/Cesare Bardelli/Tito Gobbi. Conductor: Dimitri Mitropoulos
November 8, 19	New York Metropolitan	*Madama Butterfly* Eugenio Fernandi/Barry Morell, Mario Zanasi Conductor: Erich Leinsdorf
November 15, 24 December 9, 20, 28	New York Metropolitan	*Otello* Mario Del Monaco, Leonard Warren/Tito Gobbi Conductor: Fausto Cleva
December 3, 22 January 17 (1959)	New York Metropolitan	*Manon Lescaut* Richard Tucker, Frank Guarrera, Ezio Flagello/Salvatore Baccaloni/Fernando Corena Conductor: Fausto Cleva
December 10	New York	Concert with the New York Philharmonic Conductor: Leonard Bernstein
December 12 January 1, 14, (1959)	New York Metropolitan	*La Bohème* Heidi Krall, Eugenio Fernandi/Barry Morell/ 20 Carlo Bergonzi, Mario Zanasi/Mario Sereni, George Cehanovsky/Clifford Harvuot, Nicola Moscona/Cesare Siepi/Giorgio Tozzi Conductor: Thomas Schippers

1959

January 5	New York Metropolitan	*Tosca* Eugenio Fernandi, Walter Cassel Conductor: Dimitri Mitropoulos
January 12	New York	Televised Concert ("Telephone Hour")
February 1	Washington Constitution Hall	Concert (with pianist Giorgio Favaretto)
February 7	Cleveland Public Auditorium	Concert (with pianist Giorgio Favaretto)
February 10	Ann Arbor Hill Auditorium	Concert (with pianist Giorgio Favaretto)

235

Renata Tebaldi

February 11	Kalamazoo High School Auditorium	Concert (with pianist Giorgio Favaretto)
February 15, 17	Chicago Rosary College	Concert (with pianist Giorgio Favaretto)
February 20	Toronto Massey Hall	Concert (with pianist Giorgio Favaretto)
February 23	Montreal Forum	Concert (with pianist Kurt Adler)
February 26	Philadelphia Academy of Music	Concert (with pianist Giorgio Favaretto)
March 1	Boston Symphony Hall	Concert (with pianist Giorgio Favaretto)
March 15	Havana Auditorium	*Adriana Lecouvreur* Myriam Pirazzini, Umberto Borsò, Enzo Sordello, Fernando Corena. Conductor: Napoleone Annovazzi
March 17	Havana Auditorium	*La Bohème* Cristina Carrol, Barry Morell, Enzo Sordello, Henri Noel, Fernando Corena Conductor: Napoleone Annovazzi
March 20, 23	Havana Auditorium	*Manon Lescaut* Umberto Borsò, Enzo Sordello, Fernando Corena Conductor: Napoleone Annovazzi
March 26	New York Hunter College	Concert (with pianist Giorgio Favaretto)
April 8, 10, 12, 15	Naples Teatro San Carlo	*La Bohème* Bruna Rizzoli/Adriana Martino, Giuseppe Gismondo, Giuseppe Taddei/Giulio Fioravanti, Saturno Meletti, Fernando Corena Conductor: Angelo Questa
April 23, 26, 29 May 3, 16	Rome Teatro dell'Opera	*Madama Butterfly* Giuseppe Gismondo, Giulio Fioravanti Conductor: Angelo Questa/Ugo Catania
May 21	Rome Teatro Sistina	Concert (with pianist Giorgio Favaretto)
June 5, 8	Paris Opéra	*Aida* Rita Gorr, Dimiter Uzunov, René Bianco, Giorgio Tadeo. Conductor: Georges Sebastian

Chronology

June 12, 30	Vienna State Opera	*Tosca* Eugenio Fernandi, George London, Tito Gobbi, René Bianco, Giorgio Tadeo Conductor: Georges Sebastian
June 15, 19	Vienna State Opera	*Otello* Carlo Guichandut, Tito Gobbi Conductor: Herbert von Karajan
June 22, 27	Vienna State Opera	*Aida* Giulietta Simionato, Eugenio Fernandi, Tito Gobbi, Arnold Van Mill Conductor: Herbert von Karajan
September 9, 12	Vienna State Opera	*Tosca* Eugenio Fernandi, Tito Gobbi Conductor: Herbert von Karajan
September 21, 23	Livorno Teatro La Gran Guardia	*Tosca* Franco Corelli, Anselmo Colzani Conductor: Mario Parenti
October 28	Bologna Teatro Comunale	Concert Conductor: Oliviero De Fabritiis
November 5, 8, 10	Barcelona Teatro Liceo	*Manon Lescaut* Umberto Borsò, Manuel Ausensi, Alfredo Mariotti. Conductor: Angelo Questa
November 14, 19, 22	Barcelona Teatro Liceo	*Tosca* Giuseppe Gismondo, Giangiacomo Guelfi Conductor: Angelo Questa
November 17	Barcelona Teatro Liceo	*La Bohème* Gianni Raimondi, Agostino Ferrin, Ester Mazzoleni. Conductor: Armando La Rosa-Parodi
November 26	Naples Teatro San Carlo	*Adriana Lecouvreur* (only a dress rehearsal) Giulietta Simionato, Franco Corelli, Ettore Bastianini, Antonio Cassinelli Conductor: Mario Rossi
December 9, 12, 16, 19, 27, 30	Milan La Scala	*Tosca* Giuseppe Di Stefano/Gianni Raimondi, Tito Gobbi/Dino Dondi Conductor: Gianandrea Gavazzeni

1960

January 8, 11, 15, 17, 20	Milan La Scala	*Andrea Chénier* Mario Del Monaco/Franco Corelli, Ettore Bastianini/Ugo Savarese Conductor: Gianandrea Gavazzeni

237

RENATA TEBALDI

March 4*, 12, 23 April 13	New York Metropolitan	*La Forza del Destino* Mignon Dunn, Richard Tucker/Kurt Baum/Carlo Bergonzi, Leonard Warren/Mario Sereni/Aurelio Oppicelli, Salvatore Baccaloni/Gerhard Pechner, Jerome Hines/William Wildermann/Cesare Siepi Conductor: Thomas Schippers/Kurt Adler
March 9	Philadelphia Academy of Music	*Simon Boccanegra* Richard Tucker, Frank Guarrera, Ezio Flagello, Giorgio Tozzi. Conductor: Dimitri Mitropoulos
March 15 April 7	New York Metropolitan	*Simon Boccanegra* Richard Tucker, Frank Guarrera/Anselmo Colzani, Ezio Flagello, Giorgio Tozzi/Jerome Hines. Conductor: Dimitri Mitropoulos
March 18, 26	New York Metropolitan	*Andrea Chénier* Richard Tucker, Ettore Bastianini Conductor: Fausto Cleva
March 30	New York Metropolitan	*Tosca* Barry Morell, Hermann Uhde Conductor: Dimitri Mitropoulos
April 2, 10	New York Metropolitan	*Madama Butterfly* Eugenio Fernandi/Barry Morell, Clifford Harvuot/Mario Sereni Conductor: Dimitri Mitropoulos
April 4	New York Carnegie Hall	Concert (with pianist Leonard Bernstein)
April 10	Miami Dade Auditorium	Concert
May 5, 8	Rome Teatro dell'Opera	*Tosca* Daniele Barioni, Giangiacomo Guelfi Conductor: Armando La Rosa Parodi
May 12	Bologna Palasso dello Sport	Concert Conductor: Arturo Basile
May 16	Münich Kongresshalle	Concert Conductor: Carlo Felice Cillario
May 21	Hamburg Musikhalle	Concert Conductor: Carlo Felice Cillario
May 25	Wiesbaden Kurhalle	Concert Conductor: Carlo Felice Cillario
May 30	Stuttgart Liederhalle	Concert Conductor: Carlo Felice Cillario

(*) performance suspended after Act III due to the death of Leonard Warren

Chronology

June 10, 13, 15	Paris Opéra	*Tosca* Albert Lance, Gabriel Bacquier Conductor: Georges Prêtre
June 20, 23	Vienna State Opera	*Tosca* Giuseppe Zampieri/Eugenio Fernandi, Ettore Bastianini. Conductor: Herbert von Karajan/ Berislav Klobucar
June 26, 29	Vienna State Opera	*Andrea Chénier* Franco Corelli, Ettore Bastianini Conductor: Lovro von Matacic
August 5	Rimini	Concert Conductor: Arturo Basile
October 29	Rome RAI Studios	*La Wally* Pinuccia Perotti, Jolanda Gardino, Giacinto Prandelli, Dino Dondi, Silvio Maionica Conductor: Arturo Basile
November 11, 14, 19	Chicago Lyric Opera	*Tosca* Giuseppe Di Stefano, Tito Gobbi Conductor: Gianandrea Gavazzeni
November 23, 25	Chicago Lyric Opera	*Fedora* by Giordano (debut in the lead) Jeanette Scovotti, Giuseppe Di Stefano, Tito Gobbi. Conductor: Lovro von Matacic
November 30 December 3	Chicago Lyric Opera	*Simon Boccanegra* Richard Tucker, Tito Gobbi, Renato Cesari, Ferruccio Mazzoli. Conductor: Gianandrea Gavazzeni
December 14	New York Metropolitan	*Madama Butterfly* (Act II) Clifford Harvuot. Conductor: Jean Morel
December 19 January 6, 12 (1961) February 18	New York Metropolitan	*Simon Boccanegra* Richard Tucker/William Olviz, Frank Guarrera, Ezio Flagello, Giorgio Tozzi. Conductor: Nino Verchi
December 24 January 9 (1961) February 9, 14, 26	New York Metropolitan	*La Bohème* Laurel Hurley/Elisabeth Söderström/Heidi Krall, Eugenio Fernandi/Richard Tucker/Barry Morell,Clifford Harvuot/Frank Guarrera/ Lorenzo Testi/Mario Sereni, Roald Reitan/ Clifford Harvuot, Nicola Moscona/Cesare Siepi/ Jerome Hines. Conductor: Thomas Schippers/George Schick
December 29	New York Metropolitan	*Manon Lescaut* Richard Tucker, Lorenzo Testi, Fernando Corena Conductor: Fausto Cleva

239

1961

January 2, 18 February 5, 21	New York Metropolitan	*Madama Butterfly* Eugenio Fernandi/Nicolai Gedda, Theodor Uppman. Conductor: Jean Morel
January 6	New York	Televised Concert ("Telephone Hour")
February	Miami Dade Auditorium	*Andrea Chénier* Umberto Borsò, Ettore Bastianini
March 5	New York Carnegie Hall	Concert
March 8	Philadelphia Academy of Music	*Madama Butterfly* Eugenio Fernandi, Theodor Uppman Conductor: Jean Morel
April 6, 9	Genoa Teatro Carlo Felice	*Manon Lescaut* Gastone Limarilli, Mario Stecchi, Giorgio Tadeo Conductor: Guiseppe Capuana
April 20, 22, 26, 30	Rome Teatro dell'Opera	*Manon Lescaut* Giuseppe Di Stefano, Afro Poli, Vito De Taranto Conductor: Arturo Basile
May 25	Berlin Deutschlandhalle	Concert Conductor: Giuseppe Patanè
May 29	Baden Baden	Concert Conductor: Giuseppe Patanè
June 3	Stuttgart National Theater	*Tosca* Eugene Tobin, George London Conductor: Giuseppe Patanè
June 10	Parma Teatro Regio	Concert (with Luigi Ottolini and Aldo Protti) Conductor: Arturo Basile
June 17	Lucca	Concerto Pucciniano (with Flaviano Labò, Guiseppe Valdengo). Conductor: Arturo Basile
July 8	Rome RAI Studios	*La Fanciulla del West* by Puccini (debut in the role of Minnie) Daniele Barioni, Giangiacomo Guelfi. Conductor: Arturo Basile
August 10	Fermo Teatro dell'Aquila	*Adriana Lecouvreur* Paola Mantovani, Luciano Panzieri, Saturno Meletti. Conductor: Arturo Basile
August 25 September 3		Tour of Concerts in the German Republic
September 28	Tokyo N.H.K. Hall	*Andrea Chénier* Mario Del Monaco, Aldo Protti Conductor: Franco Capuana

October 10	Tokyo N.H.K. Hall	*Tosca* Gianni Poggi, Giangiacomo Guelfi Conductor: Arturo Basile
October	Osaka	*Andrea Chénier* Mario Del Monaco, Giangiacomo Guelfi Conductor: Franco Capuana
October	Osaka	*Tosca* Gianni Poggi, Giangiacomo Guelfi Conductor: Arturo Basile
November 17, 20, 25	Manila Araneta Coliseum	Concert Conductor: Arturo Basile
November 23	Manila Philamlife Auditorium	Concert Conductor: Arturo Basile
December	Copenhagen Falkoner Theater	*La Bohème* Renato Cioni, Ottavia Garaventa, Lorenzo Gaetani. Conductor: Arturo Basile
December 14, 17, 19	Naples Teatro San Carlo	*Fedora* Sofia Mezzetti, Giuseppe Di Stefano, Mario Sereni. Conductor: Arturo Basile

1962

January 7, 10, 14	Parma Teatro Regio	*La Bohème* Silvana Zanolli, Renato Cioni, Enzo Sordello, Otello Borgonovo, Giorgio Tadeo. Conductor: Arturo Basile
February 10	Langhirano	Concert Luigi Ottolini, Otello Bersellini Conductor: Ferdinando Guarnieri
April 11, 14, 18, 21, 26	Rome Teatro dell'Opera	*Adriana Lecouvreur* Fiorenza Cossotto, Nicola Filacuridi, Renato Cesari. Conductor: Gabriele Santini
May 5, 9, 13	Turin Teatro Nuovo	*Adriana Lecouvreur* Fiorenza Cossotto, Plinio Clabassi, Gastone Limarilli, Giuseppe Valdengo, Carlo Badioli Conductor: Franco Capuana
May 23	Bern Casino	Concert Conductor: Manrico De Tura
June 22, 27, 30*	Florence Teatro Comunale Maggio Musicale Fiorentino	*La Bohème* Jolanda Meneguzzer, Renato Cioni, Rolando Panerai, Giorgio Giorgetti, Nicola Zaccaria Conductor: Tullio Serafin

*In June 30th performance, Tebaldi was replaced after the first act by Alberta Pellegrini.

RENATA TEBALDI

September 1	Berlin Deutsche Oper	*Otello* Hans Beirer, William Dooley Conductor: Giuseppe Patanè
September	Bilbao Teatro Coliseo Alba	*Adriana Lecouvreur* Dora Minarchi, Enzo Tei, Renato Cesari Conductor: Manno Wolf Ferrari
September	Bilbao Teatro Coliseo Alba	*La Forza del Destino* Luciana Piccolo, Flaviano Labò, Mario Zanasi, Renato Cesari, Giuseppe Modesti Conductor: Arturo Basile
September	Oviedo Teatro Campo Amor	*Adriana Lecouvreur* Dora Minarchi, Enzo Tei, Renato Cesari Conductor: Manno Wolf Ferrari
September	Oviedo Teatro Campo Amor	*La Forza del Destino* Luciana Piccolo, Flaviano Labò, Mario Zanasi, Renato Cesari, Giuseppe Modesti Conductor: Arturo Basile
September 28	Amsterdam Concertgebouw	Concert: "Grand Gala du Disque" Conductor: Arturo Basile
December 1, 5, 9	Naples Teatro San Carlo	*Falstaff* Mirella Freni, Fedora Barbieri, Fernanda Cadoni, Agostino Lazzari, Tito Gobbi, Renato Capecchi, Enrico Campi. Conductor: Mario Rossi
December 15, 19, 23	Napoli Teatro San Carlo	*La Bohème* Mariella Adani, Renato Cioni, Mario Zanasi, Renato Cesari, Italo Tajo. Conductor: Arturo Basile

1963

January 21, 28 February 1, 5, 9, 23	New York Metropolitan	*Adriana Lecouvreur* Irene Dalis/Biserka Cvejic, Franco Corelli, Anselmo Colzani, William Wildermann/Lorenzo Alvary. Conductor: Silvio Varviso

1964

March 10	Philadelphia Academy of Music	*La Bohème* Mary Jennings, Regolo Romani, Richard Torigi, Bonaldo Giaiotti. Conductor: Anton Guadagno
March 14	New York Metropolitan	*La Bohème* Laurel Hurley, Sandor Konya, Frank Guarrera, Clifford Harvuot, Jerome Hines Conductor: Fausto Cleva

242

March 22, 26, 30	New York Metropolitan	*Tosca* Franco Corelli/Barry Morell, Tito Gobbi Conductor: Fausto Cleva
April 4, 9, 30 May 9	New York Metropolitan	*Otello* James McCracken, Anselmo Colzani/Robert Merrill. Conductor: Nello Santi
April 15	Boston Music Hall	*La Bohème* Laurel Hurley, Richard Tucker, Calvin Marsh, Jerome Hines. Conductor: Fausto Cleva
April 25	Cleveland Public Auditorium	*La Bohème* Jean Fenn, Franco Corelli, Calvin Marsh, Ezio Flagello. Conductor: George Schick
May 15	Atlanta Fox Theater	*La Bohème* Jean Fenn, Franco Corelli, Calvin Marsh, Jerome Hines. Conductor: Fausto Cleva
May 21	Minneapolis Northrop Auditorium	*La Bohème* Laurel Hurley, Richard Tucker, Calvin Marsh, Jerome Hines. Conductor: Fausto Cleva
May 25	Detroit Masonic Temple	*La Bohème* Jean Fenn, Richard Tucker, Frank Guarrera, Cesare Siepi. Conductor: Fausto Cleva
November 8, 12, 17, 24	Chicago Lyric Opera	*La Bohème* Luisa De Sett, Renato Cioni, Sesto Bruscantini, Renato Cesari, Bruno Marangoni Conductor: Pierre Dervaux
November 29	New York Metropolitan	*La Bohème* (Act I) Carlo Bergonzi, Calvin Marsh, Clifford Harvuot, Cesare Siepi. Conductor: George Schick
December 9, 19 January 6, 30 (1965)	New York Metropolitan	*Simon Boccanegra* George Shirley/Giuseppe Campora, Anselmo Colzani, William Walker/Justino Diaz, Giorgio Tozzi/Jerome Hines. Conductor: Fausto Cleva
December 12 January 12, 18 (1965)	New York Metropolitan	*Tosca* Barry Morell/Richard Tucker/Flaviano Labò, Robert Merrill/Anselmo Colzani Conductor: Nello Santi
December 15	Philadelphia Academy of Music	*Tosca* Giuseppe Di Stefano, Louis Quilico Conductor: Anton Guadagno
December 23, 29	New York Metropolitan	*Otello* Dimiter Uzunov, Robert Merrill Conductor: Kurt Adler

1965

February 5	Cleveland Music Hall	Concert Conductor: Charry
February 8	Washington Constitution Hall	Concert Conductor: Julius Rudel
February 19	Toronto	Televised Concert
February 26	Montreal Place des Arts	Concert Conductor: Anton Guadagno
March	New York	Televised Concert ("Telephone Hour")
March	New York	Televised Concert ("Ed Sullivan Show")
March 31	New York Metropolitan	*La Bohème* (Act I) Franco Corelli, Calvin Marsh, Clifford Harvuot, Cesare Siepi. Conductor: George Schick
April 22	Boston Lyric Opera	*Otello* Dimiter Uzunov, Anselmo Colzani Conductor: Fausto Cleva
April 26	Cleveland Opera Theater	*Tosca* Sandor Konya, Robert Merrill Conductor: Joseph Rosenstock
April 30	Cleveland Opera Theater	*Otello* Dimiter Uzunov, Anselmo Colzani Conductor: Kurt Adler
May 7	Atlanta Civic Center	*Otello* Jon Vickers, Robert Merrill Conductor: Kurt Adler
May 11	Memphis Municipal Auditorium	*Tosca* Franco Corelli, Anselmo Colzani Conductor: Joseph Rosenstock
May 15	Dallas State Fair Music Hall	*Tosca* Richard Tucker, Anselmo Colzani Conductor: Joseph Rosenstock
May 18	St. Louis Opera Theater	*Otello* Jon Vickers, Anselmo Colzani Conductor: Kurt Adler
May 22	Minneapolis Northrop Auditorium	*Tosca* Sandor Konya, Anselmo Colzani Conductor: Joseph Rosenstock
May 26	Detroit Masonic Temple Auditorium	*Otello* Dimiter Uzunov, Anselmo Colzani Conductor: Kurt Adler

May 29	Detroit Masonic Temple Auditorium	*Tosca* Franco Corelli, Anselmo Colzani Conductor: Joseph Rosenstock
June 21	New York Lewisohn Stadium	Concert Conductor: Fausto Cleva
September 10, 16 October 2	San Francisco Opera	*Andrea Chénier* Richard Tucker/Joao Gibin, Ettore Bastianini Conductor: Francesco Molinari-Pradelli
September 19, 23, 29	San Francisco Opera	*La Bohème* Jolanda Meneguzzer/Marie Collier, Sandor Konya/Franco Corelli, Raymond Wolansky, Joshua Hecht. Conductor: Piero Bellugi
October 8, 13, 16, 18	Chicago Lyric Opera	*Mefistofele* Elena Souliotis, Alfredo Kraus, Nicolai Ghiaurov Conductor: Nino Sonzogno
November 5, 8, 11	Dallas Civic Opera	*Tosca* Franco Tagliavini, Giuseppe Taddei Conductor: Nicola Rescigno
November 16	Los Angeles Music Center	*Andrea Chénier* Franco Corelli, Ettore Bastianini Conductor: Francesco Molinari-Pradelli
November 20	Los Angeles Music Center	*La Bohème* Marie Collier, Sandor Konya, Raymond Wolansky, Joshua Hecht Conductor: Piero Bellugi
December 4, 10, 14, 30	New York Metropolitan	*La Bohème* Annelise Rothenberger, Franco Corelli/Sandor Konya, Frank Guarrera/Theodor Uppman, Robert Goodloe, Bonaldo Giaiotti/Jerome Hines Conductor: George Schick/Fausto Cleva
December 21, 27	New York Metropolitan	*Tosca* Sandor Konya, Gabriel Bacquier Conductor: George Schick

1966

January 7 February 26	New York Metropolitan	*Tosca* Sandor Konya/John Alexander, Gabriel Bacquier/ Tito Gobbi. Conductor: George Schick
January 11, 15	New York Metropolitan	*La Bohème* Heidi Krall, Franco Corelli/Sandor Konya, Mario Sereni/Theodor Uppman, Clifford Harvuot, Robert Goodloe, Nicolai Ghiuselev Conductor: George Schick/Fausto Cleva

Renata Tebaldi

January 22	Philadelphia Academy of Music	Concert Conductor: Georges Prêtre
January 25	New York Carnegie Hall	*Mefistofele* (in the roles of Margherita and Elena) Carlo Bergonzi, Nicolai Ghiaurov Conductor: Lamberto Gardelli
January 30 February 5, 10, 15	New York Metropolitan	*Andrea Chénier* Franco Corelli/Carlo Bergonzi, Anselmo Colzani/ Sherrill Milnes. Conductor: Lamberto Gardelli
March 1, 4	Philadelphia Academy of Music	*La Bohème* Maria Candida, Franco Tagliavini, Franco Iglesias. Conductor: Silvio Varviso
March 8	Montreal	Concert Conductor: Malcolm Sargent
March 15	Baltimore	Concert Conductor: Kurt Adler
March 18	Grand Rapids Auditorium	Concert Conductor: Karapetian
March 21	Milwaukee Pabst Theatre	Concert Conductor: Brown
March 25	Chicago	Concert Conductor: Anton Guadagno
March 28	New Orleans	Concert Conductor: Werner Torkanowsky
April 2	Vancouver	Concert Conductor: Müller
April 16	New York Metropolitan	Concert: "Last Night at the Met" Conductor: Fausto Cleva
April 19	Boston War Memorial Auditorium	*Andrea Chénier* Franco Corelli, Mario Sereni, Conductor: George Schick
April 26 May 1	Boston Back Bay Theater	*La Bohème* Adele Leigh, Placido Domingo, Peter Glossop, Boris Carmeli. Conductor: Vincent La Selva
June 21, 25	Montreal Place des Arts	*Otello* Mario Del Monaco, Tito Gobbi Conductor: Alberto Erede
July 1	New York Lewisohn Stadium	*La Bohème* Laurel Hurley, John Alexander, Russell Christopher, John Macurdy. Conductor: George Schick

Chronology

August 13	New York Stadium	Concert Conductor: Lamberto Gardelli
September 18	New York	Televised Concert (with Franco Corelli)
September 22 October 10, 22, 29 November 3, 10, 14, 23, 29 December 11	New York Metropolitan	*La Gioconda* by Ponchielli (debut in the role of La Gioconda) Biserka Cvejic/Mignon Dunn, Mignon Dunn/Belen Amparan/Ruza Baldini, Franco Corelli/Richard Tucker/Cornell MacNeil/ Anselmo Colzani, Cesare Siepi/Bonaldo Giaiotti/ Giorgio Tozzi. Conductor: Fausto Cleva
October 18	Philadelphia Academy of Music	*La Gioconda* Mignon Dunn, Lili Chookasian, Franco Corelli, Anselmo Colzani, Joshua Hecht Conductor: Anton Guadagno
December 15	Philadelphia Academy of Music	Concert (with Licia Albanese, Franco Corelli, Flaviano Labò, Bonaldo Giaiotti) Conductor: Anton Guadagno

1967

January 1	New York	Televised Concert ("The First Ladies of Opera," with Birgit Nilsson, Leontyne Price and Joan Sutherland)
January 17	Philadelphia Academy of Music	*Tosca* Gianni Raimondi, Gabriel Bacquier Conductor: Fausto Cleva
Febuary 24, 27 March 6	Boston Back Bay Theatre	*Otello* Claude Heater, Ramon Vinay Conductor: Osbourne McConathy
March 11	Washington Constitution Hall	Concert Conductor: Howard Mitchell
March 14	Boston War Memorial Auditorium	Concert
March 18, 22 April 7, 11	New York Metropolitan	*La Bohème* Jean Fenn/Marie Collier, Barry Morell/Franco Corelli/George Shirley, Theodor Uppman/Mario Sereni, Robert Goodloe, Bonaldo Giaiotti/Cesare Siepi. Conductor: Fausto Cleva
March 27 April 15	New York Metropolitan	*La Gioconda* Rosalind Elias, Belen Amparan, Franco Corelli/ Barry Morell, Cornell MacNeil, Bonaldo Giaiotti/Cesare Siepi. Conductor: Fausto Cleva

247

April 3	New Haven	Concert Conductor: Brieff
April 18	Boston War Memorial Auditorium	*La Gioconda* Rosalind Elias, Belen Amparan, Barry Morell, Cornell MacNeil, Cesare Siepi Conductor: Fausto Cleva
April 24	Cleveland Public Auditorium	*La Gioconda* Rosalind Elias, Belen Amparan, Franco Corelli, Cornell MacNeil, Justino Diaz Conductor: Fausto Cleva
May 1	Atlanta Fox Theater	*La Gioconda* Rosalind Elias, Belen Amparan, Franco Corelli, Cornell MacNeil, Bonaldo Giaiotti Conductor: Fausto Cleva
May 8	Memphis Ellis Auditorium	*La Gioconda* Rosalind Elias, Belen Amparan, Franco Corelli, Cornell MacNeil, Bonaldo Giaiotti Conductor: Fausto Cleva
May 12	Dallas Fair Park Auditorium	*La Gioconda* Rosalind Elias, Belen Amparan, Franco Corelli, Cornell MacNeil, Bonaldo Giaiotti Conductor: Fausto Cleva
May 17	Minneapolis Northrop Auditorium	*La Gioconda* Nell Rankin, Belen Amparan, Franco Corelli, Cornell MacNeil, Bonaldo Giaiotti Conductor: Fausto Cleva
May 26	Detroit Masonic Temple Auditorium	*La Gioconda* Rosalind Elias, Ruza Baldani, Franco Corelli, Cornell MacNeil, Bonaldo Giaiotti Conductor: Fausto Cleva
June 3	Philadelphia Civic Center	*La Gioconda* Rosalind Elias, Ruza Baldani, Franco Corelli, Cornell MacNeil, Bonaldo Giaiotti Conductor: Fausto Cleva
June 15, 20	New York Metropolitan	*La Gioconda* Rosalind Elias, Belen Amparan, Richard Tucker, Cornell MacNeil, Bonaldo Giaiotti Conductor: Fausto Cleva
August 25	Newport Festival	*Otello* Jon Vickers, Peter Glossop. Conductor: Kurt Adler
August 27	Providence	*Otello* Jon Vickers, Peter Glossop Conductor: Kurt Adler

Chronology

September 21, 25, 30 October 6, 27 November 18, 22, 29	New York Metropolitan	*La Gioconda* Biserka Cvejic/Nell Rankin/Rosalind Elias/ Rosalind Elias/Belen Amparan/Joann Grillo, Flaviano Labò/Barry Morell/Franco Corelli, Sherrill Milnes/Anselmo Colzani, Bonaldo Giaiotti/John Macurdy, Jerome Hines Conductor: Fausto Cleva
October 21, 31 November 4, 9, 13	New York Metropolitan	*Manon Lescaut* Richard Tucker/George Shirley, William Walker/ John Reardon,Raymond Michalski Conductor: Francesco Molinari-Pradelli
December 5, 8	Philadelphia Academy of Music	*Otello* Pier Miranda Ferraro, Jon Vickers, Louis Quilico Conductor: Anton Guadagno
December 26, 30 January 3, 7 (1968)	Naples Teatro San Carlo	*La Gioconda* Franca Mattiucci, Margherita Rochow, Gianfranco Cecchele/Renato Cioni, Anselmo Colzani, Paolo Washington Conductor: Lamberto Gardelli

1968

February 15	Hartford Bushnell Memorial	*Manon Lescaut* Placido Domingo, Enzo Sordello Conductor: Anton Guadagno
February 24 March 2	New York Metropolitan	*La Gioconda* Fiorenza Cossotto/Mignon Dunn, Belen Amparan/Lili Chookasian/Joann Grillo, Franco Corelli/Carlo Bergonzi, Cornell MacNeil, Bonaldo Giaiotti, John Macurdy, Jerome Hines Conductor: Fausto Cleva
March 6, 13	New York Carnegie Hall	*La Wally* Isabel Penagos, Deborah Kieffer, Carlo Bergonzi, Peter Glossop, Andrzej Saciuk Conductor: Fausto Cleva
March 16	New York Metropolitan	Concert: *La Regata Veneziana* by Rossini Conductor: Thomas Schippers
March 18 April 13, 18	New York Metropolitan	*Tosca* John Alexander/Franco Corelli, Cornell MacNeil/ Anselmo Colzani Conductor: George Schick/Zubin Mehta
March 23, 29 April 3, 10	New York Metropolitan	*Manon Lescaut* John Alexander/Richard Tucker, William Walker, Frank Guarrera/Mario Sereni, Raymond Michalski. Conductor: F. Molinari-Pradelli

| September 16,
21, 28
October 2, 8,
16, 25, 29
November 4 | New York
Metropolitan | *Adriana Lecouvreur*
Irene Dalis/Elena Cernei/Regina Resnik, Franco
Corelli/Placido Domingo, Anselmo Colzani,
Morley Meredith, Lorenzo Alvary
Conductor: Fausto Cleva |

1969

March 8 April 3, 7	New York Metropolitan	*Tosca* Sandor Konya/Placido Domingo/Barry Morell, Anselmo Colzani Conductor: Francesco Molinari-Pradelli
March 14, 20, 24 April 19	New York Metropolitan	*Adriana Lecouvreur* Nell Rankin/Regina Resnik/Irene Dalis, Placido Domingo/Franco Corelli, Anselmo Colzani, Morley Meredith, Lorenzo Alvary Conductor: Fausto Cleva
April 12, 16, 28	New York Metropolitan	*La Bohème* Clarice Carson/Judith De Paul, Barry Morell/ Franco Corelli, Frank Guarrera/Mario Sereni, Gene Boucher/Russell Christopher, Bonaldo Giaiotti. Conductor: Francesco Molinari-Pradelli/ Kurt Adler
April 25	Boston War Memorial Auditorium	*Adriana Lecouvreur* Regina Resnik, Franco Corelli, Anselmo Colzani, Lorenzo Alvary. Conductor: Jan Behr
May 2	Cleveland Public Auditorium	*Adriana Lecouvreur* Irene Dalis, Franco Corelli, Anselmo Colzani, Lorenzo Alvary. Conductor: Jan Behr
May 8	Atlanta Civic Center	*Adriana Lecouvreur* Nell Rankin, Franco Corelli, Anselmo Colzani, Morley Meredith. Conductor: Jan Behr
May 15	Dallas State Fair Music Hall	*Adriana Lecouvreur* Irene Dalis, Franco Corelli, Anselmo Colzani, Morley Behr. Conductor: Jan Behr
May 23	Minneapolis Northrop Auditorium	*Adriana Lecouvreur* Nell Rankin, Franco Corelli, Anselmo Colzani, Lorenzo Alvary. Conductor: Jan Behr
May 27	Detroit Masonic Temple Auditorium	*Adriana Lecouvreur* Nell Rankin, Franco Corelli, Anselmo Colzani, Lorenzo Alvary. Conductor: Jan Behr
June 2	New York Metropolitan	*Tosca* Franco Corelli, Anselmo Colzani Conductor: George Schick

Chronology

June 7	New York Metropolitan	*La Bohème* Clarice Carson, Franco Corelli, William Walker, Russell Christopher, Bonaldo Giaiotti Conductor: Carlo Franci
October 17	New York Philharmonic Hall	Concert Lucine Amara, Shirley Love, Richard Tucker, George Shirley, John Alexander, Cornell MacNeil, Paul Plishka, William Walker
December 2	Philadelphia Academy of Music	*La Bohème* Franco Corelli, John Darrenkamp Conductor: Anton Guadagno
December 13	Cleveland Public Auditorium	Concert: *Simon Boccanegra* Richard Tucker, Cornell MacNeil, Ezio Flagello Conductor: James Levine
December 31 January 3, 7, 10 (1970)	New York Metropolitan	*Tosca* Sandor Konya, Cornell MacNeil Conductor: Francesco Molinari-Pradelli

1970

January 15, 24	New York Metropolitan	*La Bohème* Colette Boky/Clarice Carson, Ion Buzea/Richard Tucker, William Walker, Gene Boucher, Cesare Siepi. Conductor: Fausto Cleva
February 11, 21, 25 March 2, 14	New York Metropolitan	*La Fanciulla del West* by Puccini (debut in the role of Minnie) Sandor Konya, Giangiacomo Guelfi, Anselmo Colzani Conductor: Fausto Cleva/Jan Behr
March 19	Miami Auditorium	Concert (with Franco Corelli)
April 11	New York Metropolitan	*La Gioconda* (Act II) Rosalind Elias, Richard Tucker, Cornell MacNeil Conductor: Kurt Adler
April 20	Boston Civic Auditorium	*La Bohème* Colette Boky, Carlo Bergonzi, Mario Sereni, Robert Goodloe, John Macurdy Conductor: Francesco Molinari-Pradelli
October 9, 14, 19, 29 November 15, 23, 28 December 15, 23, 28	New York Metropolitan	*Andrea Chénier* Carlo Bergonzi/Placido Domingo/Richard Tucker, Anselmo Colzani/Cornell MacNeil Conductor: Fausto Cleva/Kurt Adler

251

1971

January 5	Philadelphia Academy of Music	*Otello* Jon Vickers, Peter Glossop Conductor: Anton Guadagno

1972

February 25 March 2, 7, 15, 18, 23 April 1	New York Metropolitan	*Falstaff* Jeannette Pilou/Judith Blegen/Roberta Peters, Regina Resnik/Lili Chookasian, Joann Grillo, Luigi Alva, Geraint Evans/Tito Gobbi, Kostas Paskalis/Matteo Manuguerra, Richard Best. Conductor: Christoph Von Dohnanyi
November 27	Memphis	Concert with Franco Corelli (with pianist Geoffrey Parsons)
December 1	New Orleans	Concert with Franco Corelli (with pianist Geoffrey Parsons)
December 6	San Antonio	Concert with Franco Corelli (with pianist Geoffrey Parsons)
December 10	Columbus (Ohio)	Concert with Franco Corelli (with pianist Geoffrey Parsons)
December 15	Washington	Concert with Franco Corelli (with pianist Geoffrey Parsons)
December 20	Philadelphia Academy of Music	Concert with Franco Corelli (with pianist Geoffrey Parsons)

1973

January 2, 5, 8	New York Metropolitan	*Otello* James McCracken, Sherrill Milnes Conductor: James Levine
February 13	Birmingham Municipal Auditorium	Concert
February 21	Tempe (Arizona) Grady Grammage Auditorium	Concert
February 26	Los Angeles The Pavillion	Concert (with pianist Peter Schaaf)
March 1	San Francisco Opera House	Concert (with pianist Martin Katz)
March 11	Seattle Opera House	Concert

Chronology

March 16	Vancouver Queen Elisabeth Hall	Concert (with pianist Martin Katz)
March 23	Boston Symphony Hall	Concert (with pianist Martin Katz)
March 27	Syracuse Loew's Theater	Concert (with pianist Martin Katz)
April 1	New York Carnegie Hall	Concert (with pianist Martin Katz)
April 6	Ottawa National Arts Center	Concert (with pianist Martin Katz)
April 11	Philadelphia Academy of Music	Concert (with pianist Martin Katz)
April 17	Liberty Gano Hall	Concert
May 3	Jackson Municipal Auditorium	Concert
May 8	New Haven Woolsey Hall	Concert (with pianist Martin Katz)
July 7	Cincinnati Music Hall	Concert with Franco Corelli Conductor: Anton Guadagno
July 12	Ambler (Pennsylvania) Temple University Festival	Concert with Franco Corelli Conductor: Ling Tung
October 9	London Albert Hall	Concert with Franco Corelli (with pianist Gordon Jephtas)
October 14	Vienna Musikverein	Concert with Franco Corelli (with pianist Gordon Jephtas)
October 23, 27	Manila New Music Center	Concert with Franco Corelli
October 31	Manila Araneata Coliseum	Concert with Franco Corelli Conductor: Luis C. Valencia
November 7, 24	Tokyo Auditorium Bunka Kaikan	Concert with Franco Corelli Conductor: Tadashi Mori
November 10	Osaka Osaka Festival Hall	Concert with Franco Corelli Conductor: Tadashi Mori

November 14, 17	Seoul Sport Palace	Concert with Franco Corelli
November 21	Tokyo N.H.K. Hall	Concert with Franco Corelli Conductor: Tadashi Mori
November 24	Mito Ibaragi-Kenritsu Kemmin Bunka Center	Concert with Franco Corelli Conductor: Kotaro Sato
November 27	Hong Kong	Concert with Franco Corelli

1974

February 12	Palm Beach	Concert with Franco Corelli
February 23	New York Brooklyn College	Concert with Franco Corelli (with pianist Eugene Kohn)
February 26	Miami Auditorium	Concert with Franco Corelli
March 10	Washington	Concert
May 5	Long Island Post College	Concert with Franco Corelli
May 15	Milan Piccola Scala	Concert (with pianist Martin Katz)
May 20	Milan La Scala	Concert (with pianist Martin Katz)
May 30	Mantua Teatro Sociale	Concert (with pianist Eugene Kohn)
June 3	Como Teatro Sociale	Concert (with pianist Eugene Kohn)
June 7	Turin	Concert (with pianist Eugene Kohn)
June 12	Pavia Teatro Fraschini	Concert (with pianist Eugene Kohn)
June 21	Reykjavik Sport Palace	Concert Conductor: Vladimir Ashkenazy
June 28	Vienna Musikverein	Concert with Franco Corelli (with pianist Eugene Kohn)
July 7	Rimini Tempio Malatestiano	*Stabat Mater* by Pergolesi Lucia Valentini Terrani Conductor: Carlo Zecchi

October 11, 14	Paris Espace Cardin	Concert (with pianist Martin Katz)
October 17	Anvers Koningin Elisabethzaal	Concert (with pianist Martin Katz)
October 20	Mannheim Rosengarten	Concert (with pianist Edoardo Muller) Inaugural concert for the theater
November 12	Amsterdam Concertgebouw	Concert (with pianist Edoardo Muller)
December 4	Barcelona Palau de la Musica	Concert (with pianist Edoardo Muller)
December 11	Madrid	Concert
December 19	Valencia	Concert (stopped after the first part)

1975

September 27	Martina Franca	Concert (with pianist Edoardo Muller)
October 5	Warsaw Philharmonic Hall	Concert (with pianist Edoardo Muller)
October 9	Kiev Palace of Culture	Concert (with pianist Edoardo Muller)
October 17, 20	Leningrad Philharmonic Hall	Concert (with pianist Edoardo Muller)
October 13	Moscow Hall of Congress	Concert (with pianist Edoardo Muller)
November 15	Naples Teatro San Carlo	Concert (with pianist Edoardo Muller)
December 15	Novara Teatro Coccia	Concert (with pianist Edoardo Muller)
December 19	Biella Teatro Odeon	Concert (with pianist Edoardo Muller)

1976

January 16	New York Carnegie Hall	Concert (with pianist Martin Katz)

255

Renata Tebaldi

February 6	Brooklyn	Concert
February 19	New York Carnegie Hall	Concert (with pianist Martin Katz)
March 27	Brescia Teatro Grande	Concert (with pianist Edoardo Muller)
April 25	Busseto Teatro Verdi	Concert (with pianist Edoardo Muller)
April	San Marino	Concert
May 23	Milan La Scala	Concert (with pianist Edoardo Muller)

✦Discography of the Operas✦

ADRIANA LECOUVREUR *Cilea*	1962 DECCA	Del Monaco, Fioravanti, Simionato Orchestra and Chorus of The Academy of St. Cecilia of Rome. Conductor: Franco Capuana
AIDA *Verdi*	1952 DECCA Reprinted 1966, 1970	Stignani, Del Monaco, Protti, Caselli, Corena Orchestra and Chorus of The Academy of St. Cecilia of Rome. Conductor: Alberto Erede
	1958 DECCA	Simionato, Bergonzi, MacNeil, Van Mill, Corena Philharmonic Orchestra of Vienna Conductor: Von Karajan
ANDREA CHÉNIER *Giordano*	1953 CETRA Reprinted 1967	Soler, Savarese, Ferrein Orchestra and Chorus of the RAI of Turin Conductor: A. Basile
	1957 DECCA	Del Monaco, Bastianini, Cossotto, Maionica Orchestra and Chorus of The Academy of St. Cecilia of Rome Conductor: G. Gavazzeni
LA BOHÈME *Puccini*	1951 DECCA Reprinted 1961, 1967, 1970	Prandelli, Inghilleri, Corena, Ariè, Luise, Guden Orchestra and Chorus of The Academy of St. Cecilia of Rome Conductor: Alberto Erede
	1959 DECCA	Bergonzi, Bastianini, Cesari, Siepi, Corena, D'Angelo Orchestra and Chorus of The Academy of St. Cecilia of Rome Conductor: Tullio Serafin
UN BALLO IN MASCHERA *Verdi*	1970 DECCA	Pavarotti, Milnes, Resnik, Donath, Monreale, Christon Orchestra and Chorus of The Academy of St. Cecilia of Rome Conductor: B. Bartoletti
CAVALLERIA RUSTICANA *Mascagni*	1958 DECCA Reprinted 1974	Björling, Bastianini, Danieli Orchestra and Chorus of the Maggio Musicale Fiorentino Conductor: A. Erede
DON CARLO *Verdi*	1965 DECCA	Bergonzi, Ghiaurov, Fischer-Dieskau, Bumbry, Talvela Orchestra and Chorus of Covent Garden of London Conductor: G. Solti

LA FANCIULLA DEL WEST *Puccini*	1958 DECCA Reprinted 1970	Del Monaco, MacNeil, Tozzi Orchestra and Chorus of The Academy of St. Cecilia of Rome Conductor: F. Capuana
LA FORZA DEL DESTINO *Verdi*	1955 DECCA Reprinted 1959, 1970	Del Monaco, Bastianini, Siepi, Corena, Simionato Orchestra and Chorus of The Academy of St. Cecilia of Rome Conductor: F. Molinari Pradelli
GIANNI SCHICCHI *Puccini*	1962 DECCA	Corena Lazzari, Danieli Orchestra and Chorus of The Academy of St. Cecilia of Rome Conductor: L. Gardelli
LA GIOCONDA *Ponchielli*	1967 DECCA	Bergonzi, Horne, Merrill, Ghiuselev, Dominguez Orchestra and Chorus of The Academy of St. Cecilia of Rome Conductor: L. Gardelli
MADAMA BUTTERFLY *Puccini*	1951 DECCA Reprinted 1959, 1967	Rankin, Campora, Inghilleri Orchestra and Chorus of The Academy of St. Cecilia of Rome Conductor: A. Erede
	1958 DECCA	Cossotto, Bergonzi, Sordello Orchestra and Chorus of The Academy of St. Cecilia of Rome Conductor: Tullio Serafin
MANON LESCAUT *Puccini*	1954 DECCA Reprinted 1971	Boriello, Del Monaco, Corena, De Palma, Zagonara, Ribacchi Orchestra and Chorus of The Academy of St. Cecilia of Rome Conductor: F. Molinari Pradelli
MEFISTOFELE *Boito*	1957 DECCA Reprinted 1970	Siepi, Del Monaco, Cavalli, Danieli Orchestra and Chorus of The Academy of St. Cecilia of Rome Conductor: T. Serafin
OTELLO *Verdi*	1954 DECCA Reprinted 1970	Del Monaco, Protti, De Palma Orchestra and Chorus of The Academy of St. Cecilia of Rome Conductor: A. Erede
	1960 DECCA	Del Monaco, Protti, Romano Philharmonic Orchestra of Vienna, Chorus of State Opera, Vienna Conductor: Von Karajan

Discography

SUOR ANGELICA *Puccini*	1962 DECCA	Simionato Orchestra and Chorus of the Maggio Musicale Fiorentino Conductor: L. Gardelli
TABARRO *Puccini*	1962 DECCA	Merrill, Del Monaco, Ercolani, Danieli Orchestra and Chorus of the Maggio Musicale Fiorentino Conductor: L. Gardelli
TOSCA *Puccini*	1952 DECCA Reprinted 1962, 1970	Campora, Mascherini, Corena Orchestra and Chorus of The Academy of St. Cecilia of Rome Conductor: A. Erede
	1959 DECCA Reprinted 1971	Del Monaco, London, Corena Orchestra and Chorus of The Academy of St. Cecilia of Rome Conductor: F. Molinari Pradelli
LA TRAVIATA *Verdi*	1954 DECCA Reprinted 1964, 1966, 1970	Poggi, Protti Orchestra and Chorus of The Academy of St. Cecilia of Rome Conductor: F. Molinari Pradelli
IL TROVATORE *Verdi*	1956 DECCA Reprinted 1971	Savarese, Simionato, Del Monaco, Tozzi Orchestra of the Grand Théâtre of Geneva, Chorus of the Maggio Musicale Fiorentino Conductor: A. Erede
TURANDOT *Puccini*	1953 DECCA Reprinted 1958	Bork, Del Monaco, Zaccaria, Corena, Ercolani, Carlin Orchestra and Chorus of The Academy of St. Cecilia of Rome Conductor: A. Erede
	1960 RCA	Nilsson, Björling, Tozzi, Sereni, Frascati De Palma Orchestra and Chorus of the Rome Opera Conductor: E. Leinsdorf
LA WALLY *Catalani*	1968 DECCA	Diaz, Cappuccilli, Del Monaco, Malagù, Marimpiandri Orchestra of the Monte Carlo Opera, Chorus of Turin Conductor: F. Cleva

259

❧Index❧

Index

261

Index

Photo Sources

E. Pesci (1), Giovanni Barbieri - Langhirano (5), Castagneri - Parma (7), Montacchini - Parma (10), Bruno of Hollywood - New York (11), Erio Piccagliani - Milan (12, 40, 81, 100, 101), Archivo fotografico, La Scala - Milan (14, 15, 16), Foto troncone - Naples (18, 62, 63), London Records, *A Tebaldi Festival* (19, 28, 35), Louis Mélançon, Metropolitan Opera - New York (21, 31, 34, 47, 50, 51, 56, 59, 64, 65, 66, 69, 70, 72, 88, 92), Charles Rossi - New York (22), James Woods (24), Sedge LeBlang, courtesy Metropolitan Opera Guild (25, 27), Metropolitan Opera Archives - New York (26, 32, 33, 46), from the collection of Robert Tuggle - New York (29, 48 - UPI photo), Carlos Perez de Rozas - Barcelona (39), *Time* Magazine (41), Atelier Dietrich - Vienna (42), Nancy Sorensen - Chicago (44, 45), UPI photo (48, 73), Farabola - Milan (49), Fayer - Vienna (53), *Washington Post* (57), Ansa - Milan (58), Don Soucy - New York (67), Margaret Norton - Boston (74), D. Minghini - Rimini (95, 97), Gianni Galloni - Langhirano (106), Dalmazio - Busseto (104, 107), Lelli and Masotti, La Scala - Milan (111).

Other photographs are from the private collections of Renata Tebaldi, Connie DeCaro, Carlamaria Casanova, Cole Lassen, Judith Goldberg, Graziella Merendino and Andrew Farkas.

265

MY BROTHER HAS
AIDS

MY BROTHER HAS
AIDS

DEBORAH DAVIS

A Jean Karl Book

ATHENEUM 1994 NEW YORK

Maxwell Macmillan Canada
Toronto
Maxwell Macmillan International
New York Oxford Singapore Sydney

Copyright © 1994 by Deborah Davis

Atheneum
Macmillan Publishing Company
866 Third Avenue
New York, NY 10022

Maxwell Macmillan Canada, Inc.
1200 Eglinton Avenue East
Suite 200
Don Mills, Ontario M3C 3N1

Macmillan Publishing Company is part of the
Maxwell Communication Group of Companies.

First edition
Printed in the United States of America
10   9   8   7   6   5   4   3   2   1
The text of this book is set in 12 point Transitional 521

Library of Congress Cataloging-in-Publication Data
Davis, Deborah.
My brother has AIDS / Deborah Davis.—1st. ed.
p.   cm.
"A Jean Karl book."
Summary: When her older brother returns home because he is dying of AIDS,
thirteen-year-old Lacy deals with changes in her family life, in relationships with
classmates, and in her commitment to her swimming team.
ISBN 0-689-31922-3
[1. AIDS (Disease)—Fiction. 2. Brothers and sisters—Fiction. 3. Family life—
Fiction. 4. Swimming—Fiction.] I. Title
PZ7.D28586My 1994
[Fic]—dc20   93-38889

**For Dwight,
with much, much love**
_____

CHAPTER
1

Lacy dived a shallow dive off her friend's dock into the warm lake. Her arms churned, each hand entering the water as if sliding under tight bedcovers, the way Coach had taught her.

Why didn't Jack write to *me?* she wondered, and the question hurt. She swam harder. Swimming could make her forget her disappointments, at least for a while.

Stretch, pull, stretch, pull—her arms found a rhythm, but the image of the letter that arrived with the morning mail intruded: the address written to her mother and father only, more legible than usual, no nicknames, no colored inks.

I hate it when he leaves me out, she thought. It wasn't the first time he'd done it, and she resented it every time. She kicked hard and a pain shot through her lower leg, a warning to warm up slowly.

Pull, kick, glide. The hurt eased, but her curiosity remained: What's he writing about *this* time?

Reaching another dock, she turned, switching to butterfly for the forty yards back to Emma's. Nearing it, she heard voices calling her name and she waved to her friends before turning again to swim another lap of crawl.

When she climbed onto Emma's dock and walked toward her friend, she felt awkward and ungainly, a land creature again. She inched her shoulders forward and tugged at her bathing suit, feeling that it didn't quite cover.

"Can't wait for swim practice to start, huh, Lacy?" Emma waved a half-eaten Mars bar at her. "Bite?"

Lacy shook her head. "I'm just getting a head start so I can knock some of the competition out of the pool this year." Lacy dropped onto a towel beside Emma, pulled off her bathing cap, and shook out her brown curly hair. "Em," she said quietly, glancing at the three boys throwing a Frisbee on Emma's lawn, "my parents got another *private* letter from my brother."

"Private? He left you out?"

"Yup. It came this morning, addressed to 'Mr. and Mrs. Mullins' only, and they're still out on the boat, so I haven't had a chance to read it." She looked out toward the sailboats and powerboats cruising the lake.

"Maybe this time he's writing about a *girl*friend."

"I doubt it. I don't think he's dated a girl since he took Wendy to their junior prom."

"Was that a scam, him and Wendy going to the prom together?" Emma asked. "Did she know about Jack?"

"Maybe. Or maybe he was really hot for her."

"I'll bet they were just doing each other a favor. I know! Maybe he's got a new boyfriend and he wants to bring him home to meet you all."

"And dump Lincoln? They're practically married. I just hope Jack does come for a visit—with Lincoln, with a girlfriend, whatever. I haven't seen him in four years. Shhh. Here come the boys."

Eddie cannonballed into the water beside Lacy, soaking her with spray.

"You twit, Eddie!" she yelled.

Bjorn dropped onto his towel and closed his eyes, mumbling, "Did you guys know Lacy misses the pool so much she wears chlorine as a perfume?"

"I heard she sleeps in her racing suit, in a tub full of water," Kerry teased.

"Yeah—wearing fins and a bathing cap, too," said Bjorn.

"*And* goggles," Kerry added.

"Cut it, you guys," Lacy said.

Bjorn rolled over. "She dreams about lanes. Not memory lane, not lovers' lane, but Lacy's lane. It's a loop, so she can swim forever."

"Excellent idea!" Lacy exclaimed. She stood up. "C'mon you finless freaks. Beat you to that other dock!"

CHAPTER

2

Bicycling home from Emma's, Lacy followed the narrow two-lane road that skirted the lake, passing stretches of woods, trimmed and overgrown lawns, cottages and rambling houses. For a few moments she missed Jack the way she did when she was five and he left home to go to college and she cried at the top of the jungle gym every day during recess for a week. She thought of the gifts Jack had brought her each Christmas: a copy of *The Velveteen Rabbit*, which Jack patiently read to her three times in a row without pause; a red and white checkered stuffed bear that she named Mr. Huggins; and her first pair of swim goggles, which she unwrapped and insisted on wearing all through dinner.

A quarter-mile from Emma's she turned into her own driveway and wheeled her bicycle under the porch.

She found her mother in the kitchen, staring at a cup of steaming coffee. The letter from Jack lay on the counter, tucked halfway into its torn envelope.

"What's up with Jack, Mom?" She reached for the letter.

Her mother spoke sharply. "He wrote just to your father and me!"

Lacy withdrew her hand. "Well, *excuse* me. I just wanted to know how he's doing."

When her mother picked up her coffee mug, Lacy saw her mother's hand was trembling.

"What's wrong?"

"Nothing, Lacy. I just need a few minutes alone." Her mother smoothed the graying hair above her ears.

"Must be a big nothing." She waited, shifting from one foot to the other uneasily. Her mother smoothed her hair again, a familiar, nervous gesture. "Okay," Lacy said, talking over her shoulder as she retreated to her room. "I'll be upstairs, studying. Second week of school and we're having a test already. And I need to talk to you. My bathing suits are getting too small. And Julia's mother wants to split the driving to swim meets."

In her bedroom, one corner of the poster of Olympic swimmer Janet Evans had sprung loose. She searched for a thumbtack and fixed it. Opening a *National Geographic* magazine to an article on African primates, she laid it on the floor, then took a framed snapshot of herself and Jack off the bureau and stretched out beside the magazine on the carpet.

The photo was taken the summer before Jack left

for college, when he took a job cooking meals and doing household chores for feeble Mr. Bowler. She remembered sitting on the back porch that summer, overhearing her father and Jack in the kitchen. Her father asked Jack to work in one of his two hardware stores for the rest of the summer. Jack answered "No," and her father got angry.

"I've got at least a dozen guys working for me whose sons are dying to come work in my stores," her father said.

"Great," answered Jack. "Then you don't need me."

"How do you think it feels that my son doesn't want to work there? Doesn't even drop by?"

"I'm busy with my own stuff," protested Jack.

"Your own *stuff*. Being a housemaid for an old man?" Her father's voice was icy. "I think your stuff is for sissies."

Jack burst through the door and ran past Lacy down the porch steps. Scared and upset by her father's temper, Lacy ran around to the front door to find her mother.

Later her mother sent her across the neighbor's yard to Mr. Bowler's to tell Jack their supper was ready. She stood outside the kitchen window unseen. Frogs cheeped in the fading light. The old man held his head in his hands. Jack leaned forward, hands clasped in front of him on the table, talking earnestly. A pizza steamed between them. Lacy watched the old man lift his head and listen intently to her brother.

Lacy heard her mother climbing the stairs, and she put the photo back on her bureau.

"Lacy . . ." Her mother paused outside the door, "I need to talk to you . . . about Jack." Her mother came in, sat on the bed, and gazed out the window. Lacy looked down at the magazine photographs of baboons, then back to her mother, who was now rubbing one hand with the thumb of the other. Then her mother looked straight at her, and Lacy saw a strange twist to her mouth.

"Lacy, there is something I need to tell you." She paused.

It's about time, Lacy thought. Her mother looked so uncomfortable that Lacy felt a little sorry for her.

"I already know, Mom."

Her mother looked surprised and alarmed. "You do?"

"About Jack being gay?" She spoke in a rush. "I already figured that out, after we saw him in Colorado. It wasn't difficult." Her mother stared at her. "And"—Lacy looked away, feeling a little sheepish—"I read the letter he wrote after that trip. The one where he told you about him and Lincoln. I know it wasn't addressed to me." She looked at her mother. "But I don't get what the secret is. It's not such a big deal, Mom. Come out of the dark—"

Her mother shook her head. Lacy waited, curious, a small tightness in her belly.

"Jack has AIDS."

Lacy drew in a breath sharply. "What?" She fought off a sense of horror, hoping she had heard wrong.

Her mother's voice sounded scratchy, as if the words were being pulled out. "He's got AIDS, Lacy."

Lacy felt like the wind had been knocked out of her. "So he's going to die?"

"No!" Her mother cut her off harshly, then softened her voice. "I don't know exactly what will happen to him." She went back to staring out the window and rubbing the spot on her hand.

Lacy took a deep breath, trying to slow her racing heart. "I can't believe it. How did he get it?"

Her mother bit her lower lip. "His damn boyfriend. Lincoln." She shook her head slowly.

"Lincoln?" exclaimed Lacy. "How could he? How could he have given it to Jack? I mean, why would he? Weren't they . . . I mean, why didn't they . . ." She stopped, stunned. "Mom, what *happened*?"

Her mother stood up and began pacing back and forth, wringing her hands. "Lincoln was infected by a previous, uh . . . boyfriend. When he and Jack started to . . . date, Lincoln didn't know he'd already been infected, until he showed signs of being sick. And by then"—she practically spit out the words—"it was too late. He'd infected Jack." She stopped pacing and rubbed her forehead. "Lincoln is dead, and Jack wrote that he is very ill. He wants to come home."

"Wow. I can't believe it," Lacy murmured.

Her mother walked over to the window and ran a finger along the venetian blind. "I need to dust in here," she said.

"Mom! Who cares about the stupid dust! *Is* he coming home?"

Her mother wiped her hands on her pants. "Your father and I are discussing it now."

"Just the two of you? What about what *I* think?"

Her mother hesitated. "Honey, we'll do what's best for Jack."

"But I want to decide with you!"

"Please stay in your room for now. I'll call you when dinner is ready." Her mother's jaw trembled as she turned away.

She doesn't want me to see her cry, Lacy thought, and she closed the door after her mother went downstairs. She leafed through the baboon pictures: primates snarling, picking lice, cuddling babies, and munching on fronds.

It was so hard to believe.

She'd heard that the disease was rampant in Africa, killing adults and children, that it was spreading in cities like San Francisco, New York, and Boston. She never thought it would affect her, here in Wilton, a small Maine town. Or Jack, who lived in a small town in Colorado.

She headed for the phone in her parents' bedroom. Her mother picked up the extension downstairs before Lacy had finished dialing Emma's number.

"Lacy, who are you calling?"

"Just Emma."

"Lacy, I don't want you to tell anyone about Jack yet. I'm not sure I'm . . . ready," she stammered. "It's a lot to tell someone, and, well, people need to be prepared."

"Nobody prepared me," Lacy snapped.

Her mother's voice became calm and firm. "I'll let you know when it's okay to tell people."

"Mom, when I didn't want to go out on the boat with you and Dad this morning, you said that was fine, that I'm old enough to do what I want." Her voice rose. "You said that to Dad. Remember?" She wished she weren't sounding so shrill. She wished she could sound calm and logical.

"Lacy, that was this morning. This is different. I mean it."

"I'm thirteen, Mom, not three!"

"Lacy, that's enough."

Lacy slammed down the phone.

CHAPTER

3

When her mother called her down for dinner, her father was seated at the table, a drink in his hand. Lacy sat down and couldn't resist mashing the soft peas with her fork. Her mother served pot roast and potatoes.

Lacy put her fork down. "I want Jack to come home."

Her parents looked at each other, then at her. Her father pursed his lips. She felt as if she had said the wrong thing.

"We have some concerns," her father said. He took a bite of roast.

Lacy watched him chew, her own appetite absent. "Like what? I can't believe you have to *think* about it." She waited impatiently while her father swallowed, cleared his throat.

"We need to get more information, Lacy. AIDS is a deadly disease."

"I *know* that. Why don't you want him home? Don't you know we'd have to be pretty stupid or strange to get it from him?"

Her father held up his hand. "Just a minute. Are you aware that some health-care workers—nurses and such—have been infected by patients? We need to know if we'll be safe caring for him here, and what kind of medical facilities he'll need nearby. Our little hospital may not be equipped for this problem, and the Portland hospital is fifty miles away. Jack may need to be closer than that to good medical care. Maybe he would need to be in Boston. So, you see, our decision is not that simple."

Lacy pushed potatoes around her plate and poked at her meat. She felt as if something in her burned. "I know this isn't simple!" she burst out. "I know what's going on."

"I'm not sure you do," her father replied.

"Then explain it to me!"

"Well . . ." He hesitated. "There's really nothing to explain yet. I know some people at the hospital, and I'll talk to them."

"Like who?" Lacy asked.

"Such as Dr. Langdon, the head of infectious diseases. But Jack's not the only issue. I'm not sure how it will impact on you to have your brother here. How other kids will treat you. Anyway, don't you worry about anything. Just keep on swimming and studying and having a good time with your friends. Aren't you going to have swim practice three days a week?"

"Five. Monday through Friday. Like last year. And the year before. *And* the year before that."

Her father scowled at her. "*Sarcasm* comes from Greek words meaning 'to cut flesh.'"

"Well, maybe you should tattoo my schedule into your arm so you'd remember it."

"Lacy, stop," her mother snapped. "Your father has enough on his hands with his own complicated schedule, never mind anybody else's."

They ate without speaking, and then her father broke the silence. "Lacy, are you trying out for the swim team this year?"

She rolled her eyes and tried to keep the edge out of her voice. "Dad, anyone can be part of swim club. There are no tryouts, not anywhere in the whole country, for any of the U.S. Swimming clubs. Only high school teams have tryouts."

"Huh. I guess I forgot. So what are your goals this year?"

She stared at her father. "You mean my swimming goals? You want to hear them *now*?" Lacy asked.

Both parents nodded. She felt like a rabbit flushed out of the safety of its hole. Usually she didn't talk about her goals until she had swum for a few weeks, and then she would tell Jack first, in a letter, even before she talked to Coach about it.

But where would Jack be in a few weeks? she wondered. Maybe this was the perfect opportunity to tell them what she was aiming for. Maybe it would ease the tension in the room.

"Regionals," she announced. "I want to qualify in at least two different events for Regionals next spring."

"Is that the big meet you didn't make last year?" her mother asked.

Lacy nodded.

"Wonderful," said her mother as she got up from the table, removing her half-full plate, which she scraped into the garbage. She busied herself at the sink.

"Good," said her father. "You'll be so busy you won't have time to think about Jack. This is his problem, not yours." He continued eating.

She wanted to believe her father. Just swim, study, have a good time. But she felt uneasy, as if the ground were shifting as she walked on it.

CHAPTER

4

On Monday morning, Lacy bicycled the two miles to Wilton Middle School as usual. Emma waited by her locker.

"You're so late! How'd it go yesterday?"

Lacy smiled. "Gunnison's was a blast. I found Kerry and Bjorn and we rode the Tornado Twister three times. I thought I was going to throw up. They made me sit in the middle." She tried the combination lock on her locker, but it wouldn't open.

"Your Sunday sounds a whole lot better than mine," said Emma. "Gram fell asleep at the table, before we brought the cake out. My cousins watched baseball and my sister spent two hours on the phone with her boyfriend. At least I got to hear Gram tell again how she was born in a tent."

Lacy tried the lock again, but it held tight. "Darn this thing. Did she tell the same story as last year?"

"The same, but better. This year she added Great-Gram's moans and groans. Everybody came running, thinking she was kicking off for sure." Emma watched Lacy struggle. "I'd better get to homeroom. Why don't you get a new lock?" Emma spun around and started to run off, then stopped. "Hey. Did you find out what was in your brother's letter?"

Lacy felt her mouth go dry. She swallowed and shrugged. "Just . . . news." She turned back to her stubborn lock, trying the combination slowly, and was relieved when Emma ran down the hall.

The lock released. Inside was a plastic sandwich bag full of mints. Lacy smiled. Emma was the only one who knew the combination. She must have scooped them out of the bowl her Gram kept in her dining room.

The bell rang. She grabbed her books, ran down the hall to Room 24, and slipped into a seat next to Emma.

Ms. Fremont stood before the rows of desks, biting the tip of her pen with her front teeth. "That was close, Lacy."

Eddie started a chant from the back of the room. "She's late, she's late, she's late . . . !"

Lacy glanced around, breathing hard from her run. Most of the kids darted looks at her, then at the teacher, then at her again. She twisted around to glare at Eddie, and he smirked at her. She wanted to throttle Eddie for making her the focus of all the commotion.

Feeling herself blush, she hoped no one noticed.

She was sure her curly hair was sticking out at odd angles, that the freckles spattered across her cheeks and nose were standing out more than usual, and that her nostrils, which she thought flared as wide as a house, were noticeably flapping.

The homeroom teacher bit harder on her pen and yanked the cap off. "Enough. Let's get started." The class quieted. Relieved, Lacy settled into her seat for the tedious repetition of names, announcements, and pledging allegiance to the flag.

She wrote a note to Eddie: I will get revenge. But how? She could never seem to get his goat. She saw the teacher looking at her and stuffed the note into her pocket.

Emma hissed at her, attempting to hand her a folded piece of paper.

"I'm in enough trouble already," Lacy whispered back. But she couldn't resist snatching the note when the teacher turned her back.

> *Forgot to tell you—When you were sick last week Mr. Hall assigned a 6- to 10-page report due in October. Any topic, so long as it's about health.*

Lacy grimaced at Emma, who just shrugged. The bell rang and Lacy jumped up. "I'm going to kill him."

"Mr. Hall?"

Lacy scowled. "No. Eddie."

Emma tugged at her sleeve. "Don't do it in school. It makes the teachers nervous."

During fourth period study hall, Lacy got a pass to go to the library. She searched for books on AIDS and was disappointed to find that the few books on the shelf focused on how kids could avoid getting it.

"Mrs. Marshall, do we have any books on AIDS besides these?" she asked the librarian. She felt her face flush and she was surprised and annoyed at herself. She breathed slowly, trying to stop her heart from racing. But she knew her face was turning pink.

"Uh, wait. I'll—I'll be right back. I'm going to the bathroom, okay?" Before the librarian could reply, Lacy rushed out of the library and down the hall.

The bathroom smelled of fresh cigarette smoke. Lacy careened into an empty stall and leaned against the wall, her heart pounding.

A half-smoked cigarette smoldered in the sink. She doused it with tap water, rinsed her hands, and splashed cool water on her face. Just as she picked up the soggy cigarette butt to throw it away, the door to the hall opened. Tossing the butt into the trash, she spun around.

"Lacy—" The librarian spoke from the doorway.

"I'm coming, Mrs. Marshall. Just need to dry off."

She followed the older woman out into the hall.

"I didn't think you smoked, Lacy."

"I didn't. I don't! Someone left that one burning."

The librarian stopped in front of the library door, blocking Lacy's way, and she felt trapped.

"Is something wrong, Lacy?"

Lacy slid her hands into her pockets and felt the

note from Emma. She looked at Mrs. Marshall. "Can we talk in your office?"

The librarian nodded. "Sure."

Lacy followed her to the back room, where they sat down. Suddenly Lacy felt like her arms and legs were too long for her body and she was too big for the chair. "Mrs. Marshall, I want to write a report for health class on AIDS."

The librarian looked pleased. "Oh. Is that all?" She leaned forward, resting her arms on the desk.

Lacy nodded her head. "Yes. That's all. And, well, I didn't really find what I was looking for, so I wondered if we have other books about AIDS." Lacy thought her voice sounded hollow. But she didn't have to—no, *couldn't* tell Mrs. Marshall any more. Mom's orders. She forced a smile.

"What do you want to write about?"

Lacy felt her cheeks get warm, but she kept going. "Well, a little about how you get it, and prevention. But I think a lot of kids know that stuff. I want to know more about what happens to a person who gets it. You know, the symptoms and all."

Mrs. Marshall leaned back in her chair. "Someone in another class just checked out some of the other books we have, and unfortunately the new books I've ordered haven't come in yet." She got an encyclopedia and looked through it. "Lots of basic information here," said Mrs. Marshall. "But not what you're looking for, and I know Mr. Hall would want you to use other sources." She closed the book. "You picked a good topic,

Lacy. I don't think anyone else in your class has chosen it."

"Yeah, well, you know, it seems like people are either terrified they're going to get it or they think there's no way it will ever happen to them. Maybe I could write a report that would make some people more aware and others not so afraid."

Mrs. Marshall put the book down and wrinkled her brow slightly. "Are *you* afraid, Lacy?"

Lacy caught her breath. "No!" she burst out, trying to laugh and looking away. "Why should I be? Hey, do you think the public library has more books on AIDS?"

"They should. I'll call and see what's there."

"Mrs. Marshall—would you not use my name when you call, please?"

The librarian looked at her questioningly. "Certainly, if you don't want me to." She made the call and wrote several titles on a scrap of paper. Lacy stood up to leave.

Mrs. Marshall said gently, "Lacy, the new counselor seems very nice and I'm sure she'd be happy to talk to you about AIDS, if you want."

Lacy shifted from one foot to the other. "What for? I'm just doing a report."

"Well, you do seem a little, well, anxious. Anyway, you could interview her. She'd be a terrific source of information."

"Oh, yeah." Flustered, Lacy stood there awkwardly, eyeing the paper in Mrs. Marshall's hand. The librarian seemed to have forgotten it, but then she handed it to Lacy.

"The public library has quite a bit. These might be good to start with. Good luck."

Lacy folded the paper, put it into her pocket, and turned to leave, eager to get away. When Mrs. Marshall called to her, her stomach lurched, and she feared the librarian would ask more probing questions.

"Yes?"

"Have you seen this article on the Olympic swimming trials? Every time I notice it, I think of you."

Relieved, Lacy reached for the magazine Mrs. Marshall offered to her.

CHAPTER
5

"Work on these geometry problems with a partner." Mrs. Holstrum handed out a stack of work sheets. Lacy looked over at Kerry, who was raising his eyebrows at her. She nodded eagerly, and he dragged his chair to her side.

Math was Lacy's last class that day. She and Kerry bent their heads together over the work sheet, drawing and plotting and adding up angles. She noticed the reddish gold highlights in his hair, a pimple behind his left ear, and the unevenness where the barber shaved the back of his neck. A six-inch tail, usually braided, hung loose along his spine.

She brought her attention back to the work sheet. "Not like that!" she chided. "Look. Do it this way." Lacy worked a problem while Kerry watched. She enjoyed the simple logic of angles and numbers that always added up to the same 360 degrees.

"See?" She looked up at him, but he was watching her, not the paper. She felt her face getting warm.

"I don't get it." He smiled at her.

"Well, *look* at it." She stabbed the paper with her pencil. "You're not stupid. You're the only geek on this planet who actually looks forward to taking chemistry in high school and who studies weeks before a test."

"You don't do so bad yourself. Straight B's, right?"

"Wrong. I got a C last year. In singing."

"Really? How'd you do that? You sing great."

Lacy felt herself blushing again.

"Do you two need more problems to do?" Mrs. Holstrum came up behind them.

"Not yet. We're making good progress, though," Kerry reassured her. She moved on.

They laughed, caught a harsh look from the teacher, and went back to work. Lacy considered asking what he meant when he said, "We're making progress." But the bell rang and instead she tossed Kerry a quick, "Gotta go!" as she gathered her books and dashed down the hall to get her gym bag from her locker. She hurried across the street toward the new recreation center.

Eddie stood on the sidewalk, talking to Bjorn. Lacy came up behind him and swatted his butt with her gym bag.

"You're dead meat," she hissed at him, hurrying on.

"Hey!" He laughed. "Big threat, coming from you. What are you going to do next, whup me with a pair of fins?" Lacy turned her face away so he wouldn't see her laughing, too.

A girl with long brown hair caught up with her. "You and Eddie remind me of me and my little brother."

"We went to nursery school together, Nina. It's almost the same thing," Lacy said. She held the spotless glass door to the rec center for Nina and followed her in. They went through another set of doors marked Women's Locker Room.

Lacy began to anticipate the water, its warmth and buoyancy, and the lull of doing stroke after stroke. I'm like a dog salivating for a bone, she thought.

A toilet-paper banner spanned four adjacent lockers. Reserved for the Kick-Butt Relay Team—State ~~Chimps~~ Champs! Lacy read aloud, smiling. A second banner hung below it listing the names of the girls who had won the 400-meter medley three years in a row: Megan, Nina, Julia, Lacy.

After changing into her suit, Lacy padded out to the showers and then to the pool. Most days last year she had just bounced a few times to stretch her hamstrings and back and swung her arms in a few circles before getting into the water. Today she carefully followed the girl who led their stretching routine. She wanted to start off right, in case Coach was watching. And anyway, she told herself, this year, shortcuts were out.

Coach Mayo, a balding man in his early fifties with a barrel chest and wispy graying brown hair, emerged from the pool office. "Six hundred-meter freestyle warm-up!" he called out, and he began to pace slowly around the pool.

"Typical," Nina whispered to Lacy. "First day back and he tells us to swim even before he says hello."

Lacy shrugged. "Yup. That's him. Swim first, talk later." She liked it that way and eagerly stepped onto the block in lane three, adjusted her goggles, and dove. The first lap was easy, as usual. Her shoulders were loose, her arms limber. A swimmer in green stripes pulled by her, and Lacy resisted an urge to speed up. She would hate to pull a muscle on the first day of the eleven-month swimming season.

After the warm-up Lacy sat with ten other kids on bleachers beside the pool. Coach Mayo paced before them.

"This is the year when talent won't be enough," he said, "especially for you thirteen-year-olds." He looked directly at Lacy.

"No more coming to practice just when you feel like it, Lacy Mullins. This is the year that separates the swimmers who really want to win from the ones who are here for other reasons." He stopped again. "It's okay if you don't care about winning. But if you just want to have a good time, Sunday afternoon family swim might be enough for you. The way you'll get the most out of practice is if you show up every day and work to become the best swimmer you can be." He put his hands on his hips. "Enough talk. Into the pool for a game of butterfly tag. Barbara, you're it."

"Tag?" said Barbara, the girl who had passed

Lacy during warm-up. "I thought we were here to work."

"You are," said Coach. "And sometimes to work, you've got to play. Into the pool. Butterfly stroke only." Several kids groaned.

"Aren't we going to talk about goals?" Lacy asked.

"Not so fast, Lacy. We'll get to those in a week or two."

They played the game and swam 200's and 400's and laps of pulling or kicking only. When her arms were full and strong and she wasn't thinking about anything except how to flow smoothly and efficiently from one end of the pool to the other, Coach called out, "Sixteen fifties on the minute!" Lacy's heart skipped ahead in anticipation. She finished her first lap in 42 seconds, leaving 18 to rest before the next sprint. Coach crouched beside her.

"Lacy, I want you to move into lane two."

"Aw, just when it's getting easy!" But she didn't try to hide her smile.

"Aw, get over there!" he said.

Her heart skipped again: lanes one and two were for the fastest swimmers, who did 50's at 50-second intervals instead of at 60. Lacy hoped she could keep up with them. In lane three she was usually the fastest. In lane two she might be the girl gulping air between laps while other swimmers passed her.

Julia nodded to Lacy as she slipped under the lane divider into lane two. Lacy watched Julia's crawl: she used choppy, powerful strokes. Like a boxer, Lacy thought, Julia attacks the water ferociously. Lacy pushed off her end of the pool when Julia was at the far end and the clock read zero. She knew Julia's and her own swimming styles were different. "Power is nothing without grace," Coach liked to tell them. Julia had boxer power. Lacy knew she had the grace, but she was less certain about her power.

She checked the clock when she finished the lap. Forty-two seconds, like before. She was surprised at how easily she breathed. She took a deep breath at 48 seconds and pushed off again. This time she felt even stronger and more coordinated. The water seemed to make way for her. Kick from the hips, she recalled, and it seemed she was moving faster, much faster than a girl in lane three.

She finished the lap and checked the clock: 43. She was surprised and a little disappointed. She couldn't be slowing down already.

But she was. Each of the next six laps was a second slower than the one before, and then she added three seconds to the lap after that. Julia was now just half a length behind her. Lacy started lap nine short of breath and imagined she was a boxer type of swimmer, punching into the water fiercely. The water bubbled from her choppy movements, and she thought she was making good time until she sensed a swimmer immediately behind her.

Who's that? she wondered. Not Julia. I can't be going that slow; I'm swimming just like she does. But as she pounded to the end of the lap Julia glided past her, touching the wall just before Lacy.

They leaned back against the side of the pool, both of them winded.

Lacy panted and tried to smile. Julia smiled back and it was time for Lacy's next lap. She felt self-conscious, aware that Julia was probably watching her. I'd better swim like *me*, she thought. Don't want her to think I'm copying her. Didn't work too well anyway.

My best Lacy stroke, she thought. It became an inner chant: Best Lacy stroke. Best Lacy kick. It carried her to the far end of the pool where she did a smooth flip turn and shot back to the start. Best Lacy stroke. Best Lacy turn! Best Lacy stroke! She felt supercharged and her breathing was deep but not labored. Her inner chant switched: All in synch, all in synch. She almost didn't care about the clock because the swimming felt so good.

The lap ended too soon. The clock read 42 seconds. She bent forward, resting her hands on her thighs, inhaling and blowing out hard, keeping an eye on the clock. Just before she swam again she glanced at Julia, who was now two-thirds of a pool length behind.

Her twelfth lap was 42 seconds. The thirteenth was the same. On lap fourteen she let her mind wander: What was Kerry doing now? That lap was slower: 44 seconds. Gulping air, she bent over. Four seconds to breathe, take an extra deep breath, go! Last lap, last lap. Her lungs burned. Last lap, best stroke. She passed the swimmer in lane three. Best stroke, best pull, best kick, best Lacy, best, best, reach, reach, easy, flip, push hard! Best stroke, best Lacy, burn, best, burn, best . . . she touched the wall and in one motion snapped her head out of the water and tore her goggles off: 39!

She tossed the goggles into the air and backstroked slowly to cool down and catch her breath. Then she saw Coach standing by lane two, smiling and nodding his head and jiggling her goggles in the palm of one hand.

"Did you see what I did?" Lacy yelled.

"I saw!" He kept grinning. "You did great!"

CHAPTER
6

"Tomorrow? There's an outline for health class *due tomorrow?*" Lacy glared at Emma.

"Don't look at me like that. I *told* you about it."

Lacy shrugged. "I guess I didn't hear you. Or just forgot. I don't know when I'd have done it, anyway. I was so tired after practice, all I could do was go home, do the homework for today, eat something, and fall asleep." Lacy sighed. "Now I'll have to skip practice and go to the public library."

"Well, don't take it out on me. Can't you go to the library tonight?"

"If I go to practice, I'll barely stay awake through dinner."

"What are you doing it on, anyway?"

Lacy hesitated. "AIDS."

"Intense, Lace! Why'd you pick that?"

Lacy shrugged, hoping she looked nonchalant. "I thought it might be interesting. What are you doing?"

"Medical problems caused by bungee-jumping."

"Are there any?"

"Tons. But probably not as gruesome as the ones from AIDS."

Lacy's mouth felt dry. "Yeah, well, that's what I'm going to find out, I guess."

"You don't look like you really want to. Why don't you pick something else?"

"Like what?"

Emma shrugged. "I don't know. I had a hard enough time coming up with something I wanted to do."

"Well, I think it's too late to change," Lacy mumbled, anxious to end the conversation.

As she rode her bicycle the half-mile across town, Lacy rationalized skipping practice: Sometimes Coach says, Hey, just take a break. Take the day off.

But not, of course, the second day of the season.

I can't tell Coach everything that's going on, she thought, and if I give him half-truths he'll send me to the pool. So I'll give myself the permission: Take a break, Lacy. Yeah. Take a break.

Despite her resolve, guilt niggled at her. Maybe she should turn around and try to get to the library later, she thought.

But by then she had reached the public library. Hot and damp from her ride, she welcomed the cool and quiet inside the old stone building. After checking out several books, she found a quiet corner to look them over.

From the library she bicycled to the 7-Eleven. Leaning her bicycle against the side of the building, she went inside for a can of soda. Kerry tapped her on the shoulder as she was paying for it.

"No swimming today?" He scratched an area of small red welts on his leg. "Poison ivy," he said, looking embarrassed.

"Don't scratch it. It'll leave scars."

"Sure. No problem." He kept scratching. "Actually, I get this every year. I'm an expert at scratching and not leaving scars. Some people call me over just to scratch their poison ivy for them."

Lacy giggled. She left the store with Kerry close behind her. He asked again, "So what are you doing out on the streets today? I thought you'd be in practice."

She was flattered that he was thinking about her. "I needed a break. And I had something kind of important to do."

"Oh yeah?" He looked interested. "Must be really important for you to skip swimming." He held her book-filled knapsack while she put on her helmet. "What have you got in here, rocks?"

I could tell him, she thought. I could tell him about the report and Jack and how strange it is not to go to swim practice. How it feels right and not right. She glanced around. Afternoon shoppers and kids just let out of school streamed by them. Wrong time, wrong place. And she had promised not to tell others yet.

"Yes." She took the knapsack from him. "I collect rocks." She faced him, the bicycle between them, then bent to retie her shoe, which didn't need retying. She remembered the first time she and Emma saw Kerry lying in the sun at the public beach. Emma went and stood over him.

"You're tan enough," she said. "Come talk to us. Who are you?"

They found out he was from Florida and he was bored.

Kerry quickly became part of their group, and for a year Lacy had listened to him talk about his parents' divorce, the house he grew up in that they had to sell, and all the friends he'd left behind.

He tells me a lot, Lacy thought, retying her other shoe. But she knew that if she told him just a little, maybe about doing the report on AIDS, it would be hard not to tell him the whole thing.

"Do you need any more shoes to tie?" Kerry interrupted her thoughts.

Flustered, she got on her bicycle. "I've got to go," she said, and rode away, not sure where she was going, just needing to get away. She pedaled furiously across town, counting the number of people she had lied to or hidden from: Emma, Kerry, Mrs. Marshall, Coach. This is stupid, she thought. She stopped at the curb and considered going back to find Kerry.

Then she noticed the stationery store nearby. Leaving her bike outside, she went in and bought two extra fine felt-tip pens and a journal, a blue and green cloth-covered book, the kind with a lock and key.

CHAPTER

7

I'm not supposed to tell ANYONE Jack has AIDS. I feel like I've been shut into a box. One of those soundproof, padded places. It had better be padded, because I feel like kicking the walls.

It's hard to believe Jack is sick, and that there's not supposed to be any cure. He has always been so strong and healthy. He doesn't play hockey anymore, but he's nuts about climbing mountains and riding his bike, and he rides for hours. He wears these black and yellow biking shorts. I laughed when he sent us a picture. He looked like a bee. He goes off for long rides in the mountains, wears a helmet and all. He's always careful, but he's a real speed demon. I guess he's lucky he didn't wreck himself whizzing down one of those steep Colorado mountains.

I feel awful keeping a secret from Emma. I've never lied to her before! I can't believe I did it. Could she tell? We've been friends since we were babies. We're like two halves of one brain.

When I ran into Kerry and he wanted to know what was so important that I skipped practice, I couldn't say. I felt like an idiot.

I'm scared I'm going to do the wrong thing or say a little too much. I don't like to feel this way, like I'm walking on a tightrope. Maybe Kerry felt this way when he first moved here and he didn't know if anybody would like him. But I can't even ask him about it.

I hope Coach isn't mad at me.

I hope Jack comes home. I think.

I won't tell anyone about this journal except maybe Emma.

CHAPTER
8

Emma was waiting for her after swim practice.

"I can't leave yet, Em. I have to talk to Coach. He said he'd be in his classroom."

"I can wait." Emma walked with Lacy toward the middle school. "Why'd you snub Kerry yesterday? He was whimpering to me like a pup."

Lacy stiffened. "I didn't snub him."

"He said he asked you what you were up to and you bolted. Said you must be in training for a biathlon."

"I just didn't feel like talking to him."

"Since when don't you feel like talking to Kerry?"

Lacy didn't know how to answer that. "I felt . . . shy," she offered.

"What for? That boy would listen to anything you tell him. Why, he'd hold you, he'd listen, he'd help you forget all your problems." Emma giggled. "I'm sure of it."

Lacy started to laugh, too. "I don't know, Em."

"Know it, girl. Know it."

"What I know is that right now I need to talk to Coach about skipping practice yesterday. Wait for me." She left Emma in the hallway and found Coach in his lab getting ready for the next day's classes. He stood up from his desk and pulled out a chair for her.

"What's up?"

She took a deep breath. This is getting complicated, she thought. Fending off Emma's questions, she had no time to plan what to say to Coach. Deciding to start on a positive note, she leaned forward, sitting on the edge of the chair. "I can't believe I'm in lane two! You know what?"

"Tell me." Coach leaned forward, too.

"I felt supercharged Monday *and* today!"

He laughed and punched the air. "Yes! You've got it!"

"It?" She hadn't expected him to be so enthusiastic, too. "Is 'it' more than just swimming fast?" Coach nodded. "Is it about being so excited when I compete with myself—and win?"

"You got it, again."

She sat back, smiling, and wondered if she needed to talk about yesterday at all.

"How are things going in school and at home, Lacy?"

His question surprised her and, starting to jiggle

her foot nervously, she made herself stop. "They're okay. Why?"

"Mrs. Marshall is concerned about you. She told me you smoked a cigarette in the bathroom at school—"

"What a liar!"

Coach didn't say anything, and Lacy couldn't read his expression.

She shook her head. "It's not true." She kept shaking her head. "I'd like to cream her with one of her dumb books."

Coach laughed. "I believe you, Lacy. And that's what I told Mrs. Marshall. I said, 'If Lacy said she didn't smoke in the bathroom, why don't you believe her? Lacy may not always tell a person everything, but she doesn't lie.'"

"You know that about me?" She felt pleased, but also disconcerted. That used to be true, she wanted to add, but not anymore.

"I also told Mrs. Marshall," continued Coach, "that it didn't make any sense to me that you would smoke because you're one of those swimmers who *has* to swim—not just wants to or likes to but that it's in your blood, or you're half fish—and that if you smoked it would cut your time down so fast and make it so hard to breathe that you'd have to quit swimming, which you could never do."

"You know *that*, too?"

He shrugged. "I've been at this a long time."

Lacy stared at Coach Mayo. If he understood that much about her, she thought she ought to give him some explanation for her absence. "Do you want to know why I wasn't at practice yesterday?"

He put up his hand, his palm facing her, and shook his head. "Lacy, I trust you."

"What do you mean?"

"You don't have to explain. From the way you swam today, I know you made a good decision yesterday."

She shifted uneasily in her seat, wondering what he would think if he knew she skipped practice just because she had to do an assignment.

"Lacy, you want to qualify for Regionals, right?"

She nodded, wondering what *didn't* he know?

"Look, I'm not a policeman. If you want to get to Regionals, it's up to you. When you're here, I'm going to do whatever I can to help you improve your times. When you're not here . . ." He sat back and made a gesture of helplessness with his hands. "It's up to you. How much do you want to get to that meet?"

CHAPTER

9

"I don't just *want* to get to Regionals, Em. I *have* to. Everyone thinks I can do it, including me. I've got no excuses. If I don't make it, I'll feel like I'm letting a lot of people down—Mom, Dad, the relay team, Coach, and me." And this year it feels more important than ever, she thought.

"Okay! So you *have* to swim. It just seems like a lot of work, that's all," said Emma. "And time." Emma sat on the wide oak swing at Lacy's after practice the next day.

"I've never told *anybody* about how I *have* to swim. And Coach understands! He is a really cool guy."

"Especially since he stood up to Mrs. Marshall for you."

"Yeah." Lacy dropped onto the swing beside Emma. "I'm beat. I'm glad there's no meet this weekend."

"Your practice schedule sounds brutal," said Emma.

"It really is fun, though," Lacy insisted.

"Don't you get jealous sometimes of kids who can just hang out after school?"

"Sometimes," Lacy admitted. "Sometimes I see girls in the bathroom doing each other's makeup or yakking about dates and dances and stuff and, you know, I don't do a lot of that. I get a tingly feeling when I head for swimming practice, and it has nothing to do with who's going steady with who."

"C'mon. Pump! Let's make this swing move!"

"You do it. I'm too tired."

Emma got off the swing and began pushing it. "What won't I do for you?"

Lacy tilted her head back, and the motion of the sky made her dizzy.

"Em, maybe Jack's not the only gay person in our family."

"Who else, then?"

"Well, I spend all this time swimming and not putting on makeup . . ."

"You think that makes you gay?" Emma stopped pushing the swing. "Maybe you're right," she agreed, giving the swing a shove. "Maybe everyone else on swim team is gay, too. Have you wondered about them?"

Lacy laughed. "Not yet."

"Jeez, Lace. I think there's more to it than that. When did your brother know?"

"By high school, at least. No, earlier. He said he always knew. It just took a while to do something about it."

"Okay. Try this. Close your eyes. Picture yourself in the lake. It's midnight and there's a full moon. The air smells like roses and the water is warm. Your sweetheart—"

"Who?"

"—swims up to you and gives you a big juicy kiss."

"What sweetheart?"

"That's just it. You've got to close your eyes and let your mind fill in the blank." Emma came around to the front of the swing. "Just do it."

Lacy closed her eyes. She saw the water ripple in front of her. A boy's head popped up. It was Kerry. Emma poked her in the ribs.

"You're blushing. Who's the sweetheart?"

"Hey! We didn't get to kiss yet." Lacy opened her eyes. "It was the usual. The K-man."

Emma leaned against a tree and clasped her hands over her heart. "Sounds like another case of boy-girl love to me. I think you just flunked the gay test."

"Yeah." Lacy settled into a slow, easy swing. "Speaking of flunking, I don't know if I can do this AIDS report. I tried reading one of those books. It's really confusing. All this scientific stuff about T cells and invader cells and HIV. It didn't even talk about AIDS in the first part, which is one hundred fifty pages long!"

"Oh yeah? Move over." Emma grasped the swing rope and wiggled on beside Lacy.

"Em, I skipped ahead to another chapter that did talk about AIDS and I read a paragraph about dementia, about how some people who have AIDS *lose their minds*. Damn. I don't think I could stand to watch that."

"Well, why would you have to?"

Lacy felt her stomach jump. "I wouldn't. I just meant, if I *had* to." She didn't dare look at Emma. "Maybe I should talk to that counselor at school."

"You got a problem?"

"No! For the report, Emma. Mrs. Marshall suggested I interview her about AIDS."

"Oh. Eddie had to see her. He hates her."

"He hates a lot of people. And besides, he wasn't doing research. He had to go for counseling."

"Well, maybe you should, too."

Now Lacy looked at her. "Why?" she challenged.

"You're so . . . edgy."

Lacy looked away and sighed. "Thanks a lot, Em. I'm just tired. And I have a lot on my mind."

"Hey, Lace, you'll love the video I'm getting for tomorrow night."

Lacy felt her stomach lurch again. "Oh no, Em! I forgot to tell you. We have company coming over tomorrow, so we can't have video night at my house."

Emma stared at her. "If you go see that counselor, tell her you're not only jumpy but also forgetful. Maybe this swimming thing is getting too intense for you."

"Maybe it is," Lacy said, relieved that Emma was guessing wrong.

"Well, shoot, Lacy. Since Mom sold our VCR, you're the only one who has one—that works, that is."

"What about Bjorn's?"

"His parents don't like having a bunch of kids over."

"And Kerry's?"

"Still in the shop. They can't afford to get it out. Who's this important company, anyway?"

Lacy thought she could answer this one without lying. "An old friend of my family. A doctor." She jumped off the swing and started to walk away. "I'd better go." She wanted to get away before she said too much. "If you see any of the guys tomorrow, will you tell them I'm sorry?"

CHAPTER
10

"Don't you have homework to do?" Lacy's mother asked her after greeting Dr. Langdon at the door Friday night. The doctor and her father were already seated in the living room.

"Yes, but it's Friday, Mom. I have the whole weekend—"

"Well, why don't you study for a half hour or so and then you can join us?"

Lacy stomped up the stairs. "If you don't want me there, why don't you just say so?" she called over her shoulder. She slammed the door to her room before her mother could respond.

She crumpled her list of questions for Dr. Langdon into a ball and threw it on the floor. Sounds of crying wafting up through the floor heating vent distracted her. Studying was futile. She crept downstairs and sat on the bottom step. Through the closed living room doors she heard her mother apologizing, and Dr. Langdon's calm reply, "Don't be silly, Sylvia. Of course you're upset."

"So if he comes, it should be soon?" her father asked.

"Well, you don't know how much longer he'll be able to travel. I wouldn't delay."

"What's the danger to us?" Her father sounded angry.

"None, if you follow the precautions we spoke about earlier."

There was a moment of silence.

"I just don't like it."

"What are we going to do, Jim? Leave him out there to die alone?" Her mother sounded angry, too.

"He's not alone. There's a whole community of—" Her father hesitated. "He's got friends out there. People just like him. Who understand him and what he's got and who are used to taking care of people with this disease."

"Jim, he needs us! It's our responsibility."

"Sylvia, my responsibility for Jack ended a long time ago."

More silence. Lacy leaned closer to the door.

"I understand you and Jack have had your differences, Jim." Lacy heard Dr. Langdon's quiet voice. "I'll tell you what I've told other families. There will be plenty of time for differences after he's gone. And if you have to argue, you might as well have it out while he's still around to argue with."

Lacy heard her mother crying again. She slipped back upstairs and sat on her bed with a book on her lap. She was just about fed up with waiting when she heard her mother's light footsteps. She jumped off the bed, knocking the book to the floor, and opened the door. "Can I join you now?"

Her mother shook her head. "We've already decided. We're going to ask Jack to come home soon." She leaned against the doorway. Her face was pale, and her red-rimmed eyes didn't seem to be focused on anything. Lacy heard her father and Dr. Langdon exchanging good-byes.

"You said I could join you!"

"Don't whine, Lacy. The doctor didn't have much time."

Lacy ran by her mother, down the stairs, and past her father, ignoring him when he called out, "Where are you going?"

"Dr. Langdon—" She was breathless. He was in his car, hands on the wheel, his car engine running. She'd forgotten her list of questions. She had so many. Now she couldn't separate one from another. All she could think of was Jack on his bicycle, speeding down the dry mountains.

"Just one question?" she pleaded, feeling shy, thinking the gray-suited man had more important places to go.

"Sure, Lacy." He took one hand off the wheel and rested it on the emergency brake beside him.

"When Jack comes home, it's okay to hug him, right?" She bit her lip.

Dr. Langdon smiled and released the brake. "Yes. Of course it is. You do that, Lacy. Is that all?" He put his hand back on the wheel. She wanted to ask more. Her father came up beside her and put his arm around her shoulder.

"Lacy, the doctor has to go."

Lacy looked up at him. "But—"

"Thanks again, Frank." Her father waved at the doctor as if to say "enough" rather than good-bye. Then he steered Lacy toward the house. She went reluctantly, listening to the car engine roar all the way to the end of their quiet street, then pulled away from his arm and faced him, legs slightly apart, one fist clenched at her side.

"Why didn't you call me?"

"The doctor had to go to the hospital to make rounds—"

"It's not fair! You said I could join you. I didn't get to ask him anything! What do you expect me to do, keep smiling all the time and pretending that nothing's wrong? I've been reading about AIDS. I know that some really awful things can happen. I know that my brother might get rashes and scabs and vomit a lot and maybe even lose his mind"—her voice rose and quivered—"and you're not the only ones who need to know what's happening to him!" She felt her nails digging into the palm of her clenched hand. Glaring at her father, she unclenched it and shoved both hands into her jeans pockets.

Her father glanced around at the neighbors' houses before reaching for her again. "Let's go into the house, Lacy."

"No!" She wrenched away. "Tell me what the doctor said."

"Let's go inside, first," he said firmly, holding his arm out to her again. She let him put it around her as they walked through the door that her mother held open.

Sitting between her parents on the couch, Lacy folded her arms across her stomach and waited for one of them to speak. Her father looked apologetically at her mother, who returned his gaze with a sympathetic one.

He sighed. "Lacy, I've wanted to protect you. Maybe that's wrong, but to me you're very young—"

"I am not!"

"Wait! You don't need to be burdened with a lot of . . ."—he shook his head—"medical details. Besides, we want Jack to see Dr. Langdon, just to be sure what we're dealing with."

"What?" Lacy stared at him, confused. "Did Dr. Langdon think it might be something else?" she asked hopefully.

He spread his hands wide. "We just want to be sure. Now, I'm going to turn off the sprinkler before I drown the lawn." He got up and went into the dining room. Lacy heard the liquor cabinet open and the clink of bottles. Lacy leaned against her mother, who stroked her head for a few moments before going upstairs to lie down.

Her mother's footsteps receded. She heard her father go outside. Her stomach was slightly queasy and she had a tight, burning feeling in her throat. She rose and went up to her parents' room. Her mother was watching television, and Lacy sat down on the foot of the bed.

A young housewife on TV turned on her electric mixer and got a face full of thick, lime-colored liquid. An invisible television audience laughed and applauded. Lacy and her mother stared at the screen.

"Mom, why can't I tell anyone yet?"

Her mother readjusted the pillows behind her back. "Lacy, we think it's better this way. Just wait a little longer. Until he's actually here. Then we'll see."

Her father appeared in the doorway.

"See what?" Lacy continued. "How bad he looks? See whether we can keep it a secret any longer?"

"Lacy," said her father, "your mother and I need a little more time—"

"For what?" Lacy demanded.

"Planning. And adjusting to the . . . news. Meanwhile, you don't need to concern yourself—"

"Well, I already am. I'm doing a report for health class on AIDS."

"Aw, Lacy, honey, you don't need to do that." Her father shook his head.

"I *want* to!" Lacy stalked back to her own room and sat on the floor, leaning against her bed, holding a pillow close to her belly. Her mother came and stood in the doorway.

"Mom, you still haven't told me anything about how Jack's doing or what's going to happen to him."

"Honey, we don't know exactly what's going to happen." She sat down next to Lacy.

With her mother on the floor beside her, Lacy felt herself softening. "I guess I know that." She pointed to the two books on her desk. "From reading those."

"Well, here's what I do know." Her mother put her arm around Lacy and began to describe Jack's condition. Lacy listened and asked questions: Why doesn't he sleep well? Why can't he digest food easily? Why is he losing his hair? Her mother's answers were brief and sometimes sounded uncertain.

"I don't understand it all myself," her mother apologized. Her vagueness frustrated Lacy, but her mother looked so weary that Lacy just hugged the pillow tighter. Her mother got up to leave.

"Let's keep this in the family just a little longer, Lacy, okay? I know this is hard for you to understand, but it's really best this way."

That pleading voice again, Lacy thought. She tossed the pillow aside. "Sure, Mom." Her voice was flat. She wouldn't look at her mother, who then walked over to Lacy and kissed the top of her head.

"You're a trooper, kiddo. I know you can do it." Her mother left the room, closing the door softly behind her.

Lacy took out her geometry homework. She drew solid lines, squares, triangles, rectangles, rhomboids. She retraced each line until it was bold, thick, and sturdy. Painstakingly she labeled each problem with block letters and numbers, using a different color for each one. It was more than the teacher wanted, but for a short time it occupied her mind.

CHAPTER

11

Saturday, September 21

I can't stand this. I'm lying to my best friend! How long do I have to keep this crazy secret? Now Jack is coming home for sure and I have to pretend that he isn't. It's like pretending that you don't have a broken leg, or that your house wasn't just painted pink, or that you don't have an elephant living in your kitchen. At least that's what it *feels* like. I'm sick of waiting and hiding and holding everything in and getting these stupid mixed messages: We love you, but don't talk. You're a little girl, but be a "trooper."

Troopers aren't little and they certainly aren't quiet. They don't wait around talking about sports or the weather. They don't play on the swing set while some enemy is tearing down their homes and villages. They look for the enemy before it finds them. They dig their heels into their horses, yell at the top of their giant trooper lungs, and charge!

CHAPTER

12

"Em, I've got something I can't tell you."

"So why'd you call? Just to torment me? Why are you whispering?"

"My mom swore me to secrecy. But if you guessed, it would be okay, as long as I don't tell."

"Kerry asked you on a date?"

"No!"

"You bought those patent leather cowboy boots?"

"*You* want those, not me."

"I know. You've grown watermelon-sized boobs?"

"No way! Be serious."

"I give up."

"Jack . . ."—she hesitated—"is coming for a visit. I think."

"Oh yeah? So gay J *is* coming home?"

"I think so."

"Alone? Or with someone?"

"Uh, alone."

"So, if he comes, when will it be?"

"I'm not sure."

"Girl, you're not making sense! Is he coming or not?"

"I won't know until they decide."

"What's there to decide about? Is your dad still mad about Jack being gay?"

"Not exactly. It's more than that."

"More. Well, what's the mat—Oh. Oh no, Lacy. Has Jack got AIDS?"

"Yes." She felt a rush of relief, and her heart beat faster.

"Really? He does?"

"My parents are acting so weird, Emma," she whispered.

"Well, you've been kind of strange yourself, Lace. Why didn't you tell me before?"

"I . . . They swore me to secrecy. They say they need some time before people know."

"I'm sorry, Lacy. Wow. I'm sorry."

"Well, don't tell anyone what I told you."

"Of course not! We'll just keep this under wraps for now, you and me, okay?"

"Thanks. I just wish I could talk to someone who knows a lot about it, so I could ask questions."

"How about the counselor in school?"

"Em, it was hard enough keeping it a secret from

you. If I start asking her questions, I know she'll guess."

"Yeah, she just might. I knew *something* was wrong. Well, what about talking to Jack?"

"You think I should bother him? I mean, he didn't even want me to know."

"He must. He wants to come home. Maybe he just wanted your parents to tell you."

"My mom thinks I shouldn't bother him. And my dad says I should try to cheer him up."

"What are you, a clown? Live home entertainment? More likely, he doesn't want to be a bother to *you*."

"You think so? Gosh, I would hate to have him feel that way."

CHAPTER

13

Saturday, September 21

Dear Jack,

I am really, really sad that you are sick. I know a little about what's happening to you, but would you tell me more? Mom and Dad don't tell me a lot, and what they do tell me doesn't always make sense. Mostly they say just to keep swimming and studying. I'll do that, but it would help to understand more so I wouldn't worry so much.

I don't mean to be nosy. I don't want to bother you or hurt your feelings or anything. It's okay if you don't want to write back or if you aren't feeling well enough.

One more thing. I read you can get AIDS through sex with an HIV-infected person or contaminated IV needles or blood transfusions. I guess it doesn't really matter how you got it. But I know you're gay, and some people say that's connected with getting AIDS, and I don't really understand what being gay has to do with it.

I'm really sorry you're not feeling well. If there's anything I can do, please tell me. I love you.

Lacy

P.S. If this is none of my business, just say so.
P.P.S. I'm glad you want to come home.

CHAPTER

14

Saturday, September 28

Jack just called. He's coming home—in four days!

I also got a letter from him today that explained A LOT.

This whole week has been better, knowing that Emma knows about Jack. But hearing from Jack, knowing he's coming, makes it great.

And today we had our first meet, and we were hot! I dropped seconds in every event I swam! And the relay team placed first in the 400 medley. What a way to start the season!

Since the meet was at home, Em, Bjorn, Eddie, and

Kerry came to see me swim. Even though Eddie's a pain, I was glad he was there.

But Mom wasn't there. I don't expect Dad to show up, but Mom never misses a home meet. When I got home, she was cooking enough lasagna and soups and stews for a mob and freezing it all. It seems weird, because Jack says he can't eat a lot. But she's worried that she won't have time to cook much when Jack comes home. What does she think she'll be so busy doing instead?

She reassured me at least twenty times today that none of us will catch it from him.

What's he going to look like? Will I recognize him? It's been four years. Will he look different? Will he want to do any of the things we used to do together?

Well, that's stupid. I'm much older now. He's not going to make up stories for Mr. Huggins or help me learn to ride a bike without training wheels. Dr. Langdon says that if there's one thing we can expect with this disease, it's that we can't expect anything. So in the meantime, we'll just do whatever we can to help him.

Whatever that is.

Dad's being kind of strange, too. Right now he's watching TV. So I asked him, "What's the plot?" He said, "I'm not paying attention." But he was sitting there looking at the TV as if it was the most interesting thing in the world.

Sometimes I am a TV slug like him. It's one of the

things we do together. But I didn't want to tonight. I went into the kitchen to read one of the AIDS books. When Dad found me later in the kitchen, I offered him the book I was reading. He surprised me. He took it.

CHAPTER
15

"Grab a rag, Lacy, and help me out." Her father was polishing the deck of the outboard.

Lacy shielded her eyes from the late afternoon sun and tried to see her father's face. He was bent over the deck, and the sun glinted off his glasses. "Dad, I was on my way to Emma's," she complained. "Didn't you just polish the boat a couple of weeks ago?"

Her father stopped making circles with his cloth and stood up straight. "We may need to sell it."

"To get a new one?" They had always had a boat, since she could remember. Every three or four years her father traded it for a new model. But this one was only a year old. And it was the first one she was allowed to drive, though only when her parents were in it and no other boats were around.

"No, Lacy. If we sell this one, we'll probably hold off on getting a new one for a while."

"Why?"

Her father hesitated. He scrubbed a spot that already gleamed.

"Why, Dad?" This was strange, to sell the boat.

"To help pay for Jack's medication," he said. "It's very expensive."

Feeling ashamed of the anger that rose up in her, she took a rag and began to rub the caked polish onto the smooth blue and white fiberglass deck. Even though she was spending less time on the boat, she hated to think about not having it. It seemed unfair. "Dad, how much does his medication cost?"

Her father stopped polishing and sat on the fore-deck, shaking his head and looking out across the lake. "Almost four hundred dollars a month. More"—he resumed polishing—"than your mother and I keep around."

Four hundred dollars sounded like a lot to her, though she had no idea how big a chunk that would take out of her father's income. They didn't usually talk about family finances, and the sharpness in his voice was a warning to her not to ask too many more questions.

"Maybe I could get a job after school and on week-ends," she offered.

When he looked at her again, she thought his eyes looked wet, but maybe it was the way the sun hit them.

He laughed. "That's sweet of you to offer, but it's

CHAPTER
17

Lacy was awake, reading under her sheets with a flashlight. She heard the car in the driveway and jumped out of bed. Her mother was watching TV and didn't hear her patter down the stairs and out the door.

Jack and her father sat in the car, talking. Lacy opened Jack's door and tugged on her brother's arm.

"C'mon, Jack! Are you spending all night in the car?"

The tall lean man laughed. "Hi, Lacy!" He hauled himself out of the car, slower than she expected. He used to spring out of a car. She threw her arms around him, and her exuberance surprised them both.

"You're skinny!" she exclaimed, feeling his ribs in her tight embrace, then feeling embarrassed that she'd spoken out.

His laugh didn't seem to come from inside. "Your arms are longer, Lacy." But it's not just that, she thought. I can feel your ribs real plain.

She tried to take Jack's bag from her father, who shooed her away. She took Jack's arm instead and tugged. "Wait'll you see what's in your room!"

She chatted as they ambled toward the house. "My second swim meet is a week from Saturday, and I want you to be there—if you feel okay. Emma remembers you, and she says welcome home. She wants to come by and say hi." Jack seemed to be concentrating hard on her words, as if it was an effort to understand her. His appearance shocked her. His eyes looked sunken into their sockets, he had dark gray patches under each eye, and she didn't remember the bones of his face being so sharp.

She shivered, a quick fearful quiver that started deep in her chest. It was more than his skeletal thinness that made her afraid. She kept talking to cover her dismay: school, teachers, Gunnison's, the team. Not only his eyes had receded. She sensed that Jack had somehow withdrawn into his own body, that she was looking at a shell. She felt a need to reach him, to draw him out. Here he was finally, but he was still distant.

They reached the top of the front steps, where she held the door for her father. Jack waited on the porch. She stopped talking, and they looked at each other.

"You're so quiet," she whispered.

"I'm just tired, Twitch. And—I can't get a word in edgewise." He smiled widely for the first time, and shadows cast by the porch light deepened on his taut skin. Wrinkles appeared at the corners of his eyes, deep lines creased his face from either side of his nose to the corners of his mouth. He laughed, and she laughed with him, and this time his laughter sounded real to her. They hugged, and his boniness was no longer such a shock.

Their mother came to the door and drew Jack inside. "Welcome, Jack!" She held him for a long time while her father carried Jack's bags upstairs. "You're so thin!" her mother said. The three of them stood awkwardly in the entry. Lacy didn't comment on his receding hair line. A barrage of rifle shots peppered them from the television in the other room. Her father returned.

Her mother asked, "Did you eat anything on the plane?"

"I'd love a cup of tea, Mom." Lacy watched her brother follow her parents into the kitchen. His pants and jacket hung limp and baggy on his frame. She followed, too.

"Can I have some milk and pie, Mom?"

"No, Lacy. It's almost midnight. Say good night to your brother, please. You need to go to sleep."

"But, Mom—"

"Listen to your mother, Lacy," her father concurred.

Lacy lay awake listening to the murmur of the television set and later heard Jack's light step on the carpet. When she heard him cross the hall to his old room, she slipped out of bed to watch him. He turned on the light and stood quietly gazing at the six-foot spread of newsprint over his bed. She'd drawn a lobster, a starfish, assorted birds—a seagull, loon, and blue heron—all smiling and saying in bubbles that drifted above their mouths, Welcome home, Jack! At the back of the crowd was a girl wearing swimming goggles, waist-deep in water, arms held up and out, grinning from ear to ear. She'd signed it, Love, Lacy.

He turned around, smiling. "It's beautiful, Lacy. I feel really welcome now."

CHAPTER

19

"Just broth, Mom." Jack handed his bowl to Lacy to pass to her mother. She ladled the steaming beef broth into it, and Lacy placed it on the center of his plate.

"Bread?" She offered him the basket.

"I got it fresh from the bakery," said her mother.

Jack shook his head. "It smells delicious. This soup will be plenty for now." He looked at her with an apologetic expression. "I'll have a better appetite after I've rested a few more days."

Lacy saw her father glance at Jack's bowl of soup, then look down at his own bowl, which he dipped his spoon into. She looked at Jack and he smiled and blew on a spoonful of soup to cool it down.

"Is it too hot for you?" her mother asked Jack.

"It's okay," Jack reassured her. "A little spicy, maybe."

Lacy dipped a corner of her bread into her soup and ate it. "This bread tastes regular to me. Actually, Jack, you're not really missing much. They make this other kind with dark and light swirls that's much better."

They sipped their soup, dunked their bread, all in silence. What do we talk about? Lacy wondered. She wanted to ask what had happened to Lincoln. She felt too awkward to ask Jack anything about himself. She waited for her parents to say something. But her father sipped spoonful after spoonful without pause. Her mother buttered a slice of bread carefully, making sure all the edges were covered. Jack blew on his soup. No one looked at anyone else, except for Lacy, who looked from one to the other.

"Who's covering your cases while you're here, Jack?" Lacy broke the silence.

"The firm is large, Lace. Several other lawyers have divided up my load." He swallowed a spoonful of soup, grimacing slightly.

It hurts him to swallow, Lacy noted. Something to ask about later. "Were you in the middle of any good ones?"

"Lacy, how about letting Jack eat?" her mother interrupted. "He doesn't need to think about work right now." Her mother stood up, took a large bowl of salad off the counter, and selected a bottle of dressing from the refrigerator. "Does anyone want salad now, or do

Lacy shrugged. "No matter. Probably wasn't for me, anyway." She sat in the rocking chair beside his bed and noticed how sallow his skin was. They smiled at each other, half smiles. She wondered if she'd ever really known him, or else why did he seem like a stranger now?

She stood up. "Do you want to come down to the kitchen with me to get a snack?" She was pleased and surprised when he said yes. She watched him push himself upright and ease his feet onto the floor. He sat for a moment, slightly hunched, before he stood up. She had an urge to take his arm, not just because he looked weak and frail, but because she wanted him to move faster. He'd climbed out of the car that first night home faster than he got off the bed now. He looked up at her and saw she was staring and she turned away, embarrassed.

"I'll be down in a minute, Lace."

But it was fifteen minutes before he shuffled into the kitchen. She was on her sixth cookie, stalling for him by taking crumb-size bites.

Jack took slow bites of toast. Lacy pushed the cookies away and reached for an apple. The refrigerator hummed. "How come you and Dad didn't talk much before you got sick?" she asked. "Was he mad just because you're gay?"

Jack shook his head. "There was more. We had a big fight when I was a junior in college."

"I was eight then."

"Yes. Dad wanted me to come into the hardware business. I wanted to stay in Denver and go to law school." Jack chuckled. "He's a nuts and bolts sort of guy, you know, Lacy?"

"What do you mean?"

"People will always need nuts and bolts, he told me. For happy things: building homes, fixing bicycles. They're happy to buy and you can sell with an honest smile. Lawyers, on the other hand"—Jack's voice became stern, imitating their father—"don't get that kind of appreciation. Repeat customers for a lawyer are probably bad news. Lawyers help tear things apart: families, businesses." His voice became his own. "Dad couldn't appreciate that I liked working with people more than with wing nuts and gutter drains. For a long time I was his only kid. And I kept turning out different than he pictured his boy would be."

"I like you just fine, Jack."

He smiled. "I know, Lace."

She reached for another cookie and nibbled it. "Jack?"

"Twitch?"

"What's it like?"

He put his toast down. "Well, you know, I'm tired a lot and my throat hurts all the time." He paused and grimaced. "And you know I've had to go to the bathroom a lot."

She nodded her head. "The damn diarrhea."

"Yes. That."

"But I don't mean just that, Jack. Not just your throat and your stomach and being tired."

Jack looked at her for a moment, then leaned back in his chair. "I used to think I'd just received a death penalty and wonder what I had done wrong. It was like waking up from a good dream, only to find out I was living in a nightmare. I felt separate from everything, like I no longer belonged anywhere." He pushed his plate away, leaving a crust uneaten.

"Yeah, separate. And I felt scared to go out, scared to touch anything or anyone. Anything I touched would shrivel and disappear—or maybe *I* would."

Lacy held her apple, forgetting about eating it. Jack's face, pale when he was lying in bed and paler still when he first came into the kitchen, now had a pink flush.

"Then I started noticing little things," he continued. "The nubby beige fabric of my couch. The creases in my leather shoes. The way a black woman's fingers curled around the handle of her shopping bag as she rode the bus. The mix of emotions in my friends' faces."

He shifted in his chair and leaned over the table. "One day I saw this old drunk on the bus. It was rush hour and people were standing in the aisles. Every seat was taken but the one beside him.

"He reeked of wine and urine. His skin was dark, dark brown against his white and gray hair. Every few minutes he had a coughing spasm. When he coughed, his face would scrunch up and wrinkle. When he stopped coughing, his face was still wrinkled but he looked like a newborn baby. Like the babies I used to see in the hospital. There was always an old man or woman

MY BROTHER HAS AIDS

in each of those babies, and there was a newborn baby in that old man."

Lacy bit firmly into her apple. "Jack?" she spoke as she chewed.

"Yes?"

"You've been out West too long!"

Jack laughed. "What's it like, Twitch? I get angry. I feel sad. I get scared. I think it's really unfair. I think I'm going to die and then I think I'm going to live another fifty years. I start feeling really sorry for myself and don't want to go anywhere or see anyone. I lose my appetite. For"—he opened his arms—"everything." He got up slowly and walked to the sink. Leaning heavily on it, he looked out the window.

"I get mad at Lincoln, at myself, at everybody. I stay up all night going over the past, trying to change it so I don't have to be where I am today. I get exhausted from all that trying. And then I notice all those little details— how the light shines on someone's hair or shines through the leaves of a tree—and I know it doesn't matter if I live a hundred years or just another five minutes. Just so long as I take in as much as I can today—and try to share it with another human being."

Their mother appeared at the kitchen door, her arms full of groceries. Lacy jumped up to let her in.

"Nice 'do, Mom," Lacy crooned.

"Elegant, Mother," Jack concurred.

She touched her newly coiffed hair. "Thanks, you two." She eyed the cookies.

"I only ate three . . . at a time."

Her mother raised her eyebrows and hung her coat in the closet. Lacy and Jack winked at each other.

"With that new hairdo you look like a young babe," Lacy called to her mother, and she and Jack burst out laughing. Her mother looked puzzled but pleased.

"C'mon, you two. Now who's going to help me put these things away and start dinner?"

CHAPTER
22

Saturday, October 5

Well, now they know. Bjorn, Eddie, and Kerry all know. I wanted to tell them, but I didn't think I'd do it so soon. But then it seemed like the right time.

It took us forever to row out to Swift Island. We were all squeezed together in Emma's skiff. I could have stayed that way all night.

Bjorn offered me a bite of his apple, and I practically yelled at him. I was nervous, it was 2:00 A.M., I thought Mom might have heard me leaving the house. And I thought I shouldn't share food with anyone, just in case. Even though I *know* AIDS doesn't spread that way.

When Bjorn asked me what was bugging me, I told them. I told them all about Jack.

Eddie said he was glad it wasn't *his* brother. Bjorn told this long story about his favorite aunt dying of cancer, and how no one would talk about what she had, even when they visited her in the hospital and she was connected to a bunch of tubes. I've never heard him say so much at once.

Kerry asked me to sit really close between him and Emma, and he put his arm around me and my heart started flip-flopping like a goldfish out of its tank. He said he was glad I told them.

I didn't want to leave the island. I wanted to stay out there with those guys (except for Eddie) and make shelters and catch fish and share the catch and watch fires every night.

Emma didn't think I'd last more than a day knowing that swimming practice was going on without me.

CHAPTER
23

Thursday, October 10

Last night I helped Jack tack some pictures on the wall
by his bed: Jack covering Lincoln with sand on the
beach in Hawaii; the two of them hiking in the mountains and leaning against each other; Jack beaming at
the camera and Lincoln smiling at Jack.

I've seen Kerry smile at me like that. I got a lump in
my throat looking at that picture.

Jack said he misses Lincoln so much that he hasn't
wanted to look at those pictures in a long time. I asked
him why he took them out tonight. He said you can't
ignore the people you love for too long.

He knows Mom and Dad aren't telling people about

him. He says it makes him mad, but he thinks they need some time. Dad came in with a refill of one of Jack's prescriptions. I saw him look at the pictures and look away. While Dad gave us tonight's basketball scores, I got a Nerf ball from my room and a hoop you can hang from the molding. Dad and I sat on either side of Jack's bed, and we all took turns shooting. I won, hands down. Then Dad and I played one-on-one and he beat me but he cheated, holding me with one arm while he shot with the other. Jack got out of bed and tickled Dad and I got free and we were both on him. Mom came up to see what all the hollering was about, and Jack sat on the foot of the bed and he and Dad teamed up against Mom and me. To make it fair, I sat in the chair next to the bed. Mom didn't know the rules, and Dad wouldn't follow any, so the game ended up looking like a cross between basketball and football.

Then Mom noticed the pictures. She asked Jack when each photo was taken. Dad was tossing the ball up and down. Then he tossed me the ball and asked Jack, just like I did, "Do you miss him?" Jack crumbled like a house of cards that the wind knocked down and he cried in Mom's arms. Dad just watched, looking really sad.

I started to bawl when I got into bed. I felt lonely. I'm missing Jack already. I thought about getting up to find Mom, but I must have conked out, because next thing I knew it was morning. My eyes were puffy and I felt like I'd slept for eight minutes instead of eight hours.

I didn't go to swim practice. I dragged around school all day like I'd spent the night running a marathon. Just climbing stairs made my legs ache. When school was over, I couldn't imagine swimming for two hours. I guess last night kind of wiped me out. So I went over to Emma's instead, and we made cocoa and talked. Well, she talked mostly. It seemed like every time I tried to talk about Jack, she changed the subject. She wants us to plan costumes for the Halloween Dance. You'd think it was tomorrow, not three weeks away. To me, it feels like it'll be three years.

CHAPTER

24

Lacy woke from a dream and lay in the darkness, willing herself back to sleep, back into the dream. A dog lay moaning by the side of the road and she had to get to it. Its paw was crushed and bleeding. In her sleepiness, eyes still closed, she didn't know that the moans were real, until one moan rose and became a shriek. She bolted upright, staring into the dark, her heart pounding.

She threw back the covers and slid out of bed. As she opened her door she saw the bathroom door slam and then her mother was outside it, knocking and asking, "Are you all right?"

Lacy waited, unseen, for an answer.

"I'm okay," came Jack's voice weakly through the closed door. Her mother turned around and leaned against the door frame with a sigh. The moans continued, more subdued. Then she noticed Lacy.

"Go back to bed, Lacy. It's only four in the morning." She turned back to the door. The moans had stopped.

Lacy stepped inside her room and closed the door most of the way. She listened at the open crack.

"Jack, did you make it to the toilet?"

Jack's voice was low with defeat. "No, Mother, I did not."

Lacy saw her mother go downstairs and return with a pail, mop, rags, and rubber gloves. Her mother pulled on the gloves and then saw Lacy's open door. Lacy jumped into bed and pulled up the covers.

"Good night, honey." Her mother spoke firmly as she shut the door.

Lacy heard the bathroom door open, Jack's and her mother's hushed voices, water running in the shower and the sink. Her shoulders felt tense. She was fearful Jack's moaning would start again. Instead, the voices became murmurs that lulled her back to sleep.

The dream dog stood up now in the middle of the road. Its head hung but it began to run in graceful, loping strides. It picked up its head and Lacy watched it run, only it did not get farther away. She realized she loped effortlessly alongside it, unsure of her own physical form, but strong and graceful nonetheless. And then she *was* the dog and she couldn't understand how her foot could be twisted, crushed, and bleeding while she continued to race across the land.

Her radio blared. The dream vanished. She lay heavy with sleep, pressed into her mattress and pillow, tangled in bed covers.

Only her father joined her for breakfast.

"Jack had a rough night," he said to her as he poured himself a mug of coffee. "Your mother is still sleeping." He read the newspaper while he sipped coffee and ate a raspberry Danish. Lacy ate two. She sneezed, and her father said "God bless you!" and put the paper down, as if he had just remembered she was there.

"Do you have swim practice today?" he inquired.

His question irritated her. "Every day, like always. But I'm kind of tired. I may not go." She drank a glass of milk and stood up, putting her dishes in the sink. Her father continued reading. Lacy sat down again, reconsidering.

"Dad, I hope Jack is well enough to come to my swim meet next week."

He looked up from his paper. "Your meet? Don't count on it, honey. Besides, it's probably better if he doesn't mix with the people at your school."

"Because he's sick? Or because he's gay?"

"It's not that." He closed the newspaper and cleared his throat. "Just so there isn't any question—"

"Dad, I don't get it. Why are you so ashamed of Jack?"

"I'm not."

"What's he done wrong?"

Her father stared at her. Then he opened up the

newspaper again, but his eyes moved across the pages so quickly that Lacy knew he wasn't reading.

"Dad, what is it about Jack that bothers you?" Her voice was quiet but insistent. She saw a muscle in the side of his head twitch, and a vein stood out on his forehead. He looked up from the newspaper and across the room.

"Dad?"

"I didn't want him to get hurt." He shook his head.

"You mean you knew he might get sick?"

He shook his head. "Before that. Back when I sensed Jack was, uh, different. Kids like that get beat up." He looked up at the ceiling.

She waited, following his gaze. Several dead flies lay behind the iced glass of the light fixture, and a cobweb stirred gently in a light air current she could not feel.

"I beat up a kid like Jack." Her father enunciated each word like he was using it for the first time, and his face was slightly contorted.

She felt like the air had been knocked out of her lungs. "What?" she whispered.

"I was seventeen." He leaned his elbows on the table and clasped his hands together in front of his chin.

"Why, Dad? Why did you do it?"

He opened both hands and looked at her. "I'm not proud of it. It was what we did, back then. If we thought a guy was a fag, we beat him up. Gave him a chance to prove he was a man." He looked pained. "That was our excuse. It was wrong. *I* was wrong. Your brother is a fine lawyer, helpful in his community. With his buddies, he was always a good friend. I see that now. But back then, if a guy was homosexual, we thought it was our job to try to straighten him out."

"Like you tried with Jack."

"I thought it was something that he could change. I wanted to protect him."

"From guys like you?"

"From guys like me."

A door upstairs flew open and slammed against the wall. Lacy froze. Footsteps pounded through the hall, the bathroom door slammed, and a muffled groan wafted down the stairs. She heard more footsteps from her parents' room, her mother's voice outside the bathroom door. Her father looked at his watch and she saw his hand tremble slightly.

"It's okay. Your mother is taking care of it. You'd better go. And so had I." But he passed by her and went upstairs.

CHAPTER

25

Thursday, October 17

My hands were freezing when I got to school today. Em offered to do the combination on my locker and I told her I could do it myself. She was standing there with Barbara and she said, "Did I just feel an arctic wind blow over me or what?" They walked away together. It took me ten minutes to get the damn thing open and I was late to homeroom, got sent to Mrs. Andrews' office, and that was just the beginning. Mrs. Andrews asked me why I was late and what was I supposed to tell her—that my hands were numb and I couldn't think straight enough to open a lock or wear gloves or ask for help? Should I have told her that my dad used to beat up homosexuals?

Or that when I left home this morning my brother's body was exploding in the upstairs bathroom?

I couldn't say any of that. Instead I did what Eddie does in her office—folded my arms and scowled at her and shrugged. If I had opened my mouth, I would have cried, and I don't want to do that. I need to stay strong.

Then I ran into Em before swim practice. She was alone. I started to tell her how Jack has changed, how he's sick a lot and we have to clean up after him, and he spends most of his time up in his old room. She kept twisting around like she was looking for someone else. Then she backed away from me. She looked mad or maybe scared. I asked her, do you think I'm going to catch it? She said, I know you're supposed to be safe, but how do you know for sure that you are? Her face got all scrunched up, as if she were in pain, or maybe disgusted. I assured her there was no way. Dr. Langdon assured us, and it says so in all this reading I've done. I can't get it—I told her that.

She took off. Said she'd call me.

I hate it. I hate the slamming doors and the races to the bathroom and the groans. I hate seeing Mom with dark circles under her eyes, worrying all the time about Jack. She doesn't remember anything I tell her. I told her I needed twelve dollars for the book sale next week and she said she'd write me a check. Later I asked her for the check and she said, "What check? For what?"

I'm studying a lot but nothing stays in my head. Sometimes I stare at the words in my books and they don't make sense.

In swimming today I felt like I was fighting the water, like I'm thrashing around just to stay afloat, never mind move forward. I don't know what's happening to me. This time of year I'm usually making steady improvements, but the past week or so my clocked times have been terrible. I try harder and I go slower. I even had to go back to lane three! It's so embarrassing.

Today I finally found a way to swim that worked. Each time I took a stroke I pictured a face. Em. My mom. My dad. Mrs. Andrews. Dr. Langdon. Even Jack. I made each stroke a punch that knocked the stuffing out of each person I saw.

CHAPTER
26

Saturday, October 19

Mom left the swim meet today after just half an hour, and then she was late picking up Julia and me. She's NEVER late! I didn't know what to tell Julia. They locked the school where the meet was held, and we had to wait in the freezing rain for forty-five minutes.

We lost the relay because I was slower than a pollywog. And I really choked in the 200.

After we dropped Julia, Mom told me she had called home from the meet because she had this funny feeling, and sure enough, Jack had been throwing up since we left the house. And when she called Dad at the store to go home to be with Jack, Dad had just left to meet someone who's buying the boat.

I threw a fit. He said he would try not to sell it!
Mom says we have no choice.

It's just a boat. A stupid boat. And Jack won't be sick forever.

I'm awful. Already looking forward to my brother being gone so we can have a boat again. Have a normal life. Have everything come back that's slipping away.

Well, almost everything?

CHAPTER
27

Approaching the end of her lane, out of breath, Lacy did a flip turn too early, missed the wall, breathed at the wrong time, and took water up her nose. Coughing, she hung onto the edge of the pool, waiting for her throat to stop spasming.

Coach crouched near her. "You're trying too hard. Ease up a little."

After practice, she found Coach in his classroom. He was putting on his coat to go home, and she offered to come back another time. He took off his coat, insisting that she sit down.

"We lost the relay last weekend because of me," she said. "Maybe you should switch me to an individual event." She didn't want to slow the relay team down.

"Relax. Every swimmer has times when their performance slips a little. Besides, since when do you do the coaching?" he chided.

"I do everything you tell me," she complained. "It's not getting any easier." Not swimming, not school, not living with Jack, she wanted to say. When I ache after a hard practice, I can't take long, hot baths, because Jack needs to be able to get into the bathroom frequently. I can't play music in my room because Jack needs to try to sleep. Emma hasn't returned my phone messages in days. "I haven't improved any of my times in *weeks*, Coach. The way I'm swimming, I won't qualify for the state meet, never mind Regionals."

"You're still trying too hard," Coach repeated. "What are you trying to prove?"

She felt tears come to her eyes and she looked at the clock on the wall. That I'm okay, she thought. That nothing is wrong and I can swim as well as any of them.

"Maybe I shouldn't finish this season. Maybe I need a break from the team."

"Are you not feeling well?" Coach sounded concerned now.

She shrugged. "Just tired, I guess." Be quiet, she told herself. Go home. What are you doing here?

"Tired, or discouraged?"

She hesitated. "Both."

"Okay," he said gently. "One at a time. What is making you so tired?"

She clenched her jaws and shrugged, trying to contain the turmoil she felt inside.

"Lacy, I have seen very few girls or boys who take to

the water as naturally as you do. You've progressed tremendously—"

"I'm still not a top swimmer. I'm back in lane three! And I'm slowing the relay team down."

Coach shook his head. "For you to give up swimming, there's got to be something very, very wrong."

He waited. She stood up, aware of the chlorine smell on her skin. For the first time in her life she thought that was what was making her queasy.

"Have you ever known anybody with AIDS?" she blurted.

"I have."

His answer surprised her and made her feel bolder. "You have? What was it like? I mean, did you visit the person? Is he—or she—are they still alive?" She stopped, embarrassed. "Sorry. That's kind of personal."

"It was my brother, Lacy. He died six years ago. Very sad. A terrible thing." Coach rubbed his chin and looked away. "Left his wife and two young kids."

"Your brother!" She sat down.

"Yeah."

"How did he . . . oh, never mind."

Coach smiled. "How'd he get it? It's okay to ask. He got it from a blood transfusion during surgery. Contaminated blood." He shook his head. "A real tragedy." He looked down at the floor. Then he squinted at her. "Do you know someone with AIDS, Lacy?"

She looked away. "Yes," she said quietly, then louder, looking right at him, "Yes."

"Is he having any symptoms?"

She looked away again. "Lots. He's really sick." She shook her head. "Really, really sick."

"Who, Lacy?" He leaned forward, his chin in his hands.

She held his gaze. Coach, who doesn't lie. Who deals straight, honestly. Who treats her like an adult, trusts her choices. She took a deep breath.

"My brother. Jack. He was a varsity hockey player, before you came here." The room was slightly out of focus, all except Coach Mayo. She noticed every detail of his green and brown plaid shirt, the brown plastic buttons sewn with dark thread, the mix of gray and brown hairs in his eyebrows, dots of black stubble on his cheeks.

"I wake up every night," she said. "He is—wasting, the doctor calls it. From diarrhea. And now he has a big purple spot on his chin." She put her palm against her jaw, then drew a large circle there with her finger. "It's some kind of cancer that only people with AIDS get."

Coach was nodding. Lacy felt scared and relieved. He wasn't angry or backing away from her *or* telling her not to worry.

"He doesn't look like himself," she said, her voice wavering.

Coach Mayo kept nodding. "No, I'm sure he's changing a lot."

"There's nothing I can do for him. I want to do something, and there's nothing I can do!" Her voice shook and tears rolled hotly down her face, into her mouth. Salty, warm. Coach dug out a handkerchief and gave it to her.

"You have a lot of these?" She tried to laugh and she began to cry harder. Coach smiled sadly. She thought she saw tears in his eyes, but she wasn't sure.

"Just keep on swimming, Lacy. Keep on swimming."

"That's what my father says!" She felt annoyed. "It's not enough. It seems stupid."

Coach said nothing. She thought they sat a long time, but when she looked again at the clock, only two minutes had passed. She stood up and looked at the handkerchief, then stuffed it in her pocket. "I'll wash this and get it back to you."

He waved away her words. "No need to. It's yours. I bought a half dozen when my brother was ill. I don't need so many now."

Lacy paused by the door. "I'm supposed to give a report in health class tomorrow," she told him. "My topic is AIDS." She stopped. Coach waited. "I've taken tons of notes and now I can't make much sense out of them."

He kept nodding his head.

"I feel like I could write a whole book about Jack!" she exclaimed, then shook her head. "But I can't seem to write a stupid six-page report about his disease. The facts. I can't put them in order."

"So don't," Coach suggested. Lacy looked at him, puzzled.

"The night before a race, Lacy, you don't keep training. You get a good night's rest, and the next day, you just swim. The best you can, with the training you've got." He put on his coat. She thanked him and mulled over his words as she pedaled her bicycle home.

CHAPTER
28

Monday, October 21

It's 11:30 P.M. I can't sleep. I've got my notes spread all over the floor. I wanted to call Emma tonight, but I was scared she wouldn't want to talk to me. I told Jack I'm nervous about giving my report tomorrow. He said, "Just take your time and look 'em in the eye."

I practiced in front of the mirror for an hour. The truth is you'd probably need a telescope to see up my nostrils. I told Mom I wanted to cover up my freckles and she loaned me some of her makeup. It's weird. I put some on and I looked so different without freckles that I missed them, so I washed the makeup off.

I tried on just about everything in my closet. I didn't like any of it. Then I tried to do something with my hair. Mom helped me put some clips and combs in it. Jack came in with some cotton balls and said if I really want to look different, I should go all out and put cotton balls in my hair. He said I can tell people that living with someone with AIDS makes you do strange things. He stuck the cotton onto the combs. Then Dad brought in some fishing lures and attached them to my earrings. Mom got into the spirit by digging out her old feather boa. I complained that they weren't helping any, but I was laughing pretty hard.

Mom told me to stop worrying about how I would look. Told me to wear something really comfortable.

I sat on my bed looking at the piles of clothes all over the room. I'm going to sweat, I kept thinking.

So that's it. Tomorrow I'm wearing my favorite jeans and a sweatshirt.

CHAPTER

29

Lacy rode the school bus the next morning. She carried a medium-sized cardboard box on her lap. She wore a red sweatshirt, jeans, new earrings, and a dab of her mother's perfume. She kept the box with her all morning, setting it under her chair in each class. When she got to health class, she put it on the teacher's desk.

"I'm ready," she announced, louder than she intended. Mr. Hall asked her to remove her box until after he made some announcements. Impatiently she took it to her seat, where she set it on top of the desk and waited for him to call on her to begin.

"Lacy, you can step up here now." Mr. Hall beckoned to her. "Your topic, if I recall—"

"Is AIDS," she broke in.

Most students looked up at her. One boy snickered.

Emma sat still in the back row. Kerry leaned forward, his chin in his hands.

"Will you be reading or speaking from notes, Lacy?" Mr. Hall inquired.

"Speaking from notes," she replied.

"May I have your written report then?"

Lacy shook her head. "It's not finished."

"It was due today, Lacy. Sit down, please. You'll have to do your presentation another time. I believe several other people are fully prepared to go today."

He picked up her box and handed it to her. She stood in front of the room, looked at all the curious faces before her, and put the box down on Mr. Hall's desk.

"I'm fully prepared to present my topic now," she said firmly, trying to keep her voice from shaking. Someone called from the back, "Yeah, let's hear it *today.*"

Lacy felt her face get warm. "Mr. Hall, I just need to copy it over. I'll get it to you by the end of the day." He relented. He sat down and asked her to begin.

She took a pile of books out of the box and set them up on the desk so their titles could be seen. The plastic covers felt sticky in her sweaty hands. She pointed to the books, hoping everyone would look at them, not at her. "I have read most of these six books, all on the topic of AIDS," she began. Just then the door opened. Coach Mayo and Mrs. Andrews came into the room.

"Do you mind if we listen to your student's presentation, Mr. Hall?" asked Mrs. Andrews.

He looked surprised, but quickly rearranged two seats. "Not at all," he replied, indicating that they should sit down. Before she sat, the assistant principal turned to Lacy.

"Do *you* mind if we listen?"

Am I in trouble? Lacy wondered. Then why don't they stop me now? Flustered, she shook her head. "Uh, no. It's okay with me."

Lacy felt her jaw tighten as she faced her classmates. Most watched her, looking calm or curious or bored. Emma looked down at a piece of paper she was doodling on. Kerry gave her a quick thumb's up—so quick she wondered if he'd really done it.

"I tried to write a paper to tell you the facts about AIDS, but I decided that wasn't what I wanted to do." She paused, took a deep breath, fought an urge to drop her head forward. "Instead, I want to report on what it's like to be living with someone who has AIDS." She glanced at the adults. They were motionless, except Coach Mayo, who gave a slight, encouraging nod.

"My brother, some of you know, has AIDS. The rest of the family does not." A drop of sweat trickled down her side, underneath her sweatshirt. Except for the buzz of the fluorescent lights overhead, the room was silent. The quiet became a pool for her to dive into. She stood up straighter and began to talk.

She talked for almost half an hour, letting her nervousness propel her. She forgot to look at her notes. Words and images came by themselves, tumbling out of her: Jack's letter, the doctor's visit, her question to him,

Jack's arrival, his thin body, his balding head, his long naps. She read fragments from several books, factual statements or quotes that resonated with her own experiences. Several times she wept as she read, pausing briefly to use a handkerchief and stuff it back into her pocket. She didn't try to read the expressions of the others in the room. She knew they were listening—their silence told her that. She rushed on, certain that if she stopped she would not be able to start again, or that someone would tell her to stop.

"Last night at 3:00 A.M. Jack woke us up, calling out to my mother from his room. Usually when he calls, my mom gets there first. But this time I was the first one to his door. She gets tired. His sheets, his pajamas, they were all soaked. He has these night sweats. He was shivering and he looked sixty-five, not twenty-five. Then my parents came and we all helped him into a warm dry robe and he sat in a rocking chair in his room while my father changed his sheets and my mother went to throw the wet things in the washing machine. I stood by the rocker and Jack was holding my hand." She held up her left hand, looking at it.

"He looks young and he looks really old at the same time. He is not anything like he used to be. Except his sense of humor doesn't go away. When he got back into bed—we had to kind of carry him because when he stood up his legs buckled—he said to my dad, 'Thanks for making the bed, Dad. But—either I'm hallucinating or there are some lumpy little critters in these sheets.' And sure enough we looked and found that some socks had been clinging to Jack's sheets before my dad put them on the bed, and they were still under there, making the bed all lumpy."

She looked around the room. A few students were wiping their eyes. Emma was one of them. Kerry smiled at her sympathetically.

"If we thought—or if our doctor thought—that we'd get sick, too, we wouldn't have let Jack come home. And I wouldn't be in school—" She glanced questioningly at Mrs. Andrews and Mr. Hall, who nodded in agreement. She turned back to the class. She felt warm and the room seemed airless.

"Are there any questions for Lacy?" Mr. Hall asked the class.

Barbara was looking around the room at the others. Then her hand went up. Lacy swallowed hard and called on her.

"How do you know you haven't caught AIDS from your brother?" Barbara challenged. "Have you had a test?"

Lacy bit her lip, trying to think how to answer. Coach Mayo cleared his throat. "I'll respond to that." He stood up and walked to the front of the class, beside Lacy. "Six years ago I visited my sick brother and his family. I went for a week, and wound up staying the whole summer. I ate with him, washed him, held him. His kids were all over him. One night we ate a half gallon of ice cream together, sharing the same spoon, eating right out of the carton." He chuckled, remembering. "My brother sneezed on me. Coughed on me. Like

Lacy's brother, Jack, my brother had AIDS." He pulled out a handkerchief and blew his nose.

"A year after he died, we all got tested, just to make sure. The kids, my sister-in-law, and me. We all tested negative. We weren't infected. I wasn't surprised about the kids. But my sister-in-law? How come she hadn't gotten it? Well, she told me they had been using condoms all their married life." Some kids looked at each other and whispered. "Except when they conceived their kids, of course," he added, smiling.

"This one's for Lacy," Barbara said. "How long will your brother live?"

Lacy was taken aback. Mr. Hall intervened. "Barbara, that's an impossible question to—"

"No. I'll answer it," Lacy stopped him. "I don't know. Nobody knows. Jack gets drugs for his symptoms, but so far none of the drugs can cure him. He just fights as best he can."

"Just one more question," broke in Mr. Hall. Several hands went up. Emma waved hers back and forth.

"Me, please!"

Lacy called on her. Emma placed her hands flat on her desk and sat up very straight.

"Lacy, I just want to tell you. You are extremely courageous, strong, intelligent, beautiful, and brave." She began to clap. The other students joined her. The adults, too. Lacy stood before them, pleased and embarrassed and shaking.

CHAPTER
30

Tuesday, October 22

Thank goodness that report is over. Em hugged me after class and promised she'd call tonight—for real. While I put my books in my locker after health class, Barbara snubbed me in the hallway, but at least most kids aren't acting obnoxious. A lot of people said they're sorry about Jack. After last period Claudia came over to me and said she had learned a lot from my report. She said her grandfather lived with her family for his last few years and that my story reminded her of how hard it was sometimes.

I was late to practice because it took me almost an hour to finish copying over my report for Mr. Hall. I went only because I had promised Coach I'd be there. It's so frustrating to be swimming so slowly!

When I got into a lane for warm-up Darcy switched out of that lane. She's not in my health class, so she didn't hear my report, but she's getting to be friends with Barbara, who sure is being a jerk.

Nobody else switched out of my lane, but when I got in line behind Nina and Megan to do 100's, Nina said she heard that my brother has AIDS, and she looked mad. Julia was upset I hadn't told them sooner. Nina said she and some other girls were wondering if they can get it from me, like in the pool. Some other girls were listening. They were all nodding their heads.

I could see they weren't mad, they were just scared, so I told them they couldn't get AIDS from a pool and then I asked Coach to help me explain. He thought that was a good idea and he sat us all down for a talk. At the end he asked how many girls have had a close friend or relative—someone they love—get seriously ill. About five kids raised their hands. He asked them to remember how they felt during that time, because that's what I'm going through now.

I felt embarrassed. Maybe they didn't want to think about those times. But afterward Nina and Megan and Julia hugged me and told me to call them if I wanted to talk. Darcy still kept her distance, but I noticed she was pouting, which she does a lot, so maybe how she's acting has nothing to do with me. I even felt kind of sorry for her that so many people were being nice to me while she looked unhappy and lonely.

CHAPTER
31

"The kids at school want you to come in and talk to them." Lacy stood by the living room couch where Jack lay under a blanket, resting. She was glad to find him downstairs instead of in his bed. "Have you been here all day?"

He turned to face her. The purplish spot on his face had grown darker. She noticed another on his hand that she hadn't seen before. Her heart sank.

"No, Mom and I went to the hospital today. More tests." He coughed, and his voice was hoarse. He curled his whole body to cough, turning away from her, but she could see the grimace on his face. Light from the afternoon sun reflected off his scalp where his baby-thin hair no longer covered, and his shoulder blades were sharply outlined under the blanket. He waved a hand at her, dismissing her. "Need to sleep."

She found her father in the den, seated in the large stuffed green chair, an unopened beer on its cushioned arm. A folded newspaper lay in his lap. He stared at the blank television screen and spoke without turning around.

"Jack has pneumonia," he said, still staring at the screen.

"No . . . ," Lacy moaned, flopping down on the footstool in front of him. "Is that part of his AIDS?"

He turned toward her and nodded. She was shocked to notice that her father looked more youthful than her brother.

"Where's Mom?"

"Napping, upstairs."

"I gave my report today in school. For health class. About Jack and AIDS."

He looked at her without saying anything. She saw a slight ripple at his temple. He set the can of beer on the floor and patted the arm of the chair.

"Come here, Lacy."

She got up and sat on that cushioned arm. He put his arm around her and she leaned against him, trying to recall the last time they had sat together that way. It was awkward now. She had grown too tall to rest her head against his shoulder. She wished she were small enough to do that or to sit on his lap. Instead she eased herself away from his embrace.

"That's not comfortable, Dad. I'm too big." She sat on the couch.

"Mrs. Andrews called me," her father said. "She got

a couple of phone calls from parents of kids in your health class." He shook his head. Lacy expected a lecture. She pressed her lips together and folded her arms across her stomach.

"Just a few called," her father said. "I thought, under these circumstances, there would be a slew of parents calling. They were upset that the teacher hadn't informed them ahead of time." Lacy unfolded her arms. "Show me what else you've been reading, would you?" She got the books and watched as he leafed through them.

"Was Mrs. Andrews mad at me?" Lacy asked.

He shook his head emphatically. "Not at you. She was concerned."

"But she *was* mad?"

Her father tapped his finger on a book cover. "At me, honey. For not letting her know about your brother." He bit his lip and put the books on the floor. "Once again, Lacy, I'm sorry. I guess I've made things more difficult for you."

She relaxed, a weight lifted. Lying down on the couch, she covered herself with the quilt. "Dad, I'm thinking of quitting the team. I'm not doing well."

He got up and, pulling the quilt over her feet, sat down on the edge of the couch. "It doesn't matter how you do, sugar."

She scowled. "Just keep swimming, right? No matter what?"

"It's up to you."

"You sound like Coach. Did *he* call you, too?" Her

father shook his head. "Dad, I thought you wanted me to do well."

"I did. And I still do—only it doesn't seem so important now." He lifted her feet, slid back to lean comfortably against the couch, and laid her feet across his knees. "Maybe going to work for me is like going to practice for you."

"I doubt it. I don't get paid."

He laughed. "No, you don't, but listen. I've got all these strong, strapping young guys working for me. It tears me up inside. I hate myself sometimes, wishing it was one of them and not my own."

His words stunned her. She had never heard her father talk like that.

"Don't compare yourself to others, Lacy. Or to what others have. Or do. It does terrible things to you." He stood up, gently replacing her feet on the couch, and turned on the evening news.

How can I not compare myself in swimming? she wondered.

The doorbell and the phone rang simultaneously. She ran toward the kitchen, but the phone stopped ringing, and her father answered the door. She heard him paying a pizza delivery man, and then her mother called softly from upstairs, "Lacy, it's for you."

Lacy walked over to the kitchen phone. Her legs felt leaden.

"Lace? You were fantastic!" Emma's cheerful voice came from another world. Lacy wanted to grab it like a rope and haul herself out of her home.

"You think so? I don't remember half of what I said. I was scared! I don't think I made any sense." Her own voice sounded strangely alive in her leaden body.

"You made a lot of sense. A lot. I had no idea things had gotten so bad. I'm really sorry, Lacy. About your brother, I mean. And about me. Backing off. I didn't get it. I really didn't understand. I wanted to believe you, but I've heard different things, and I didn't know what to believe."

She wanted to tell Emma how good it was to hear her voice, but the words wouldn't come.

"Lace? Are you still there?"

Lacy began to cry. She sank into a chair and put the receiver in her lap. Emma's voice sounded small and tinny, piercing the room. "Lacy! Are you okay?"

Her mother came and gently took the receiver from Lacy's lap. "Hello? Emma? She's all right. She just can't talk right now. She'll call you back later. Thanks for calling."

She replaced the receiver and sat beside Lacy, stroking her hair. Lacy turned to her mother and let herself be held while she cried. When she could talk she said, "They asked if Jack could come to speak to all the students. In health class. They asked for him." She kept on crying. Her mother began to rock slightly.

"He's too sick, honey. He's too sick." Lacy cried harder, soaking a patch of her mother's shirt.

"Maybe when he's feeling better," her mother whispered. "Maybe next week, if he's feeling better."

CHAPTER
32

Friday, October 25

Emma, Bjorn, and Kerry biked home with me after practice today. Eddie ignored me in school today, so I wasn't surprised that he didn't come with us. When we reached the house Em pulled a bunch of daisies she had gotten at the florist out of her saddlebag and told me she wanted to give them to Jack. They were so wilted, we all burst out laughing. She threw them into a pile of old leaves, and I invited them all inside, but Jack was asleep.

We sat in the kitchen and demolished a batch of brownies. They've all decided what they're wearing to the Halloween dance next week. Bjorn and Kerry want to be Calvin and Hobbes, and they had a big tussle over who gets to be the tiger. Emma wants to wrap a shower curtain around her, carry a shower head, and have bare feet and a shower cap.

I still haven't thought about the Halloween Dance. Here are some suggestions they made for my costume.

A *toaster.*
The Statue of Liberty.
Rumpelstiltskin.
A *Gummi Bear.*

Dad came home and was surprised to see everyone, of course. He was even more surprised when Emma told him they had wanted to say hi to Jack. He asked if their parents knew they were here. Was he crazy? Bjorn reminded him that we're kind of old to be reporting to our parents every move we take after school. Dad paused then. I thought he was going to disagree, but he just looked at me funny, as if he was seeing me clearly for the first time, and he said, "Of course you are." Then he reminded us to be quiet so we wouldn't wake Jack. As if we needed a reminder. At least he didn't throw them out. Not that I thought he would—but I didn't really know what to expect. I almost asked him if we could watch a video later, but I decided not to push it.

A Gummi Bear?

CHAPTER

33

Lacy's heart ached as she watched Jack ease his stiff joints onto the kitchen chair. It was five o'clock in the morning, and neither of them could sleep.

"Jack, why didn't you come home sooner?"

The kettle shrieked, and Lacy got up to make them tea.

"I stayed to take care of Lincoln." Her brother's voice was low. "When he died, I couldn't stand being there anymore. We thought we would grow old together. Go on yearly vacations to the mountains and to Hawaii. Take a trip to some place more exotic every two or three years. Buy a house, decorate it with wall-to-wall carpet, and pipe classical music into every room."

"Just classical?" She wrinkled her nose.

"And KXYO's top ten."

"Better."

He sighed. "We had big plans. No, we had small plans. Just comfortable, run-of-the-mill American dreams and plans. We thought we might retire to Mexico, spend our last days learning how to paint watercolors, and take long swims in the ocean."

"I would have visited you often!" Lacy bit her lip. "Maybe you'll still retire to Mexico. Or to some other great place."

"Twitch, I think I'm in retirement here. Now."

She stood up, knocking the table and sloshing their drinks. "You sound like you've given up, Jack! You're here and we're helping you and anything could happen. A vaccine. A miracle cure. A new diet or something. People cure all kinds of things with herbs and diets and stuff."

She breathed hard, as if she had just finished a race. Jack mopped the spilled tea with a napkin, then took his cup in his hands.

"Twitch, I already tried the miracle cures and diets. Fruits and veggies only. Visualizing the surf on a warm spring day and my T cells multiplying. I drank nasty-tasting Chinese herb teas and said life-affirming prayers."

His lined face was relaxed, while she could feel the tension in her brow and shoulders.

"I'm dying, Lacy."

She knew it was true, but she couldn't help giving in to her outrage. "You are not! You're just sick!" She sat down hard and bumped the coffee cup onto its side.

She watched the whole cupful pour onto the floor. She didn't care; just let the tears come, fall on her bathrobe. She wouldn't look at Jack.

He set his cup down and handed her a wad of napkins. "I'm not giving up, Lacy. I'm just trying to make the best of the time I have left."

She blew her nose in a napkin. "You don't know how much time you have left!"

He nodded slowly, never taking his eyes from hers. She felt more tears and she tried to quiet her sobs.

"I shouldn't be crying. You're here and you're doing okay. You could make it."

He said nothing, just looked at her with a gentleness that made her anger fade. His brown eyes, unflinching, were so much like her own. People often commented on how similar their eyes were, how different from their parents'. Mom's were gray blue. Dad's were green with brown flecks. But Jack's and hers were brown with tawny flecks. Lion spots, she used to call them. Mustard spots, he would reply.

Now those eyes held her own, connected her to him in a way she'd never felt connected to anybody else. She and Jack were so different, had so much distance between them, yet they had this thing that connected them: Jack's eyes, so like hers, that could see her so clearly. She wanted to be able to see him the same way, but it hurt so much that she felt an urge to yell and fling the coffee cup against the wall. Instead she got up and set it in the sink. Jack's voice followed her.

"Twitch, I don't want to argue with you."

She turned to face him, leaning against the sink. "Me neither." She took a deep breath and the blood pounded in her chest. "But if you die . . ." She hesitated. "I will kill you." Jack laughed. She looked down at the floor. "And miss you." The relief she felt from saying that surprised her, and when she looked up she saw Jack smiling and dabbing his eyes with a napkin. She went around behind Jack, wrapped her arms around his shoulders, and laid her head against his.

CHAPTER
34

Monday, October 28

Peace. Quiet. Mom and Dad took Jack to the Portland hospital tonight for tests. I was kind of glad when Dad said I couldn't go with them. But now I'm restless.

And worried. Mom bought adult diapers for Jack today.

Kerry and I went to a movie together Saturday night. When Kerry called to invite me, Dad said he thought I was too young to date. Mom said she thought it was fine. She was thirteen when she first went to a movie with a boy. Jack said he thought it sounded like fun. I thought Dad was going to choke on his mashed potatoes. When he stopped coughing, he kind of growled, "What do you know about boys and girls dating?"

At first I thought he was being mean. But Jack didn't take it that way at all. He reminded Dad that he dated plenty of girls when he was younger and had a great time. Even kissed a few of them. Said he did it to make sure who he really wanted to be kissing. Then he looked at me and said, "You won't know until you try it." I know I turned bright red. Then I blew up. Told them it's none of their business if I kiss anyone or not and that I just want to go to a stupid movie with someone I happen to like. Why do they have to make a big deal out of it? If I thought I could get away with lying, I'd have told them I was going with the whole gang.

Then Mom giggled and said she knew why Dad was being so ornery. She told us that when she and Dad met they were both nineteen and she was the first girl he *ever* invited on a date. We all howled except Dad. It was his turn to blush. Jack told him to stop picking on him and me and just admit that he was a late bloomer. Which he finally did.

The movie was good. I grabbed Kerry's hand during a scary part. He put his arm around me on our walk home. I kissed him by the park and he kissed me a block from my house. We kind of took turns. It works out really good that way. Emma says she's never done it like that—taken turns. I reminded her she's never done it at all. Most people don't know that. Most people don't know that she's sort of a late bloomer. Like Dad.

I didn't think about Jack once, until I got home. For a whole evening, everything felt okay. I felt *normal*. Then I walked through our front door. Mom and Dad were upstairs with Jack, changing his sheets, cleaning up some kind of mess. When Mom saw me, all she said was, "Oh, good, you're home. Better get to bed, honey." Dad asked me if I had a good time as he passed me going downstairs to the laundry room. He didn't even stop to hear my answer.

First they make a big deal about my going out, then nobody can even listen to how it went. Mom looked exhausted and I know they're preoccupied with Jack and he's sick as a dog. But still, that was my first time going out. I got into bed, but I couldn't sleep because every fifteen minutes or so for a couple of hours I could hear Jack throwing up. I finally took Mr. Huggins off the shelf and sat with him by the window. After a while, my arms started to ache. I was squeezing him like he was a live thing that I was afraid would get away.

CHAPTER
35

She had never called Kerry before. Breathing slowly to calm the thumping in her chest, she dialed his number.

"Kerry? I just wanted to talk."

"Talk away."

"My parents are at the hospital with my brother."

"Are you scared?"

She had expected him to ask about Jack, not about her. His concern touched her. "It's just for tests. I've got a ton of homework, but I don't give a damn about it right now."

"The English is a breeze. You can copy my answers."

"Thanks." She paused. "They wouldn't let me go with them."

"Why not?"

"The usual: pretend nothing is wrong with *my* life."

"It's not bad advice."

"Thanks a lot."

Kerry was quiet. Then he said, "Before my parents got divorced, they'd argue about who was going to buy cat food. I tried to get them to talk reasonably to each other, but then they got mad at *me*. So I left them alone and went on with my life."

"This is different," she said crossly. "I can't just leave it alone!"

She heard him sigh, and then nothing. "Kerry, you still there?"

"Yeah." His voice was soft. "How about taking a taxi to the hospital?"

"It's too far away. They took him to Portland."

"How about writing a letter?"

"But he's coming home tomorrow."

"Jeez, Lace, then stay loose."

"But . . ." She remembered seeing Jack's pale, blotchy face early that morning. She was afraid he wasn't coming home.

Kerry cleared his throat. "Want me to come over?"

"You can go out now?"

"The window doesn't stop me."

She hesitated. "Better not. Some other time, though."

"Sure." There was a long pause. "How about now?"

She laughed. "Okay. Now."

By the time she made popcorn, he was there, and they watched television while doing their homework.

"Have you figured out a costume for the Halloween Dance yet?" Kerry asked.

"No."

"But you're going, aren't you?"

She thought he looked a little anxious, and that pleased her. "Yes. I'll figure something out," she said, smiling. "I've got three more days. Say, what's the answer to number six?"

"I'm not giving you any more answers."

"Why not?"

"I only give you answers if I'm sure you know how to do the problem. Then you don't have to waste your time repeating what you already know, and you're free to do other things."

"Other things?"

Kerry smiled and his eyebrows lifted for a brief moment. "I'll tell you when you figure out number six."

She chewed on her pencil eraser and regarded him calmly, but she felt her cheeks getting warm. "If you tell me the answer, we can get to the 'other things' that much quicker."

Kerry lay back with his hands behind his head. "I've got time. You'll come around."

She had an urge to lie down next to him and wrap an arm across his chest and stay that way for a long time, close and warm. Instead she looked at the geometry problem that had her stuck. "I wasn't listening when Mrs. Holstrum explained how to do this," she confessed. "Are you going to help me?"

"Multiply the radius times pi."

"Pi?"

"It's in your notes."

"I didn't take notes."

"It's in your book."

In one swift move she was sitting on his belly. "Who put you in charge here?"

He laughed, surprised, and linked his fingers with hers, their palms touching. He tried to push her off but she leaned hard on his hands.

"You're strong." He sounded pleased.

"And mean. If Jack were here, he'd tell you."

"I can't just give you all the answers. But I will make a trade."

Here it comes, she thought. What'll it be? Making out, probably. A *long* time making out. Lying down, maybe. She felt a slight dampness between their hands.

"A tour."

"What?" She sat upright, releasing the pressure on his hands. "Of what?" She felt a panic rise. Did he want a tour of *her*? She tensed to spring off his body.

He laughed. "Boy, do you look suspicious. Of your *house*, beanbrain. What did you think?"

Embarrassed, she stood up. "Why a tour?"

"This place feels like a palace. There are six of us in a seventy-foot trailer. I just wanted to see all the space." Now he looked a little embarrassed. She held out her hands and helped him up. For a moment they stood close and she thought he might hug her, but he stepped away, shoved his hands into his pockets, and waited for her to begin.

They glanced into her parents' room first, then paused in the open doorway to Jack's room. She watched his eyes move, followed his gaze as he quickly scanned the room. The photographs by the bed drew him over.

"Lincoln?"

She nodded. He looked at the pill bottles and Kleenex on the bedstand, the hoop still suspended from the molding, the shiny, stainless vomit pan and the pale pink plastic bedpan on a table on the far side of the bed. His eyes ran over the stains in the carpet where they'd been scrubbed with strong disinfectants, leaving those areas several shades lighter than the rest of the rug. He looked at the stack of neatly folded sheets on a chair in one corner, and the box of adult diapers in another. His gaze rested there, his expression serious.

She felt a need to say something, to explain. "He—can't—always—control himself." She expected him to look disgusted, but instead his eyes just widened slightly, making him look a little bewildered. She reached for the doorknob and jerked her head toward the door. "C'mon."

He nodded and walked past her. Relieved, she shut the door behind them and bounded across the hall to her own room. "Mine," she said, sitting down on the bed with her hands underneath her thighs. He sat down a few feet from her. *Wait until I tell Emma that Kerry* and I were on my *bed,* she thought. Again he looked around, took in details, but now he was smiling.

The phone rang and she ran to answer it. "My parents are on their way home," she told him as she came back into the room. "We've got about an hour before they arrive."

"They must have just dropped him off."

"They said there's no reason for them to stay. He needs to sleep. Let's go downstairs. I think we should finish the math before we complete our tour."

When their homework was done, Lacy led Kerry down into the basement.

"This basement alone is as big as our whole trailer," Kerry exclaimed. "What a lot of stuff."

Half the basement had a concrete floor. The other half was covered in painted plywood.

"Your tour continues." She took his hand and led him to the water skis leaning against the wall. "These are tongue depressors for a large species of alien."

"What are they doing here?"

"My mother is developing a new product. These are ready for shipping to Galaxia Pi Tundo, where the aliens will test them and send back a report."

"Uh-huh." Kerry pointed to an orange Hula Hoop. Cobwebs spanned the inside circle. Lacy picked it up and dusted it off with a rag.

"This is an earth balancer that the aliens gave me," she explained, having difficulty keeping a straight face. "When you use it properly,"—she put it around her hips and began to gyrate smoothly, rotating the hoop around her—"like this, it slows hurricanes down, cools volca-noes, stops rivers from overflowing. It sort of smooths out all the wild energies on the planet." Kerry watched her, his eyebrows raised.

"Is that so?" he said.

She suddenly felt self-conscious. Letting the hoop drop to the floor, she stepped out of it and handed it to him. "I forgot something important." She turned on the radio on her father's workbench. A country-western singer wailed, "Something ain't right / when a hard-working cowboy / loses his precious / to a trucker in flight." "You need this kind of music to make it work," she said.

Kerry couldn't work the hoop. He tried moving his hips side to side and backward and forward. He tried moving fast and he tried moving slow. Laughing, they switched to a rock station, but that didn't help.

"Maybe you balanced the earth enough already," he said, setting the hoop down.

"Yeah." She reached for a nearly paintless hobby-horse. "See how the alien licked off all the color? This is a cast-off alien Popsicle."

Kerry craned his head toward the horse head, wig-gling his tongue. "I want a taste!"

Lacy snatched the wooden animal away. "Ugh! Alien germs!"

She led him across a hopscotch court painted on the floor, whispering, "Alien hieroglyphics," past boxes with labels like Electric Skillet and Camping Cookware, until he tapped her shoulder and pointed to a box containing a child's baseball bat and mitt.

"What are those?" he whispered.

She was stumped. She couldn't turn them into anything.

"They were Jack's," she whispered back. She felt as if a spell had been broken.

They stood side by side, looking at the bat and mitt. She tried to keep the game going.

"They may, however, be an alien toothpick and something that was stuck between its teeth!"

Headlights lit up the high basement windows across the room.

"Oh no," Lacy groaned. "You shouldn't be here this late." She pushed him firmly toward the bulkhead door, unlocked it, and ran to turn the radio volume up. Then she strained to listen to the sounds upstairs. "As soon as you're sure they're both inside, you slip out that door, okay?"

CHAPTER
36

"Haven't they told you?" Barbara looked surprised. "I've heard they want to replace you in the relay." She rubbed her hair with a towel and switched on her hair dryer. Lacy glanced toward the showers, where Julia, Nina, and Megan talked and laughed with one another.

"My costume has real slime . . ."

"Silver streaks, heavy eyebrows, fangs . . ."

"Why do I keep coming up with such dorky ideas?"

"Dorky? Your costume will be the best at the dance!"

Lacy turned to Barbara. "Who'd you hear it from?"

Barbara's eyes were brittle. She regarded Lacy briefly before turning back to her own image in the mirror. "If you haven't heard anything, maybe nothing's going to happen. Maybe they're just talking."

Lacy dressed slowly, waiting to see if they would say anything about wanting her off the relay team. But each girl moved around her without speaking.

Fully dressed, she sat on the bench by the lockers. The girls avoided her eyes.

"Pass me my sneakers, would you, Lacy?" Megan looked at Lacy for a moment, then looked away.

Lacy picked up the black sneakers under the bench and handed them to her. Megan sat down and bent over to put them on. Barbara strode out of the room.

"What's going on, you guys? Is it true you want someone else to swim the freestyle leg?"

They exchanged worried looks, confirming Lacy's fears.

"You're not keeping up, Lace." Julia leaned against a locker, her arms folded across her stomach. "We're all getting faster, and you're slowing down." She said it simply. It wasn't an accusation, just a statement of fact, and nothing Lacy didn't already know, but she felt ashamed.

"I—I'm trying," she said.

"We know," said Nina, and the others nodded. "But . . ." She looked helplessly at Julia.

"Between the three of us, we've dropped seven seconds in the medley relay," said Julia. "And you've added almost five. It's frustrating, Lacy. We want to qualify for State again, and we're hoping for Regionals."

"So was I." Lacy examined the zipper on her gym bag. She flipped the toggle on the end of it back and forth. "What does Coach say?" She felt like the walls were closing in. Her cheeks felt hot in the overheated room.

"We haven't said anything to him. We thought we'd see how the next meet goes."

Lacy bit her lip, then took a deep breath, and made herself look into their faces.

"You don't need to wait for the next meet. I'll talk to Coach."

She took her time rubbing lotion onto her hands and face, drying her hair, brushing it. When the other girls left, she sat down and watched the clock, waiting until she was sure the bus had left before she ventured outside.

She welcomed the cold fall air. Piles of crispy leaves invited her to wade through them as they had every year since she could walk. She breathed in the crispness, the rich rot of leaves becoming earth. She walked slowly and, before she reached home, made a firm decision.

"There you are." Her mother held the door open for her. "Where have you been?"

"I walked home from practice. I missed the bus."

"You walked? Why didn't you call me?"

"I figured that with Jack coming home today, you'd be busy with him. And—I kind of wanted to. Is he upstairs?"

"They're keeping him for a few days."

Lacy's heart sank. Her mother took two plastic trays of steaming food out of the microwave and set them on placemats on the table. "How was practice?"

Lacy shrugged. "Okay."

"Did you figure out your costume for the dance tonight?"

"Not yet. I need your help, remember?" Lacy picked up the box on the counter and made a wry face. "'Low-cal cuisine,' Mom? Do we all have to starve now?"

Her mother looked at the box. "Sorry. I grabbed the wrong ones, trying to hurry."

"'Only two hundred forty calories,'" Lacy read. "I bet Coach would want me to eat about ten of these."

Her mother pushed her tray toward Lacy. "Here. Take mine."

"What are you going to eat?" She watched her mother, puzzled, as she reached for her coat.

"I'll get something at the hospital. Your father is meeting me there." She pressed her lips tight and sighed. "I'm sorry, honey, I can't help you with your costume tonight. Why don't you call Emma? She's full of creative ideas."

Lacy pushed the two trays away and stood up. "Can't I go to the hospital, too?"

"That's not necessary."

"But I want to."

"What about the dance? I don't want your life to be interrupted."

Lacy rolled her eyes. "I can't believe you're saying that. You're not the only one who hears Jack in the middle of the night. And with you always doing something for him—picking up a prescription, taking him to another doctor's appointment, cleaning up after him, changing his sheets, his clothes—do you think things are normal around here? You're either busy taking care of Jack or you're exhausted and taking a nap! You haven't come to one meet all season." Her voice started to shake. "You know, he's not your only child." She picked up the two trays and shoved them into the trash. "I don't want to go to the dance. And if I eat one more frozen dinner I think I'm going to vomit!"

Her mother winced. "I know this is hard on you—"

"How could you? Your whole life revolves around Jack. You don't see how it is in school or at swimming. You hardly hear anything I say. You don't even know I'm alive."

Her mother's lips were tight as she buttoned her coat. "That's not true." She stepped toward Lacy, putting a hand on her shoulder. "Let's talk later. I have to go." She glanced at her watch and picked up her car keys.

"Mom, let me go with you."

Her mother leaned her head against the door. "No."

Lacy felt like screaming, but she tried to keep her voice even. "What are you afraid of? I'm not going to catch it. If you go without me, I'm not going to the stupid dance. And I'm not going to answer the door for any trick-or-treaters. I'm going to read about AIDS and I'm going to call my friends and tell them what jerks you and Dad are for not letting me visit with Jack! And Saturday I'll take a bus to the city if you won't let me drive in with you." She glared at her mother's back as she straightened up and reached for the door knob, then turned around.

"Don't you have a meet on Saturday?" her mother asked.

Lacy's stomach gave a small lurch. She stepped back and sat down at the kitchen table. "I'm not going."

She saw the question in her mother's eyes and wanted to delay answering it, delay the argument that would likely follow.

"Mother! Did Jack tell you not to let me come to the hospital?"

Her mother paused. "No, he did not."

Lacy turned her hands toward the ceiling. "Then what is it?" she pleaded.

Her mother turned around and her eyes were wet. Her voice was nearly a whisper.

"It's a lot of things, honey. Jack's so terribly sick. I'm just trying to keep everything else"—she shrugged— "normal." She brushed Lacy's hair back with her hand. "C'mon. Let's get in the car."

Lacy ran to get her jacket. She's not ready to ask me about the team, she thought, feeling relieved. Or maybe she knows it would be useless to try to change my mind.

CHAPTER
37

Friday, November 1

I wanted to write in here last night but I was too tired when I got home from the hospital. I've got lots of time this afternoon, since I'm done with practice. DONE. I'm not telling anyone yet, since I want a few days to get used to it myself. Coach probably thinks I'm taking another little break. I'll go see him on Monday. When Julia, Megan, and Nina find out I'm quitting, they'll be glad. I can't say I blame them, but it stinks to not swim with them after four years. It really stinks.

The truth is, right now they stink, too.

Anyway, quitting makes sense. Didn't Coach tell me I was trying too hard? Didn't Dad say how well I swim isn't important? Besides, the relay team doesn't want me, and my individual times are slipping farther and farther from the qualifying times for the big meets.

And one more thing: Back on the first day of practice, Coach said we had to work to become the best swimmers we can be.

Or did he say just show up every day?

Whatever it is, I can't do either—show up every day or do my best.

If a ship is sinking, it's best to get out of the boat, right?

Dad sure was surprised to see me show up at the hospital. I walked right up to him and before he could say anything, I told him I had to visit. He looked at me for a long time. I thought maybe he was going to cry, but he just took my hand and Mom's and we went up to see Jack.

I was scared. It's one thing to be around just Jack, whom I know. But a whole ward of PWA's (people with AIDS)! Even though I know I won't catch it, I sometimes picture tiny viruses flying around the room, somehow escaping and leaping onto me or into a little cut on my finger that I hadn't noticed.

But they're just people, those guys with Jack. And not just guys. I saw women, too. And we walked by a nursery with babies who have AIDS. I saw Dad turn his head away. Mom slowed for a second and then sped up and took Dad's hand. It broke my heart, half a dozen or so babies in there in incubator-type things. Babies surrounded by plastic.

Jack was really glad to see me. When I walked in he

practically yelled to Luis, the guy in the next bed, Hey look who's here—TWITCH! The sister I told you about.

I wasn't so glad to see him. I mean, I was, but he looks awful. He's got a tube in his arm that connects to a sack of fluid the color of pee. When I said that to him (Mom and Dad were out of the room), he thought that was pretty funny. He turned to Luis (he's got it, too) and said something about how the doctors are so desperate that they'll try anything. Luis joked that maybe they should suggest it.

It's amazing what they find to laugh about.

It's kind of strange, but Jack seems happier in the hospital than he is at home.

Just before we left, Jack was asking me a ton of questions, until the nurse came in to give him a shot. Some questions he asked twice, so I could tell he wasn't listening to my answers. A few minutes after the shot, he sort of sank into the mattress. His eyes kept closing. The nurse came back to check on him. I helped her tuck Jack's arms under the blanket.

I asked her what she gave him. Something for pain, she said, terrible pain.

He never told me it was that bad.

CHAPTER
38

Lacy dreamed she was covered with purple spots. She had peeled them off Jack and pasted them onto her own arms, legs, and face. They were just sticky labels.

"See?" she told him. "Having AIDS isn't so bad. Where should we put these next?" They laughed together as they stuck the purple labels on the mailbox and on the white poodle next door. They put some on the ceiling, turned off the lights, and the spots glowed in the dark. Lacy turned and saw a whitish light coming out of Jack's mouth. She saw he had a mouth infection, and he said, "This one's mine, don't touch it." The purple labels fell to the floor like dead leaves and she saw that they weren't real and the white infection was and she felt afraid.

She woke up crying. Her mother was stroking her

head, tears in her eyes. Her father was sitting by her mother. When she told them the dream, her father said, "Maybe it's not such a good idea after all for you to go to the hospital."

"Don't make me stay away," she protested. "If Jack gets better, he'll go back to Colorado and I won't see him much. If he dies, I won't see him at all."

Her parents looked at each other. "She's right," her mother said softly. "She should go, as long as he's there."

CHAPTER
39

"I've got to hang up, Em. I promised Mom I'd vacuum before she gets home with Jack. We haven't cleaned at all since he went in ten days ago."

"Has he been in *that* long?"

"Yeah. Complications." She found that word came in handy, saving her from trying to describe a lot of gruesome details or remembering hard-to-pronounce new infections, some of which seemed all the more awful because they were normally found only in chickens or goats or sheep. "I'll meet you on the ice in an hour."

When she was done vacuuming she dressed warmly, took her ice skates off their hook in the closet, and walked down to the lake. The temperature had dropped suddenly and now black ice, sparsely etched with irregular white cracks, extended across the entire surface of the lake.

She'd never had much time to skate before. She'd never had much time, period. She changed into her skates and glided onto the ice, trying not to think about the swim team. When she did, her stomach did a little dance, and she wondered if she'd made a terrible mistake.

And then there was Coach. She felt bad that she hadn't gone to see him. Once he called to her in the crowded hallway of school and she pretended not to hear him. After a week of not going to practice, she wrote him a note:

Dear Coach,

You said you trusted me, so please keep trusting. I can't be on the team right now. I know it's the right decision. I didn't tell you in person because I knew you would try to talk me out of it, and I just don't need that right now.

Lacy

It worked. He didn't try to talk to her again.

She skated faster, following designs in the ice. Two girls called her name. She looked up, surprised to see Julia with Emma. They skated toward her, and the three of them joined hands, taking turns pulling one girl, swinging her around.

"No practice today?" Lacy asked Julia. The three of

them skated side by side, arms linked, Emma in the middle.

"Day off."

She knew Barbara had replaced her on the relay team. She wanted to ask how the team was doing, but was afraid she'd sound jealous or disappointed.

"We miss you," Julia said. "You should have stuck with it."

Lacy didn't say anything. Why did they miss her? And what did they expect from her? She didn't think any of them would stick around either if their times were plummeting or if they couldn't swim on the relay team after four years of swimming that same event together.

Emma slipped her arms out of the others' and drifted backward, making small loops on the ice. Julia and Lacy kept skating, but they didn't link arms.

"Lacy, we didn't think you'd quit the team altogether."

"I visit my brother in the hospital every day." She went at night, but she wasn't going to tell Julia that.

"Oh. Is he—"

"Worse." That usually stopped people from asking more questions.

Emma skated up to them, breathless, and her nose was bright pink. "There's going to be a lot of moonlight tonight. Let's come out again after dinner."

Lacy watched her mother's car arrive at her house and skated off. "I'll see if I can."

Jack was already in bed by the time she took off her

skates and walked up to the house. When she saw him, she felt a surge of anger: I don't want him home like *this*. His skin was yellow and sagged around his eyes. Later that day, he opened a letter that came from the school.

"Read it to me, Twitch." Jack wheezed when he talked. A magazine lay open in his lap, but she knew he wasn't reading it.

Dear Mr. Mullins,

You are invited to be a guest speaker at the Wilton Middle School Forum on AIDS on January 26 . . .

Lacy looked up at her brother. He was grinning at her and his eyes were bright. The grin looked out of place on his thin, sallow frame.

"Is there more?" he asked.

She skimmed the letter. "Just times, location. And it's signed by Mrs. Andrews and the chairman of the curriculum committee. Ta da! You're famous, Jack!"

"Huh. Something to look forward to." He shifted painfully. "Damn bedsores." He shook his head. "That's what Lincoln used to complain about the most. Bedsores. At the end, he was blind and his kidneys failed and all he complained about were the bedsores. Now I know why." He laid his head back and closed his eyes. "Twitch, you did a good thing there. Even if I don't get to that forum, you did a really good thing."

"You'll get there! You have to!" She tried to sound light.

Jack opened one eye. "Why?"

"Because . . ." She fished for an answer. "Because if you don't, there are a lot of lumpy critters in that school who will miss out."

Jack smiled and closed his eye. "Tell me . . . Why aren't you swimming?"

She'd been expecting him to ask, but now his question caught her off guard.

"I wanted to spend more time with you. When you were in the hospital, I couldn't do both."

He opened his eyes. "And . . . ?"

"That's true!"

"I believe you. What else?"

"I'm not good enough to get to Regionals." She paused. "And they put somebody faster on the relay team."

"I'm sorry, Lace." He closed his eyes.

She couldn't tell if he thought it was his fault or if he was just feeling sympathetic.

"Why?" she asked. "Why are *you* sorry?"

"Because you loved it."

CHAPTER
40

Tuesday, November 12

Fevers, rashes, blisters, mottled spots, all over him. I'm surprised that I'm not grossed out. He looks terrible.

But he's still, well, Jack. Last night he got really mad when he heard a news report about a Spanish-speaking woman janitor who did a great job but got fired by her new boss, who didn't speak her language. Mom says Jack keeps shining through.

I heard the team won the meet last weekend. I guess Barbara's doing better than me, but not that much better. Nina and Megan called me tonight just to say hi.

Mrs. Andrews called me into her office today to ask how Jack was doing. She had a million phone messages on her desk and her in-box was spilling over, but she wanted to know. Some kids ask me, and I can tell they are just curious. But Mrs. Andrews really cares. I could tell because she didn't ask dumb questions like do I use the same toilet as Jack or do we burn his sheets instead of wash them. She also asked about me. That's when I cried. I don't try to hide it so much anymore.

Now that I've got all this time, everyone else is busy. Em is headed for a D in English, so she's madly trying to rewrite some assignments before the end of the term. Kerry's got a job after school. His dad got laid off, and Kerry wants to make sure his little sisters get presents this Christmas. Eddie still avoids me. The swim team kids are swimming, of course. I can't even skate anymore because it snowed and then it thawed, so the ice is a mess. I feel cooped up, and I'm ready to climb the walls!

Jack swings from good days to really bad ones. Actually, even the good ones aren't so hot. Mom, Dad, and I swing with him. Up and down. We're all tired and cranky.

I used to like roller coasters. Not this one. I told Emma we should trade places because she loves those crazy rides. She said that's not totally true. All the while she's laughing her head off she's scared out of her wits and trying not to wet her pants.

This is one roller coaster I wish I could just get off.

CHAPTER

41

When Mrs. Andrews called Lacy out of study hall on November fourteenth, her heart pounded.

"Your father just called. They've taken Jack back to the hospital, and they want you to come immediately. I'm going to take you there." Mrs. Andrews touched her arm. "Lacy, they wanted me to prepare you. He may be dying."

Lacy folded her arms in front of her and looked down the hall at the light reflecting off the scratched linoleum. She moved numbly back to her desk. Eddie, sitting two seats away, looked up from the book he'd been reading.

"Jack?" he asked.

She nodded, blinking fast. She reached for her books, nervously knocked one off the desk, and papers tucked inside it scattered across the floor.

Eddie jumped up to collect them, banging his knee on the desk and looking flustered. "I'll get Em to put this stuff in your locker, Lacy," Eddie said. "Just . . . go." She opened her mouth and tried to whisper "thanks" but no sound came out. She wheeled around and walked to where Mrs. Andrews was waiting.

All the way to the hospital, Mrs. Andrews talked, but Lacy didn't listen. Her heart beat fast, and she thought the snow by the roadside looked ugly, all covered with the gray soot of car exhaust. She wished the snow would melt, or that it would snow again. She wanted it to look pretty.

"Do you want me to go in with you?" Mrs. Andrews asked, steering the car into a parking space in front of the hospital.

Lacy shook her head. She thought she should say thanks but she didn't feel thankful. "Why didn't you schedule the forum earlier? He could have made it!" She turned around and ran toward the hospital entrance, forgetting to close the car door behind her.

She got the room number at the front desk, ran to the elevator, and raced down the hall to Jack's room. The door was ajar, and she pushed it open slowly, breathing hard. Inside the lights were low, and her parents sat on either side of the bed, each holding one of Jack's hands. When Lacy came into the room, her father stood up and offered Lacy his chair. She hugged him and sat down.

Jack's eyes were closed. Lacy was shocked at how small and shrunken he looked against the white sheets.

She cleared her throat. "Hey, Jack . . ." When he didn't respond she fought down a panicky sensation that rose from her stomach to her throat, and she looked up at her mother. "Can't he hear me?" She bit her lip.

Her mother put her arm around her and drew her away from the bed. "A little while ago he asked to have the respirator and IV removed. Then he slipped into a coma. He comes in and out of it, honey. Sometimes he can say something. But he's really tired, and he can't stand the pain anymore."

Lacy held her brother's hand gently between her own, not wanting to hurt him. Her father pulled up another chair, close to her mother's, and sat beside her.

Lacy felt as though something heavy pressed on her chest. "Can he hear us?" she asked a nurse who came in to take Jack's pulse and temperature.

"Absolutely!" the woman replied, vigorously nodding her head.

They sat in silence.

"Why are the lights low?" Lacy asked.

"His eyes were sensitive to the light—it hurt him," her father replied.

Jack's hand was cool and slightly moist, but she wasn't sure if it was her sweat or his. She felt an urge to pull away, but she reminded herself that she could not catch his disease from a sweaty palm, and the urge passed. She gripped a little tighter. "Jack?" she called softly. She watched his closed eyelids and thought they fluttered slightly.

"Mom and Dad, will you go out of the room so I can say something in private to Jack?"

They looked surprised, but they stood up and left the room. The nurse came in to write on the chart at the foot of his bed.

"I want to talk to him in private," Lacy repeated.

The nurse hung the chart on its hook. "He'll like that," she said. "I'll come back later." She closed the door behind her.

Jack's mouth was open slightly and his breath came in slow, labored, uneven waves.

"You sound like an old radiator, Jack." She was glad no one else was around to hear her. "I don't know if you can hear me." She gestured toward the door. "She says you can." She watched his face closely for a response. "If you can hear me, squeeze my hand, okay?" She waited. His noisy breathing continued. His hand lay limp and soft in her own. She stood up and walked to the window, parting the curtains to look outside. A cloud scooted across the face of the sun, throwing the hospital into shade. Lacy shivered even though the temperature of the airtight room didn't change.

Returning to Jack's side, she took a deep breath and picked up his hand again, holding it briefly to her cheek. His hospital gown sleeve slipped back, revealing his thin arm. Purplish spots extended from just above his wrist to his elbow. The bones of his elbow pushed sharply against his translucent skin. She laid his arm flat and gently tugged the sleeve down to his wrist.

"Not much left of you, bro'." She swallowed, feeling a lump in her throat. "You told Lincoln good-bye; you said that helped." She shook her head and felt a tear slip down her cheek. "I don't want to say good-bye to you." She glanced back at the door and then leaned close to his ear and lowered her voice. "I'm mad at you for going, do you hear that? It's not fair." She watched again for his eyes to open, his hand to move, anything. All she noticed was that he seemed to take a deeper breath, and that he breathed a little slower.

"If you're not going to die, I feel awfully silly saying this to you." She wiped the tears away. "You were fun, Jack. I'm going to miss being silly together. And I'm glad you're gay. Because now I don't think that all gay people are weird, the way some people do. I know differently." She stroked his hand, and the movement soothed her. "And I'm glad you came home, because . . ." She thought about the sleepless nights, the tensions with her parents, the awfulness of watching him get sicker, the difficulties at school. "Well, I can't explain it, but I am. I'm glad you came home. You were brave." She heard voices outside the door, so she leaned close again and spoke softly. "In case I don't get another chance, good-bye. I love you, Jack. Good-bye." She sat back, feeling calm and spent and strangely lighter, as if she'd just taken off a heavy coat. She sat still, focusing on the sounds of air passing in and out of his fluid-filled lungs. She felt short of breath and realized she'd been trying to breathe at the same pace, and it was much too slow for her. Suddenly she felt as if Jack was already far away.

Her parents came in and sat down. She took a walk

on the ward, took the elevator down to the gift shop, looked numbly at the stuffed animals in the gift store that wore red felt hearts saying "I love you!" and "Get well soon!" For the rest of the day and into the night, she sat with her parents by Jack's bed or took walks up and down the ward. She watched his breathing get slower and more erratic. She took turns with them telling stories, beginning, "Jack, I remember when . . ." After the sun set she found it harder to talk to his closed eyes, and she began, "Mom, Dad, remember the time . . ." and she kept glancing at Jack for signs that he might be listening.

At 3:45 A.M. her mother woke Lacy as she dozed in the vinyl-covered chair by Jack's bed.

"Huh?" She sat up fast. Jack's eyes were open and aimed at the ceiling and he had a small, sweet smile that just barely turned up the wrinkles at the corners of his mouth and eyes. Lacy reached for his hand, held it lightly between hers. Her mother took his other hand, and her father laid a hand on Jack's arm.

"He's coming out of the coma!" Lacy exclaimed. Her mother was crying and her father shook his head. Lacy felt angry. "He is!"

"I'm sorry, Jack," whispered her father. Lacy looked from her father back to her brother several times, then sat back in her chair and watched her brother only. His jaw moved up and down, reminding Lacy of a fish lying on the dock with a hook caught deep in its throat. Then a deep, raspy sound came from his throat, a loud gurgle, and he lay still, eyes still open, smile gone. Her mother turned to her father and buried her face in his shoulder, weeping. Lacy got up and walked slowly to the nurse's station. The nurse looked up questioningly from her paperwork.

"He's gone," she told the nurse, her voice sounding calm and unfamiliar. The nurse came around the tall counter, put her arm around Lacy, and led her back into Jack's room. She stood alone while the nurse checked Jack's pulse, then gently shut his eyes and mouth.

CHAPTER
42

"Em, Jack died this morning." Lacy's voice was hoarse. It felt odd to speak those words into a cold, plastic phone receiver. She heard her friend sigh.

"I wondered, when you weren't in school. I'm sorry, Lace. Really sorry."

"Thanks," she mumbled. She wanted to tell Emma that this morning she had felt more relieved than sorry, but she was too ashamed.

"What have you been doing?" Emma asked.

"Well . . ." she hesitated. Opening the door to Jack's room, she thought. Her mother had shut it. Three times Lacy had opened it. She couldn't figure out what she was looking for, until the third time: She wanted to make sure he was really gone.

"Lace, are you there?"

She nodded her head. Silly, Em couldn't see her. "I baked cookies. I'm sitting around with my mom and dad a lot. I feel like a lemon."

"What?"

Lacy tried to laugh, and it came out like a snort. "I can't go near my parents without them squeezing me. Now my shoulders start to scrunch up as soon as I get near them." Why was she joking about it? Those reassuring hugs during a nightmarish afternoon.

"Lacy, are you there? Are you okay?" Emma's voice in the phone jarred her.

"Em, will you meet me on the lake?"

Emma agreed, and she hung up.

The afternoon had stretched out, endlessly. Lacy had napped after lunch. Waking up, she had entered Jack's room disoriented, in a confusing tangle of grief and terror. Her mother found her sobbing, "Will we die that way, too?" and led her out of the bedroom and down to the living room. Pressed between her parents, her face in her mother's shoulder, her sobs subsided to occasional jagged breaths.

Then, still watery-eyed but calm, Lacy asked them to accompany her to Jack's room. She heard her mother weep, heard her father clear his throat repeatedly, and felt the warm wetness on her own cheeks as she took the tacks out of the drawing she made for Jack's homecoming and carefully rolled it up.

She stood before her parents, the weight even on her feet. "Can this stay with Jack?"

Her mother nodded and smiled through tears. Her

father took it from her. "I'll call the funeral home."

The cold air pinched her nose and the sky was crystalline blue. Lacy squinted to block the glare bouncing off the pockmarked crust covering the lake. Her boots made crunching noises, and she sank a couple of inches with each step.

She met Emma a quarter mile from the shore. Emma put an arm around her and squeezed, then withdrew quickly her arm. "Sorry."

Lacy shook her head. "No, it's okay." They walked on, and Lacy began to cry. Emma handed her a packet of tissues.

"I knew you wouldn't have any," said Emma. Lacy laughed and cried harder.

They didn't talk. Lacy knew Emma looked at her occasionally, but she kept her gaze straight ahead. Her sadness rose and broke like waves against the shore.

Reaching the far side of the cove, they found a bare rock to sit on, out of the chill breeze. Looking back the way they came, Lacy saw their converging footprints formed a huge **Y**. She took off her hat, leaned against Emma's back, and let the sun dry her face.

CHAPTER
43

Sunday, November 17

Two days since Jack died. Em, Kerry, and Bjorn came to his funeral today. A lot of people cried. Even Jack's nurse from the hospital was there and she cried. Not me. I've got this big hole. It's just empty. I guess I cried so much before that now there's nothing left. It feels awful. Bawling is ten times better than this empty feeling.

I took Mr. Huggins down from the closet and now I'm holding him as I write this. I press him hard against me but there isn't enough left of him to fill the space.

There. I just threw him in the trash.

Dammit. He's all covered with pencil shavings. I'm

really sorry, Mr. Huggins. I've got him back in my lap. It's not his fault he can't sit up like he used to. Maybe I'll find some stuffing and sew him back up and give him to some little girl who will appreciate him.

CHAPTER

44

Lacy went down to the basement to bring up more soda for the friends and relatives who crowded the house. She sighed with relief to get away from her mother's tears, her father's stiffness, and the visitors' probing, sympathetic faces. She looked at the orange Hula Hoop, the paintless hobbyhorse, the hopscotch court, and the old pink couch. When she was little Jack used to toss her onto the plush, squishy cushions that seemed to have no bottom until she went *clunk* on the broken springs on the floor, and she would laugh and laugh until she almost cried.

She sat on the couch, but the dust and moldy odor drove her off. She gave an experimental hop on the hopscotch court, from the purple triangle to the orange square. It used to require a giant leap. Now she had to hold herself back from jumping too far, from skipping right over the orange square altogether.

She balanced on one foot and bent over to touch the cool painted cement floor. Thoughts of Jack boiled painfully and then the couch reminded her again of being tossed lightly and trusting and hitting the bottom that didn't hurt but only startled and made her laugh, and she had the urge to throw her arms up like she used to and say, Again, Jack, do it again!

She thought, Jack is gone. She took the Hula Hoop and crushed it, closing the gaping circle by pressing down until the two sides met. The plastic folded but didn't break. She released it and it sprang back into circle form; she hurled it like a giant Frisbee across the cluttered room. It hit a stack of cardboard boxes and clanged off a metal table before clattering to the floor, where it danced in small circles, a soft hula dance of its own, and lay still. She remembered laughing with her brother and parents because she couldn't shake her hips, her small body all one piece, head and shoulders and bottom not yet capable of moving separately.

She picked up the baseball bat, worn smooth and etched with nicks and scratches. She slipped her hand into the glove that Jack had worn and felt his young-hand shape inside, felt the eeriness of sliding her own flesh against the leather that used to cover her brother's hand, her skin touching skin that used to touch him. This is the space that Jack built, the glove that protected him, she thought.

Nothing had protected him! She picked up the bat

again and struck the couch, first the back, then the arms, and finally the cushiony pillows where she used to bounce. She swung and struck again and again, raising clouds of dust and mold spores, and she started to cough and her eyes watered. From the dust, she thought, until she realized she was crying and Emma was beside her taking the bat out of her hands and trying, gently and urgently, to hold her close.

She hugged her friend, and more arms encircled them both. Kerry and Bjorn held them tightly. Eddie stood a few feet away.

"Your mom and dad sent us to find you," Emma murmured into Lacy's hair.

CHAPTER
45

Monday, November 18

I keep expecting to see him. There's still a big box of adult diapers in the hall closet and the rubber gloves and bucket are under the sink. I thought I'd never want to hear his terrible hacking cough again, but I actually miss it.

We all stayed home today. I got out an old photo album and sat by Dad, but we never got around to opening it. I don't think we've ever agreed on so many things: We both miss Jack, we both think it's unfair, we both hurt a lot, and we're both glad he's not suffering anymore. It helped to know that Dad feels relieved, too.

I asked Dad if I could work at the store after school and on weekends. I need something to do, especially with Christmas vacation coming up. Besides, everyone's so busy and there's not much to do around here in the winter and I don't want to end up watching soaps or taking naps.

And Dad and I aren't arguing so much anymore.

He said yes!

CHAPTER
46

"I need a nut for my little boy's sled. It's off one of the runners."

Lacy took the bolt the woman held out. It was her first Saturday at the store, which was especially busy due to the upcoming Thanksgiving holiday. She looked around to find a clerk, but they were all occupied with customers. Her job was restocking shelves, not waiting on customers, but she thought she knew where to find what the woman needed. She smiled at the small boy beside her. His unzipped jacket revealed a Boston Bruins T-shirt, and he looked anxious. He smiled back shyly.

The bolt was an odd size, and after trying nuts of various sizes, none of which fit, she called her father out of the back office. He found the right washer and nut, brought the sled in from the woman's car, and knelt down to repair it.

The little boy hopped impatiently from one foot to the other. "Can you fix it?" he asked Lacy's father. "Can you fix it?"

Her father didn't answer. His hand shook as he tried to screw the nut on, and he dropped it twice. By the time the runner was secured, his face was flushed and droplets of sweat beaded his brow.

"Is it broke bad?" asked the boy.

"Don't bother the man, Timmy." The woman gently pulled her son back.

"No bother," her father said in a rough whisper as he tightened the nut with a wrench. Glancing at the boy, he said, "It's all fixed," and stood up abruptly. The boy grinned up at him, but he was looking away, so the boy smiled at Lacy instead.

"No charge, Lacy," said her father, and he walked briskly back to his office.

"No charge," Lacy repeated to the woman, wondering if she should apologize for her father's strange behavior.

The boy gripped the sled tightly as his mother thanked Lacy and carried it out of the store. Lacy wandered back to her father's office. The door was ajar and she heard muffled sounds, like someone coughing into a pillow.

She opened the door. Her father stood by the window, watching the woman load the boy's sled into an old station wagon. He shook all over now. His arms were crossed tightly in front of his stomach, his fingers clutched the sides of his shirt. He uttered sounds she'd never heard him make before: choking, gasping noises punctuated by deep sighs, and then he bowed his head, covering his face with his hands. At first she thought he was sick, and then she realized he was crying.

She stood frozen inside the doorway. Her eyes filled with tears and she leaned against the wall, knocking a framed Rotary Club award askew.

The phone on his desk buzzed, but neither of them reached for it.

A young man appeared in the doorway. "Mr. Mull— Oh. I'll come back later." He gently closed the door. The latch clicked and her father lifted his head, noticed Lacy, and drew a long breath.

"You shouldn't be here, Lacy."

"Why? Are you all right, Dad?" She took a step toward him.

He shook his head. "What a sweet—" He dropped his head again and cried, the sounds freer now, more like a boy's. Lacy stood still, feeling awkward, crying, too, and trying to be silent. He pulled a blue bandanna out of his back pocket and loudly blew his nose.

Stiffly she crossed the room. She slipped an arm around his waist and felt his body shake.

After a few minutes, his sobs quieted and he stopped shaking. He sat in his desk chair and she leaned against his desk.

"You shouldn't be here," he repeated.

She hiccuped. "Why?" She thought he didn't want her seeing him cry.

"What about swimming? Is there a meet today?"

She shrugged.

"Do you want me to take you over there?"

"No."

He picked up his jacket and laid it over his arm. "Let's go home for lunch then."

On the drive home, she began, "That little boy—"

Her father shook his head. "The T-shirt. Jack had one just like it when he was about that size." He didn't say any more.

Her mother met them at the door. "Slow day? I thought you'd have sandwiches at the store."

Lacy looked at her mother, who glanced from Lacy's face to her father's.

"Lacy, there's soup on the stove and cheese sliced for sandwiches on the second shelf of the fridge." Her mother followed her father into the living room, closing the door behind them.

The refrigerator hummed. The soup was thick, with lots of pepper. She burned her tongue tasting it. It smelled good, but she wasn't hungry. She dialed Emma's number.

"Yo! Emma here." Lacy heard sounds of a football game on television.

"Em."

"Lace? How's the big job?"

"I'm off for the rest of the day."

"Hot stuff. I'm painting my fingernails green."

"Green?"

"It looks like I dipped my fingertips in barf, according to Eddie. But what does he know? Lime Ice, it's called. One of the new winter colors."

"Anybody else there?"

"Bjorn and Kerry. It's your lucky day."

"Well, I just thought I'd say hi."

"Hold on. Kerry's trying to eat the phone."

"Lacy?"

"Hi, Kerry."

"When are you coming over?"

She looked at the closed living room doors, heard muffled choking sounds again. She was glad her mother was in there.

"I don't know. Eddie's not too fond of me these days."

"Yeah, well, we're straightening him out. Bjorn and I dragged him down to the counselor's office the other day and stayed with him while she unscrewed his twisted brain. You can still see the slot in his skull where her giant screwdriver—hey!"

"Lacy?" She heard Eddie's voice on the phone. "You gotta watch out. There's a lot of bad information going around about this AIDS thing, you know?"

"Yeah," she said, "and it's especially attracted to sponge brains. The ones that aren't filled with the usual stuff."

"Give a guy a break, huh? C'mon over here and let me dazzle you with my diamondlike brilliance. I'm gonna quote from Shakespeare while calculating the square root of a turnip that's been orbiting in the upper atmosphere—"

"Lacy!" Emma interrupted. "When are you coming over?"

"Now."

She left a note for her parents and jogged the quarter mile to Emma's. When Emma opened the door, Lacy slipped off her gloves and held out her nails. "How do you think Lime Ice would look on me?"

CHAPTER
47

Saturday, November 30

I woke at 6:00 this morning and remembered: Wilton Swimmers against Holden. I packed up my swimming gear and wrote Mom and Dad a note that I was going to the rec center to watch the meet. I almost wrote that I'd gone swimming, but I didn't. I wanted to think about it on my walk to the rec.

It was dark as night and the stars were still out. I wondered if Jack's up there with those stars, and if I should go to Sunday school and find out what happens after you die. If anyone really knows.

I got there early. I had that stuck feeling again, like something was jammed between my chest and my throat.

I sat in the bleachers and felt really stupid. What was I expecting? That Coach and the others would be happy to see me? That Coach would put me in all my old events?

Then Coach came out, set up the dividers, and saw me. He came over and sat down, and just then that stuck feeling in the base of my throat unjammed, and I started bawling. He gave me a handkerchief. I put my head on my knees, and when I looked up again half the team was crowded around us.

Coach told me he had to go start the meet. I sat there for a minute, hating the idea of watching the team swim.

Then I pictured this little scenario: Jack looks down on me from those bright stars, shakes his head and says, I'm sorry, Twitch. I say, what for? I'm sorry you're watching, he says.

I ran to the locker room to get changed.

In the locker room Barbara and Darcy stared at me like I was some kind of freak. Nina told me I couldn't swim today because Coach had all the events planned out and my name wasn't on the roster.

I stood in the shower for five minutes, hating her. Then I sat on the bench with the rest of the team.

Coach looked surprised, but he didn't say anything. I think he nodded to me, but it was so quick, maybe I imagined it. He wrote some changes on his clipboard, and when he read off the swimmers for each event, he had me in the 200-meter freestyle, a 50-meter backstroke, and—I couldn't believe it—back in the medley relay with Megan, Julia, and Nina!

I was afraid to look at Barbara. I was sure she was fuming.

Nina apologized to me just before warm-up. Said she was shocked to see me here today and didn't know what to say. Said she was sorry about Jack.

Julia walloped me on the back, her way of welcoming me. I asked her if she wasn't disappointed that Coach had bumped Barbara from the relay team. She said, Are you kidding? We'd much rather swim with someone who's willing to share the glory.

I didn't remind Julia we probably wouldn't be getting any glory, with me being so out of practice.

Coach told me to swim about three-quarters speed in the 50. I didn't understand why, but I wasn't about to start arguing. I just wanted to swim. I came in last.

Coach told me to give it *almost* my all in the 200. My time wasn't as bad as I expected, and I placed fifth.

Even though I was swimming okay, all things considered, I was really nervous when they called us up for the relay, and I don't know what made me look up. I was behind the block, shaking my arms out, waiting for the relay to start. I don't usually pay any attention to the noisy crowd—looking at all those people just distracts me.

But for some reason I looked up just as Emma led Eddie, Bjorn, Kerry, and *Mom* and *Dad* to some empty seats high up in the bleachers. Em pointed to me. Seeing all of them, my heart started whipping even faster than it usually does before a race. All season they can't get to a meet and then they come to this one, when I'm probably going to blow it.

Everything felt unreal, like I was looking at a movie set. Mom and Dad stood up and it looked like they were arguing with Eddie. I wanted to leave. I even started to back away from the block.

But I bumped into Nina, who told me I looked like I'd seen a ghost. She asked me if I was okay and she started rubbing my shoulders. It felt good. Just then the backstrokers were called into the water to take their starting positions. Megan jumped in. Nina stepped in front of me so I was fourth in line.

The gun went off. I watched Megan swim 100 yards of backstroke. She stayed up with Holden's top relay swimmer.

Then Nina dove off the block to do breaststroke. I moved forward like a zombie. I felt scared and numb at the same time. And revved. Wound up. And I had this strange I-don't-care feeling also. Why bother swimming? It's not important, when someone has just died. It won't make a difference. It won't bring Jack back.

But I also kept thinking Jack was in the room, somewhere. Down from the stars.

We were in third place when Julia started the butterfly. She was beautiful. She looked so strong, so free. I was on the block before I knew it, wanting to swim like that. I must have left Jack on the cold, wet cement behind me.

Julia touched and I dove. I didn't care that we were still in third place. I didn't care about getting to Regionals. All I wanted was to feel strong and free. I pulled and kicked and gasped for air.

It was over so fast. I hung on the wall gulping and crying. Nina and the others were dancing up and down, slapping me on the head and shoulders. Don't cry, they said, we came in second, and we were just one and a half seconds over our best time!

Everybody must have thought they were nuts, whooping and hollering over second place. We're all a long way from Regionals—in fact, we're a long way from qualifying for State, but we swam a good race.

As I got out of the pool, I had this strange thought—that I didn't leave Jack behind. I think he swam with me.

Mom, Dad, and the gang were all waiting for me after the meet. It was strange. Everyone hugged me and told me I was terrific. I didn't agree—but I didn't say anything. The hugs felt good, and I was glad to see Em and Kerry and the others. Then Mom and Dad drove me home. Good thing they were there—I was too tired to walk.

It turns out Mom and Dad had argued with Emma and Eddie about whether I should be racing, after not having practiced in so long. With all that's happened, they thought maybe they should stop me.

Eddie finally told them, "She'd rather be dead than not swim." Which was a terrible thing to say and he apologized immediately. But they knew it was true.